A Philosophy of History

B

A Philosophy of History in Fragments

AGNES HELLER

BLACKWELL
Oxford UK & Cambridge USA

Copyright © Agnes Heller, represented by EULAMA, Rome, 1993
The right of Agnes Heller to be identified as author of this work has been asserted in
accordance with the Copyright, Designs and Patents Act 1988.

First published 1993

Blackwell Publishers
108 Cowley Road
Oxford OX4 1JF
UK

238 Main Street, Suite 501
Cambridge, Massachusetts 02142
USA

British Library Cataloguing in Publication Data
A CIP catalogue record for this book is available from the British Library.

Library of Congress Cataloging-in-Publication Data
Heller, Agnes.
A philosophy of history in fragments / Agnes Heller.
p. cm.
Includes bibliographical references and index.
ISBN 0-631-18755-3 (alk. paper). — ISBN 0-631-18756-1 (pbk.: alk. paper)
1. History — Philosophy. 2. Postmodernism. I. Title.
D16.8.H4916 1993
901—dc20   92–18222
CIP

Typeset in Sabon 10/12 by
Pure Tech Corporation, India
Printed in Great Britain by
T.J. Press Ltd., Padstow, Cornwall

This book is printed on acid-free paper

Contents

Preface

Since finishing my book, *A Theory of History*, in 1980, I have increasingly become aware of having left a task unaccomplished. I first believed that the unaccomplished task was the theory of history itself, for the last chapter of the book (Part IV: 'Introduction to A Theory of History') was meagre in comparison to the preceding ones. More recently, however, I have come to an entirely different conclusion.

As I now see it, the fourth part remains a lame duck because it has simply been an appendix to the theory of history completed in the first three sections.

A theory of history is the reflection upon, and the interpretation of, historical consciousness and its various manifestations. A philosophy of history is something different; it is one of the manifestations of the modern historical consciousness, and, as such, a kind of self-reflection. Certainly, a theory of history is also philosophy; but it is not a philosophy of history.

In *A Theory of History*, I chose three major manifestations of historical consciousness: everyday historical consciousness, historiography as *episthémé* (writing histories or history) and philosophy of history; I used these as the main sources for reflection and interpretation. I think that this was the right choice, although literature or fine arts, which served only for illustration, could have also been considered.

The choice of the three major themes introduced the historical element into the discussion, for everyday consciousness is 'older' than writing history, and writing history is 'older' than philosophy of history. The process of reflection thus follows, although only very roughly, the evolution of the stages of the historical consciousness itself.

In the third chapter ('Sense and Truth in History, or Philosophy of History') I only discuss 'grand' narratives. I do not consider the possibility of the emergence of a new philosophy of history after the

demise of the old. At that time, philosophy meant for me the traditional kind, and I saw no prospect of its resurrection. Instead of new
philosophies, I recommended (in Part IV) an empty utopia on the one
hand and the ethics of an active stoicism-Epicureanism on the other.
The emphasis was on human finitude. The last sentence of *A Theory
of History* reads as follows: 'We can live an honest life – why should
we not try it?' I spent the following years of my life answering this
question. It was only after having done this (finally in *A Philosophy
of Morals*) that I could return to the other task left unfinished in *A
Theory of History*.

   This task was also prefigured in the book. *A Theory of History*
begins with the brief discussion of the stages of historical consciousness. These are: consciousness (1) of unreflected generality: the myth,
(2) of generality reflected in particularity, (3) of unreflected universality: the universal myth, (4) of particularity reflected in generality:
consciousness of history proper; (5) of reflected universality: world-
historical consciousness; (6) of reflected generality – as a task (of
overcoming the decomposed historical consciousness; planetarian responsibility). Thus consciousness of reflected generality (I term it
now, together with some others, post-modern consciousness) becomes
the *task*. This task includes two aspects, one speculative, the other
practical/ethical. Since I have already addressed the ethical component, I now turn to the speculative one.

   Some of my critics have pointed out that although I reject grand
narratives, my own rendering of the six stages of historical consciousness is itself a kind of a grand narrative. This is true to a certain
extent. The sixth stage returns to the first in the well-known Hegelian
fashion of the spiral. After taking several different forms, consciousness of unreflected generality arrives at reflected generality. To my
mind, this is not the path of a kind of universal 'progression', in that
I subscribe to Collingwood's dictum that only gains without corre-
sponding losses can be called 'progressive'. Yet I still add to this that
the very idea of progression is itself modern, and in this sense, it is
'progressive'. Actually, the story about the stages of historical consciousness is less speculative than it seems. Stage one (myth) has been
termed unreflected generality, whereas stage six (the post-modern)
has been termed reflected generality, and for very good reasons.
Insofar as 'beginning' can be discussed at all, it is presupposed that
'once upon a time' entirely unique and different cultures shared the
globe (without knowing much or anything about each other) and
manifested the same level of historical consciousness – that of myth.
Myth was thus the general form of historical consciousness, yet it
remained unreflected. Insofar as we discuss post-modern conscious-

ness at all, it manifests the recognition of difference in a world where
modernity has been (empirically) generalized. That means that for the
second time after the 'initial situation', people and cultures can share
the same temporality. The imagination of post-modern consciousness
has something in common with our own image of an initial historical
consciousness. In the present book, in chapter 6, I will return to these
issues.

When, in *A Theory of History*, I point at the consciousness of
reflected generality as a task, I write: 'The awareness of the task
stemming from the consciousness of reflected generality is again and
again countered by the awareness of the incommensurability of this
same task.' It is in the awareness of its incommesurability that I now
address myself to this task. In chapter 19 I write: 'History is the
metaphysics of an epoch which is History. The need of exactly this
kind of metaphysics is deeply rooted in our existence and we cannot
get rid of it. We can only reflect upon it.' I embarked on these
reflections in *Can Modernity Survive?* Many of the ideas I conceived
there have been developed in this book. Still, *A Philosophy of History
in Fragments* is the continuation of *A Theory of History*, and this is
precisely why it does not return to the questions of a theory of history.
It takes the results of parts I–III of the previous book for granted.

This book is not a book on history. It is a philosophy of history after
the demise of the grand narratives. The leftover of the past is historical consciousness itself; post-moderns understand themselves as dwellers in the prisonhouse of our contemporaneity/history/historicity.
This is why one cannot get rid of the awareness of historicity and
history, although one can give it a try. I have attempted this a few
times, but, on the whole, this book manifests rather the entanglement
of modern men and women caught within this prisonhouse.

Post-moderns inherited historical consciousness, but not the self-
complacency of the grand narratives. The confidence in an increasing
transparency of the world is gone. This is not a good time for writing
systems. On the other hand, it is quite a good time for writing
fragments.

The trust in universal progression created an entirely false expectation. Previously, we were told, poor philosophers or artists had to
labour in chains. In addition to constant political and religious constraints and pressures, they were limited by the strict requirements,
prescriptions, codes and canons of their genres. Now, we are told, we
are free; priests, emperors and overlords are gone; canons and norms
of literary and philosophical genres have been lifted. Nietzsche pondered that it was perhaps easier to dance in chains. I would not know

about 'easier', but it certainly was different, for the creative minds, be they giants or of a more modest size, are far from being free. The prisonhouse of contemporaneity/history has replaced the chains. One does not overcome the dialectics of *peras/apeiron*.

Since strict limitations of genre have been lifted, our time is quite favourable for philosophical fragments. I would not dare to assert that fragments alone can be written in our times, for I do not know what can be done before it has been done. At any rate, this book *has been written* in a fragmented way, for its author could not fathom a philosophy of history in any other form.

I conceived this book in a fragmented way, which does not at all mean that it is a collection of essays or conference papers, loosely assembled as an afterthought, for the purpose of publication. On the contrary, the whole composition of the book was ready before I embarked on writing the first chapter. Since ruins can be designed, I figure I can also design fragments. I merely use the freedom offered me by post-modern historical imagination. One can object that Fragment is also a genre (Kierkegaard wrote a book titled *Philosophical Fragments*), but if it is one, its limitations coincide with the walls of our prisonhouse. I have chosen the genre of fragment, because, in my mind, it fits best the task I set for myself. The idea was to disclose and to interpet post-modern historical imagination, and further to reflect upon it. Post-modern historical imagination is certainly not restricted to the topic 'history'; it encompasses the consciousness of our historical limitations to the same extent as that of our historical possibilities, our relation to the past, to the tradition(s), to culture in general and to our own culture in particular. But the same historical imagination is very much obsessed with history also, not with the 'universal' one, but with the burning shame of our own century, with Auschwitz and the Gulag.

The term 'post-modern historical imagination' can be misleading. Certainly, there are challenges common to everyone, problems that sincere minds have to face. But the very circumstance that we are not chained to, but instead, share the same prisonhouse, unfocuses philosophical inquiry. In a way, each of us 'has' a world of his or her own, though we also share one. One can duly express post-modern historical consciousness, if one does what one can anyhow not avoid doing: one describes the world according to 'him' or 'her'. Yet one can still present a multitude of manifold and shared perspectives, that is, 'different worlds', if one listens to others, and also to the conversation that happens to take place in one's own mind. It was first and foremost for this reason that the current book was conceived as a composition in fragments. The sub-sections of each chapter do not simply introduce new topics or 'ideas', but sometimes also another view or rather, another voice. It is in this way that chapters assume a dialogical character. There are no 'solutions' here. What happens to be the solution in one of the chapters or sub-sections is questioned in the next, and vice versa. In chapter 2 I experimented with the paraphrasis of a musical composition – ending with the funeral march on our century. In the second part of the last chapter (chapter 7), I accelerated the pace of the musical dialogue, changing from theme to theme in *allegro vivace*, as it befits a finale.

There are internal switches (fragmentations) within chapters that bear no necessary connection to switching from one voice to the other; I simply change altitudes. Occasionally, I begin with the discussion of an esoteric philosophical matter and switch from there abruptly to a political issue or ponder phenomena of daily life, and vice versa.

'The Question of Truth' is placed in the middle; it cuts the whole book into two equal parts, each containing three chapters. The question is whether the one in the middle is 'the One'? The last chapter (conclusion) returns to the beginning – to contingency. But it returns to the beginning in a reversed route. The first chapter deals with the cosmic wager first, and only later, in the second sub-section, with the existential choice. This sequence has been reversed in the final chapter; here, the first sub-section ('On the Railway Station') ends on the note of the existential choice, whereas the very last sub-section (on world and life) finishes with the cosmic wager. But not quite; for the last sentence points again to the prisonhouse of history. The book has been artificially left unfinished. This was the only way to conclude it.

I hope that my ten-year-old debt has now been paid.

Agnes Heller

Acknowledgements

I thank my students and colleagues from the New School for Social Research Philosophy Department with whom I exchanged many of the ideas included in this book. I am also grateful to my friends and former students from Melbourne for their reflections and remarks.

I thank Wayne Klein for the editing of the manuscript.

I thank Aaron Garrett for his work on the notes, and for preparing the bibliography and the index.

I thank my old friend, Mihály Vajda, for his conscientious reading of the manuscript and for his many useful critical remarks.

As always, I am most grateful to my best friend and husband, Ferenc Fehér, who has assisted me in my work on this book on all levels with his good advice, his criticism, his encouragement and his labour.

New York

1

Contingency

1 Chance, Telos, Contingency

I use the word 'contingency' as an existential term; it is the human condition that men and women experience and describe as 'being contingent'.

In what follows, the term 'contingent' does not mean 'accidental', although it has something to do with 'accidental'.

From everyday thinking to traditional metaphysics through sciences, the 'essence' of a substance, an event or a development is duly distinguished from its propensities or attributes, some necessary, some others accidental. Viewed from this angle, the colour of a table or the name of a king are accidental, because the essence ('being a table', 'being the king') would remain just the same were the table white instead of brown, and the king Edward instead of Charles. If the human condition itself is described as being contingent, contingency cannot be understood as a propensity which may be added to the human condition as well as not, without changing its 'essential' nature. Neither can we say that the human condition remains essentially the same, with whatever contingent (accidental) propensities it may appear. As an existential experience and description, contingency has nothing to do with this kind of 'accidental'.

Things which happen 'by chance' are also termed accidents. Accidents proper are inessential but intrinsic relationships (the table has to have a colour, the king has to have a name), whereas things that happen 'by chance' result from extrinsic relationships and can be inessential as well as essential. Everyday thinking, philosophy or sciences are equally familiar with these phenomena but describe them in different terms. They are described as sheer coincidence, or as throwing the dice from two separate and unconnected diceboxes, or as self-reproducing systems which happen to cross each other so that one of them causes decisive changes, or a series of changes, in the other. As in the first case, so in the second, natural events can also be described as 'accidents'. There are genetic accidents, cosmic accidents and the like. Since times immemorial, men were fascinated by chance insofar as chance events were supposed to have affected the affairs of single persons or of groups of single persons. *Moira* or *tyche*, *sors bona* and *sors mala*, blessing and curse, good luck and bad luck, are so many names for Chance as the Supreme Power looming large over the heads of mortals. Cross purposes, designs coming to nought, ends reversed, disproportion emerging between intention and result, actors groping in the dark – these are the oldest versions of our stories. Chance has something to do with contingency, yet contingency is also the opposite of chance. One is defeated by bad luck, one is subjected by chance to the Power of Chance. But one cannot be contingent by chance, nor is one subjected to the Power of Contingency. Chance appears as an external power, outlandish, sometimes violent, often vengeful and always whimsical. But contingency is intrinsic to the person; moreover, a person cannot but be intrinsically contingent. For the most part, the pre-modern powers (divinities) of chance are also the powers (divinities) of fate. For what else is chance for the person subjected to it but his or her fate? If your intentions are crossed by blind chance, chance could have been pre-ordained as fate; and one cannot escape one's fate. Foreknowledge of the designs of fate can give one the power over one's future, for pre-knowledge of the future changes the future itself; yet, alas, future as fate cannot be changed. This is the paradox of chance qua fate; but this is not the paradox of contingency. Contingency is not temporal, for being aware of our own contingency does not add to our knowledge of the past, the present or the future. I will not foresee my fate better in the awareness of my contingency, given that contingency-awareness implies that there is nothing to foresee, and even if there were, we would not gain anything by foreknowledge.

Contingency as an experience and as an existential description has no cognitive value at all. I do not know more or, for that matter, less, about the human condition in general or that which concerns or pertains to that condition in particular, by experiencing and describing this condition as being contingent, than I would know otherwise. This holds equally true of philosophies of contingency. Pristine existentialism has exalted contingency-awareness in the jubilation of discovering the experience and the term; it clad contingency-awareness in the robe of a higher dignity than could have been allotted to it by any traditional philosophy. Kierkegaard remarked[1] that Hegel's *Logic* might have become the greatest achievement in philosophy, had Hegel spelled out in the preface that it was meant as a thought-experiment. For an 'existing thinker', as Kierkegaared termed the kind of philosopher who is the carrier of the paradox of contingency, a philosopher of Absolute Knowledge is ridiculous if meant seriously. In presenting a philosophy of absolute knowledge, the philosopher reaches out beyond his own mental and human resources, beyond his contingency, and this is a comical gesture similar to that of George Dandin. But a philosophy of absolute knowledge presented in the spirit of Socratic irony could act out the paradox of contingency: to know that one knows nothing and, nonetheless, bet on this knowledge in absolute faith. A thinker who holds to this paradox, without relapsing either into Hegelian omniscience or into a frivolous version of scepticism, will be authentic. In all other cases, he will be inauthentic.

Up to a point, I would go along with Kierkegaard: in the last instance, no speculative thinking can sublate contingency authentically. The question is, whether 'authenticity' is as decisive a constituent in speculative thinking as it is in matters of character. Heidegger certainly is an inauthentic person; even the best friends of his philosophy, from Derrida to Rorty, discover a strongly comical streak in his philosophy.[2] The heavily comical element is due, here even more than in the case of Hegel, to the George Dandin-like pretensions of the author: a person, not less contingent than anyone else, celebrates here a *missa solemnis* of cosmic proportions around his own mental creatures. But I simply do not think that the philosophical greatness or the speculative weight of authors necessarily depends on their personal authenticity. Certainly, ironical (self-ironical) philosophers are not perceived as comic, whereas the display of earnest philosophical pathos without irony in a modern author will lend the thinker's stance a touch of the comic for everyone except the blind follower. But it does not follow from this that the thinkers who belong to the first type of attitude will also be better philosophers in sheer speculative terms. Above all, the line of division between the authentic and the inauthentic way of coping with contingency is slightly different if it is about coping with *cosmic contingency* or with *historical contingency*.

There are two kinds of contingency or contingency-awareness, and the relation between the two is dialectical (in the Kierkegaardian, rather than the Hegelian, interpretation of the term). Representative metaphors will serve us as guides, at least at the outset, to tell one from the other. 'The Zero and the Infinite' stands for cosmic, 'Being-Thrown-Into' for historic, contingency.

Contingency is the opposite of teleology; men and women become contingent beings by having been stripped of their telos. One can be stripped of something one has already possessed. One must be aware of having possessed something to discover that one has lost the heritage. A person suffers from the malaise of cosmic contingency, or, alternatively, she takes pride in it, if it dawns upon her that her life does not serve any purpose higher than being lived. But, regardless of whether one suffers from contingency or takes pride in it, one cannot experience it without bearing in mind that once, not such a long time ago, each and every person was believed to serve a special purpose in this world, and that this comfort has been lost once and for all. (Whether or not single persons or whole generations will once again return to universal teleology makes no difference.)

Contingency-awareness can come as a shock, as the culmination point of a conflict which will be presently overcome. Having eaten from the tree of knowledge, Adam and Eve discovered their nakedness. This was the moment of *aletheia*, of unconcealment, the moment of truth. Literally, nakedness stands for shame (sex is visible and should be covered), metaphorically, for contingency. What becomes visible is man's and woman's nothingness, their vulnerability, the nakedness that cannot be covered by hand. The Absolute Telos that had governed the interminable life of the first man and woman, has been lost for good. From this moment onwards, men and women must choose on their own, and they must respond, that is, they must take responsibility. Contingency is the loss of innocence. In becoming similar to God (by gaining the capacity to discriminate between good and evil, that is, by gaining reason), man also becomes the absolute difference; the absolute otherness before the face of God, the mortal, who knows that s/he is mortal; the Zero vis-à-vis the Inifinite. But contingency-awareness evaporates in the instant of shock. God's voice resounds loudly; although cursing and punishing them, he still remains the God of human creatures. He makes sure that their lives do not remain without purpose.

Contingency-awareness can also linger on the margins of a culture, stubbornly preserving a niche for the drop-outs and marginals as well as for those who ask too many questions. The Epicurean cosmos consisted of absolute necessity and absolute chance (which, in the final count, are two faces of the same coin), and many a Gnostic discovered in fear and trembling that men were thrown by a malignant demiurge into an entirely indifferent universe.[3]

At the dawn of modernity, contingency-awareness arrived with a shock that could no longer be given a cosmetic treatment, relegated to the margins. Once a marginal phenomenon, contingency-awareness moved swiftly towards the centre.[4]

Cartesianism and the emergence of modern cosmology gave an immense boost to the awareness of cosmic contingency. Actually, mechanic and mathematical world-explanations shifted the marginal phenomenon to the centre.[5] Yet the immensity of the shock could be perceived as an over-reaction. After all, the meaning of our life is not shaken by the Cartesian theory of motion nor by the Copernican description of the revolution of the celestial bodies. Epicureanism, though equally marginal, was hardly 'shocking' for a pre-Christian world. The shock came, and it was immense, because modern natural sciences were invented by Christians in a world where the teleological explanation of the universe and of each and every person's life had been taken for granted since time immemorial. For long, it had been a matter of heresy even to touch the chord of a possible contingency. The moment of truth, of *aletheia*, of unconcealment appeared – in the dominating Christian interpretation of Genesis – as the hereditary sin. Men and women were anything but contingent in medieval imagination; on the contrary, they were guided by Providence, and so was the whole universe. As far as our knowledge goes, never before had a dominating world-view been so entirely impregnated by the idea of providence, never before was teleology so universally conceived and accepted as in medieval Christianity. In this cosmos, no leaf could have fallen from a tree without having been so willed by God.

Popular Greek or Roman tradition was not teleological. If one's fate was preordained, this was so without sense or reason. This is why human decisions were made according to the proper and imaginative reading and interpretation of signs. Mere chance events (for example, birds flying above us) were such signs. This gloomy perception of the cosmos, where one could convincingly say that the best thing for a man is not to be born,[6] was challenged by philosophy, in particular, by Aristotle the first to elaborate a completely teleological vision of the cosmos. At one stage,[7] Aristotle takes note of the difficulty of designing a purely teleological universe without allowing for the immortality of the body. Criticizing one branch of Pythagoreans, he remarks:

> The view [the immortality of the soul: A.H.]. . . involves the following absurdity: they all join the soul to the body, or place it in a body, without adding any specification of the reason of their union. . . . All . . . that these thinkers do is to describe the specific characteristic of the soul; they do not try to determine anything about the body which is to contain it, as if it were possible . . . that any soul could be clothed in any body – an absurd view, for each body seems to have a form and shape of its own.

No wonder that the 'good tidings' about the resurrection of the body
were embraced fast by the 'unhappy consciousness'. Teleology was
not only restored, it was made total and perfect.[8]

Perhaps this strongly universalistic teleology had to be elaborated
in detail and also philosophically in order to suppress gnostic heresy.
Explaining Evil and pushing contingency-consciousness in the background simultaneously, called for a very complex and sophisticated
version of a strong teleological schema where everything that is senseless, void of reason and purpose, becomes teleologically in-built and
made meaningful. A new metaphor, the Will, was discovered and
elaborated by Augustine to serve this purpose.[9]

Contingency appears in the centrepoint of imagination once contingency-awareness has been moved to the centre. Since this first
happens in early modernity, contingency itself is through and
through historical. There were, and there still are, people without
contingency consciousness, although equally without strong teleological narratives. They could have been stripped of nothing in
order to lay them bare and naked. Nevertheless, cosmic contingency is un-historical, albeit not a-historical or anti-historical. It is
not a-historical, for nothing that appears historically is a-historical. It
is not anti-historical, for it neither confirms nor negates the historicity
of everything human. But cosmic contingency is still un-historical
because no direct connection with the discovery of man's historicity
transpires from its discovery. Rather, the shock comes from
the awareness of the loss of cosmo-teleology. And this is why the
attempts to cope with this shock and to overcome it do not heavily
depend on historical constellations. Once cosmic contingency has
been moved to the centrepoint, new philosophical and theological
ideas were forged in order to overcome it once again. Blumenberg
describes this rearrangement as the second round of the game in
which gnosticism is pushed back into the historical unconscious. In
theology, protestantism, particularly Calvinism, is the main case
in point. In philosophy it is Hegel, who was also the child of Luther-
anism.

The whole of the Hegelian system can be described as a gigantic
attempt to overcome cosmic contingency and, simultaneously, to
accept historical contingency, the modern human experience *par
excellence*. To cut a long story short, Hegel forged a system of overall (universal) teleology, where the teleology of single individuals
is historically suspended. The single individual remains contingent
within the overall teleological development, unless he chooses to
jump into the mainstream of universal telos. If he fails to do so, he
lives by 'accident', as a merely chance manifestation of the universal

necessity. This synthesis is made plausible philosophically by Hegel's remoulding of the concept of necessity. Necessity is no longer tantamount to the cause-effect relation, or rather, cause-effect relations are conceived as the lowest and emptiest (because merely formal) manifestations of necessity. Before finalizing his system, Hegel had already made an attempt to overcome cosmic contingency philosophically, in the famous chapter on alienation in *The Phenomenology of Spirit*.[10] Here Hegel historicizes the experience of contingency itself by bringing historical and cosmic contingency into close connection. Contingency consciousness is described as alienation which appears at a certain juncture of world-historical development. It is the experience of contingency which belongs here to historical telos and which is overcome by the historical telos itself in the present.

Hegel was not alone among the great thinkers who made an attempt at the restoration of cosmic teleology. In a far more hesitant and sceptical manner, Kant made a highly similar effort in the Third Critique and his last political writings, coming close to the young Hegel's solution. In these variations on old teleological themes, the after-effects of the original shock became widely perceived. But, notwithstanding a few major exceptions, Kierkegaard being one of them, these delayed tremblings registered lower and lower on the existential Richter-scale. The original shock experience turned into an adjustment, admittedly partial, to cosmic contingency.[11] For example, nineteenth-century positivism was quite content with accepting cosmic contingency. In yet another false prediction, it was even widely held in positivist circles that the terror of cosmic contingency had been overcome by science and that teleological visions would never return, while, ever since, forms of teleology have been creeping into the fissures of old positions. Toulmin now even discusses a 'return to cosmology'.[12] Once marginalized conceptions, gnostic, kabbalistic, orientalizing and many other different kinds, may once again enter the mainstream. In a post-modern world, both the stubborn will to live in the awareness of cosmic contingency and the attempts to overcome it can peacefully co-exist. The manifestations of cosmic contingency touch a sympathetic chord in some souls, whereas a great variety of teleological compositions ('quotations'), which aim at annulling cosmic contingency, will influence others.

To repeat, the consciousness of cosmic contingency is historical, and our present historical consciousness is pluralistic. Pluralistic historical consciousness tolerates both the acceptance and the denial of cosmic contingency, provided that they take modern forms. Given that cosmic contingency, or the lack thereof, is a 'thing in itself', or rather, *the* thing-in-itself (to subscribe to Kant's basic formula), as long as our consciousness remains post-modern, as long, that is, as no world-vision will occupy the exclusive position of domination, neither the acceptance of cosmic contingency nor its rejection can be excluded from the forms of imagination.

For example, existentialist authors can accept cosmic contingency as well as reject it. Religious existentialism, having grown out of Pascal and Kierkegaard, would not interpret 'thrownness-into' as the description of cosmic contingency or as the refutation of the poss-ibility of providence, while Sartre or de Beauvoir would. Heidegger's Being[13] wears sometimes the features of a dice-box, the allegory of cosmic contingency. Moreover, Heidegger's preference for pre-Platonic philosophy can also be understood as the manifestation of his commitment to a pre-cosmic-teleological understanding of the fate-accident connection. At some stage of his development after the 'turn', Heidegger keeps referring to the truth that comes to the persons who stand in the clearance of Being or in the draught of Being and the like, and the structure of this metaphor has a strong resemblance to the Hegelian idea of the recognition of necessity. Even Hegel's comeback might become possible, given the attraction in our times of the combination of 'being thrown into' as the expression of social contingency with cosmic teleology, or with some of its substitutes. The popularity of the later Heidegger is a case in point.

Thus, cosmic contingency consciousness can be overruled in post-modernity, but the consciousness of historical-social contingency can-not. Historical-social contingency is not a 'thing in itself'. The veracity of the assertion 'we are contingent beings' in the latter understanding depends on our interpretation or perception only as statements of fact in general. Historical-social contingency cannot be annulled by think-ing, imagination, perception, interpretation, or by any thought act or speech act in speculation. One cannot get rid of it by neatly glueing together pastiches out of old teleological images and world visions. There are only practical ways to divest historical-social contingency: by returning to one of the pre-modern social arrangements or invent-ing new ones which transcend the present state of the world. And these are precisely the attempts that post-modern men and women have become extremely suspicious of. As long as one shares this world and not another, one cannot remain an authentic person unless one faces one's own historical contingency and learns to live with it, to cope with it and to withstand the strong temptation to escape from it.

2 The Zero and the Infinite

Pascal wrote:

> When I consider the short duration of my life, swallowed up in the eternity before and after, the little space which I fill . . . I am frightened, and shocked at being here rather than there; for there is no reason why here rather than there, why now rather than then. Who has put me here? By whose order and direction have this place and time been allotted to me?[14]

A universe without telos is a universe void of reason. In a universe void of reason, neither the existence nor the non-existence of a thing has a reason. Forces of causality are blind and spiritless. Every thing determined by external efficient causes is a contingent thing. One single external cause in the chain of causation makes the result of that causal chain dependent on a mere coincidence of forces. It makes no sense to speak of sense with regard to the universe. Hegels's dictum that if you look at the world rationally, the world will also look back at you rationally[15] is tautological, since in Hegel's mind one looks at the world rationally *if* one presupposes that the world is Spirit like ourselves. Yet if the world is the infinite chain of chance events, the more we will look at it rationally, the less it will look back at us rationally.

A universe without telos is a senseless universe; a universe with telos, however, cannot be an infinite universe. The end, the goal, wherever one places it, makes all relationships within the universe finite. Infinitude needs to be eliminated in order to avoid the recurrence of the problem that was supposed to have been solved. Relying upon the authority of physics as science, it can be asserted that it is illegitimate to raise the question of 'What was before the big bang?', so deeply unscientific within the framework of the universal theory of relativity (where there is no time, there is no 'before'). But, as a rule, philosophers do not accept such interdictions. Or, alternatively, one can eliminate infinity while surreptitiously keeping it, by constructing a circular system as Hegel did, where the infinite development is nothing but the endless self-determination of the Spirit itself which goes on in circular movements.[16] If there is an eternal circle of self-determination, the end (the goal) remains a thing in itself, for we cannot have knowledge of it. At the same time, by the very supposition that we have arrived at the end (the goal) of the system, infinitude 'ends', and this contradiction cannot be sublated. The alienated spirit returns to itself *now*. If the movement starts afresh, circularity is eternity; it is also infinitude. But then, we cannot possibly know whether we (our age or our occidental culture) is not entirely contingent from the standpoint of the end. If, however, the self-development of the Spirit has come to an end in its self-recognition, and there is no next round, universal teleology remains, but infinitude has been lost.

Eternity as infinitude can be thought in terms of *causa sui*. If the Universe (the All) is conceived of as *causa sui*, 'bad infinitude' has been authentically eliminated, together with questions such as 'What was before it?' or 'What is outside of it?' Spinoza invented such a system. He made a clean sweep, too, by getting rid of 'bad infinity' and dismissing teleology, simultaneously and absolutely.[17] By injecting temporality into the system, Hegel added *telos sui* to *causa sui*, and made the substance subject. This tremendous improvement also turned out to be a tremendous liability.

Hegel distinguished, with reference to Aristotle, between internal and external teleology.[18] External teleology is but an outdated form of the external cause-effect relationship, and as such, it should be dismissed. The final cause is not external to the thing, but is inherent in the thing as its own possibility. Teleology is the self-development of possibility into actuality. But if Truth is the Whole, and the Whole is grasped (known) in the Absolute Science, then there is no other teleology but the internal one, for every possibility is inherent in the Spirit at the 'beginning' of its self-determination, which is, however, always a relative one. But if teleology is entirely internal, how can it be that not all possibilities become actuality?

Let us suppose that all of them do become actuality. In this case, teleology would not differ from an entirely deterministic conception, where whatever exists first is the cause of all subsequent things and events, of the whole chain of cause-effect relations *adinfinitum* (for example, God the watchmaker or the first mover, the primeval matter, and the like). By contrast, let us assume, as did Hegel, that not all possibilities become actuality, but only some of them. How and why is this so? The question cannot be answered in a Hegelian fashion, for it is wrongly put. In Hegel, it is actuality that explains possibility, and not vice versa. If one thing has already been actualized, we have the exclusive proof that it was exactly this end that was inherent in the thing as its own necessity, whereas all other possibilities were only contingent. This is a story, but not an explanation; taken as explanation, it is tautological. The story follows the logic of a story. The end result sheds light on the whole, the actual result proves to be the necessity among many a possibility. The metaphor of the Owl of Minerva makes it explicit that Hegel regarded the explanatory approach in ontology (metaphysics) as fruitless, a dead alley. This is why he has chosen to abandon the unpromising exercise. He is discussing the Absolute, but the story he tells is that of the limited (not the unlimited) Spirit of occidental culture or of the contingent modern individual, as the self-development of the (occidental) macrocosm and microcosm. Tell the story of the Spirit as the story of the limited Spirit, of finite self-consciousness, and everything is immediately in place. When Lukács once remarked: 'From contingency to necessity – this is the way of all problematic individuals'[19], he merely made a succinct summary of the non-tautological interpretation of Hegelian internal teleology.

All this has not been said in order to re-confirm the widely held view that Hegel's system is a kind of a *Bildungsroman*, but to instill some doubts concerning the Hegelian venture, the introduction of circular movement into teleology, which, in my mind, fares neither better nor worse than any other philosophical therapy of attempting to rid the modern consciousness of the *horror vacui* left behind once trust in providence had collapsed. No reconciliation with actuality, that is, with the utopia in the present, can remove this horror. On the contrary: the more our thoughts are focussed on it, the less it can be removed.

Pascal writes:

> Returning to himself, let man consider what he is in comparison with all existence; let him regard himself as lost in this remote corner of nature and from the little cell in which he finds himself lodged, I mean the universe, let him estimate at their true value the earth, kingdoms, cities, and himself. What is man in the Infinite?[20]

And later:

> Unity added to infinity does not increase it at all, any more than a foot added to an infinite measurement: the finite is annihilated in the presence of the infinite and becomes pure nothingness. . . . If there is a God, he is infinitely beyond our comprehension, since, being visible and without limits, he bears no relation to us. . . . Let us say: 'Either God is or He is not'. . . . Reason cannot decide this question. Infinite Chaos separates us. At the far end of this infinite distance, a coin is being spun which will come down heads or tails. How will you wager? Reason cannot make you choose either, reason cannot prove either wrong.[21]

As is well known, Pascal substitutes the rationality of the wager for the rationality of knowledge. One cannot rationally prove God's existence or non-existence, but one can rationally prove that one must put one's stake wholly on the existence of God: 'Since you must necessarily choose, your reason is no more affronted by choosing one rather than the other. . . . But your happiness? Let us weigh up the gain and the loss involved in calling heads that God exists. Let us assess the two cases: if you win, you win everything, if you lose, you lose nothing.'[22]

Pascal asserts that man is suspended between the Zero and the Infinite, that is, between the internal and external infinitude. He also remarks that the single man is the Nothing, the Zero, for a unit added to the Infinite is Nothing. The latter description is closer to the life-experience of modern men and women. On the average, modern men and women do not understand the subtleties of physics or mathematics. But as much as they understand, namely that they as single persons do not matter, that their life has neither purpose nor significance, that they were thrown by accident into the infinite Necropolis,[23] into the infinite combination of indifferent dead matter or its equivalent, fills them with horror.

The wager restores teleology, but in a way entirely different from the teleological narrative. The teleological narrative tells us that the development of the World (History) has a purpose and that this purpose can be known; but it does not comfort us with offering a purpose to the life of every single individual in its own right. On the contrary, the inevitability of betting itself springs from the need to find a sense and a purpose (happiness) for our own single individual life and existence as well as from the insight into the limitedness of our knowledge. These are the two ways to cope with the terror of cosmic contingency on a speculative level. This explains why narrative teleology and teleology-through-wager are such entirely modern philosophical props. In all probability, they are the sole philosophical visions which were completely absent among the pre-moderns. Of course, whenever the speculative ground has been abandoned, and the ethico-practical implications of the teleological narrative or of reasoning in favour of the wager are being discussed, modern solutions follow certain pre-modern (sometimes not even marginal) positions. It is through the practical domain that the speculatively novel is linked with the tradition.

Wager and teleological narrative can be mutually exclusive and extreme, but they can also be combined, as in the model case of Kant[24] and many times since. The theme can be played out in several variations, from grand narratives to *petit recit*; it can be played in different tunes, from existential pathos to irony through scepticism. But I am not familiar with any other philosophical suggestions up until now which could compete with them as challenger of cosmic contingency.

Cosmic contingency can also be accepted as our human condition. Once it has been accepted, the possibility of re-introducing some kind of teleology into one's personal life or into the arithmetic of the universe has been discarded. There is no telos, there never was; there is no order, there never will be. There is no Reason other but our fallible mind. One is, indeed, Zero in the Necropolis called Universe. It is fraudulent to accept the contingency of all things natural and insist in the same breath on History being nonetheless purposeful. To accept contingency on the one hand and still cling to the objective purposefulness of human life on the other is the inauthentic way of facing contingency. For Kierkegaard is right: there is an either-or here.

The difference between the atheist and the disbeliever is that the former does not avoid the wager: he bets on contingency. To paraphrase Pascal: the atheist is 'calling tails' that God does not exist. The disbeliever, however, does not bet for or against God or Telos at all. Between the believer and the atheist, there is a kind of deep fraternity that has been recognized both by Kierkegaard and Dostoevsky. They both knew that everything hinges on the wager. The disbelievers, the sceptics, the agnostics are not regarded as members of this fraternity.

In Pascal's view, there are no good reasons to bet on contingency. However, for modern persons who do not care for eternal happiness but for freedom alone, there are such reasons. Providence appears for them as the main enemy of freedom, as the Absolute Whim that makes men puppets, moved by strings, as 'the iron hand of necessity [that] shakes the dice box of chance' [25]. One can draw edification, even pleasure, from the idea that one's life has no objective sense or purpose, that one is actually a Zero in the Infinitude, if one has good reasons to believe that there is no higher telos than the telos of the human mind. A Telos, Spirit, God (known or unknown, manifest or hidden) obstructs man's quest for absolute freedom. We, that is the human race in general, or we, the single persons, the great individuals, can do with this Earth and on this Earth just as we please, and we will conquer it entirely and absolutely. We are Nothing, but we, the modern Titans, will become Everything. Infinitude does not scare us; rather it invites us to conquer, and the universe, this Necropolis, is an inexhaustible arsenal of our weapons.

Many men and women are still 'calling tails' that God does not exist in order to reassert their freedom. But the most emphatic motivation of this wager, the quest for the deification of man, has lost its appeal and attraction. Ever since the two most murderous political regimes of our century practised their policy of genocide in the name of human omnipotence, the kind of freedom which is generally sought for is no longer attached to the project of deification of man. The freedom one gains by putting one's stakes on contingency is the freedom from all illusions rather than the freedom to achieve all. When Rorty says: 'Freedom is the recognition of contingency',[26] where he includes cosmic contingency in the concept of contingency, he simply means freedom from illusions, from hopes, a kind of Stoic freedom that requires courage.

But what if one refuses to enter into the wager? Is betting inevitable? Or is there a second-order wager, a bet between betting and not-betting? The second-order bet is not one between 'heads' or 'tails'. It requires that we should put all our stakes on non-betting as against both bets of the first-order wager ('calling heads' or 'calling tails'). One bets for not betting, one does not play the game, one is a spoilsport. One puts one's whole existence at stake against playing this game. One is not prepared to stake one's life, freedom, happiness or anything else on the existence or the non-existence of God, Spirit or Telos. On the contrary, one puts one's whole existence at the stake of accepting our ignorance as to the final truth concerning matters of cosmic contingency or destiny.

For the players of the first-order wager, the decision of non-participation can appear a mere attempt to avoid the unavoidable. But is the unavoidable avoidable? One can certainly live without being engaged in the wager, that is, without reflection, but not as a modern person who has already accepted the challenge, and who has already experienced the terror of cosmic contingency. For the thinking, really living person, the bet is unavoidable. Otherwise, one can dismiss the gesture to call 'heads' or 'tails' and remain in the state of indecision – not about calling 'heads' or 'tails', but about participating in the wager. One can avoid engagement in the wager for reasons of indifference, mental laziness or spiritual dumbness.

However, the second-order wager has nothing to do with the avoidance of the wager, for it is, after all, a wager. The spoilsport is not a gamewrecker, for she accepts the inevitability of betting the instant she stakes her life against betting on either 'heads' or 'tails'.

Pascal would ask at this point: what do you gain by entering the wager against calling heads or tails? You could gain happiness, felicity by calling simply 'heads'; why don't you do it? And Nietzsche could say: you might gain freedom by calling 'tails', why aren't you calling tails then?

What could one gain by betting against the unavoidability of calling either heads or tails? Perhaps nothing. What kind of a wager is this, then?

There is a ballad by Schiller, telling the story of a young knight desperately in love with a proud lady. He begs the lady to accept his love. She haughtily rejects him at first, but on second thought she throws her glove into the lion's den and says: if you return with my glove, I will love you. The knight enters the lion's den, stakes his life, picks up the glove and leaves unharmed; the lady declares herself ready to lend an ear to his declaration of love. But the knight throws the glove before the lady's feet, and leaves the place never to see her again.

In calling 'heads' one stakes one's life on the truth that it is God who is sending us into the lion's den so that we can prove our bravery and our love for him. In calling 'tails', one stakes one's life on the truth that we are thrown into the lion's den to get some unidentified gloves just for nothing. When I put all my stakes against both calling 'head', and calling 'tails', I do not express my indecision between 'heads' or 'tails', but my decision not to bet on either. Anyhow, a God, a Spirit or a Telos does not require our bet, nor does it claim back the glove from the lion's den.

Pascal, Kierkegaard and others contended that we could gain happiness by calling 'heads'; one can gain happiness as well if one bets against the wager. No real lover sends you into the lion's den, but if you are valiant, she will certainly love you for what you are and make you happy. Nietzsche, Marx and others said that we could gain freedom by calling 'tails'. But if one is thrown into the lion's den, rescues the glove of honour and remains unharmed, what does it add to one's freedom to know that the whole exercise was for nothing?

What certainly makes sense is to rescue the glove of honour which is thrown into the lion's den. There is an idea and purpose involved here, even if one chooses to accept human ignorance about the existence or non-existence of a cosmic or historical telos. Moreover, one puts one's whole life at stake by believing that rescuing the glove of honour lying in the sand of the lion's den makes sense, regardless of 'heads' or 'tails'.

This is freedom, but not the kind one achieves by recognizing contingency. Neither is it the kind of freedom that results in the deification of man: we were not calling 'tails'. If the glove of honour is rescued and the knight leaves unharmed, this is also happiness. But it is finite, not eternal happiness: we were not calling 'heads'.

It seems that I have unduly overstretched the metaphor of wager, and in bad taste. Once tossed, the coin falls either on heads or on tails, and there are no other ways to win but either by calling heads or tails. But betting against the wager can be as radical as other wagers; for one puts everything on one stake. But on what does one stake everything in the cosmic lottery where there is only 'heads' or 'tails'? One stakes everything on not staking anything in the cosmic lottery if, and only if, one chooses to act as if freedom or happiness, sense or meaning were not dependent on lottery, be it cosmic, social or private. This is an old commitment; Kant called it 'the primacy of practical reason'. Or, as Pascal said: 'All bodies together, and all minds together, and all their products, are not equal to the least feeling of charity. This is of an order infinitely more exalted.'[27]

3 Being Thrown into Freedom

Historico-social contingency is the human condition of modernity. There is no wager for or against this contingency, since there is no ignorance about it. Modern men and women are aware of their contingency, even if they are entirely unfamiliar with the concept, for they experience it. Modern thinking summarizes this experience, makes it manifest, reinforces it, reflects upon it.

Sartre, as a highly sensitive writer, provided us with several graphic phenomenological descriptions of contingency-experience. Here is one example of it: 'To be is to choose oneself; nothing comes to it either from the outside or from within which it can receive or accept. Without any help whatsoever, it is entirely abandoned to the intolerable necessity of making itself be – down to the slightest detail. Thus freedom is not a being; it is The Being of Man – i.e. his nothingness.'[28] Sartre's philosophical discussion of contingency does not match the power of his descriptions for many reasons, one of them being that he failed, at least in *Being and Nothingness*, by far his best book, to distiguish between cosmic and socio-historical contingency. But if one wants to exemplify the modern experience of contingency, Sartre's books lend themselves well to this purpose.

This kind of contingency experience can also be described in terms of Nothingness, of being Zero. But the experience of having been thrown into Nothing (or being held out into Nothing, as Heidegger once said [29] merges with the experience of not-being (or being-nothing) in an entirely different sense. One is Nothing, not in the sense of being determined by sheer chance, but in that of being-entirely-non-determined, completely empty. The horror of contingency arises not only, not even primarily, from the image of being the mere plaything of external forces, but also from the sense of total abandonment, of being left on one's own without the support of external forces. The anxiety of loneliness is the anxiety of emptiness. It is this anxiety that holds sway over modern men and women when they come to discover that they, and they alone, make themselves that which they become; and it hinges on them alone whether they become

anything at all. Freedom is the name of the Curse. Freedom is also
the name of infinite possibilities. Infinitude is nothing, for it is freedom. Curse and possibilities are identical: 'the first condition of
action, is freedom'.[30]

What has been termed the accident of birth is not contingency;
contingency is a modern phenomenon, whereas the accident of birth
is a pre-modern experience. Contingency is rather the dialectical
negation of the accident of birth. To paraphrase Hegel,[31] birth remains
accidental as long as the universality of the human race is not acknowledged. Since we are all born humans, to be born master or to be born
slave is a sheer accident. Accident means here, as elsewhere, external
determination. Nothing is inherent in the person himself or herself that
makes him or her master or slave. The dice has been thrown somewhere else. Men and women are born something, not nothing – they
are born master or slave. They are not born contingent, precisely
because they have been born something. Being born by accident determines one's possibilities. As long as men and women are born by
accident, they are not yet bundles of infinite possibilities. The accident
of birth determines one as a finite being. Finite beings are not free in
the sense that Sartre described freedom (qua contingency). One can be
born as a free citizen without being free (*être libre*).[32]

Contingency does not annul the accident of birth, but sublates it;
and still, contingency is the opposite of that accident. It is easy to
point out that moderns, too, receive a *bagage* at the moment of their
birth. One can draw better or worse in the genetic lottery by being
born with a strong or weak constitution, beautiful or ugly, better or
worse equipped with certain endowments which can be developed
into highly awarded talents. Equally, one can draw better or worse
in the social lottery by being born rich or poor, in an educated or
uneducated family, in a democracy or in a tyranny, at times and places
where one's best endowments are in great or in very little demand
respectively. But all these accidents together do not add up to contingency, the less since contingency, as infinite possibility, is neither
determined nor restricted by those accidents. Historico-social contingency is ontological; it is historico-ontological. This is nothing but
the re-formulation of the initial description of contingency as the
modern human condition.

Contingency has been said to be the opposite of teleology, and not
of determination, not even of essential determination. As long as the
accident of birth was the major constituent of the human condition,
human life had an initial telos; it was exactly by the accident of birth
that men and women were allotted their destiny. For example, a boy
born of Athenian citizens had to become what free Athenian citizens

were expected to become: the perfect Athenian gentleman. One received the model, the end, the final goal of the utmost achievement of one's life as a birthday present from whimsical powers. Men were guided by their restricted, limited possibilities; but guided they were. They were not thrown into freedom, nor were they thrown into Nothingness. They were rather placed into a pattern, the possibilities and limitations of which they learned in early childhood. They knew what they could do and what they should achieve; they were made, not self-made.[33]

Yet nothing, no thing is written on the cradle of the modern person.

Pre-modern persons were like letters thrown into one of many mailboxes at random, where all letters, thrown into the same mailbox, are addressed alike – they are supposed to arrive at the same point of destination. Thus, the accidental character of having been thrown in this mailbox rather than in the other could be easily concealed. If all letters thrown in the same mailbox are addressed alike, all letters can believe (if they have the capacity of thinking) that they were thrown in the same mailbox because they were sent to the same destination by some higher dispatcher. The mystical dispatcher can have different names: *moira, tyche* or God.

The modern person is also similar to letters thrown into different mailboxes at random, yet with no address written on them: they have no destination. The letters, so to speak, need to define their own destination themselves. They become their own dispatchers, or else dispatchers will take them from one address to another, and none of them will be the proper one. The envelope is blank. This means to be thrown into freedom or nothingness.

A person is the hero or the heroine of his or her own life-story. The hero and the heroine have a name. A name obliges or does not oblige. The name of a modern person is contingent, for it does not oblige. Modern men and women can change their name without being changed themselves; just as they can change their domicile, their country and, recently, also their sex. The novel of one's life is written chapter by chapter, in brief installments. And there will be no co-herence in it (in the manner there is in fiction) unless the author and protagonist, in one and the same person, opens up and thus limits his or her possibilities in the process of becoming free. Becoming free is the self-transformation of one's being-free (as nothing) into being free as being-oneself. More about this later.

The contingent person is a historical result. It is in the process of deconstructing the pre-modern social arrangement that men and women have become contingent. That all men and women are born free, and that they are equally endowed with reason and conscience,

is the foundational creed of the new, modern social arrangement.[34]
Once born into the modern social arrangement, girls and boys learn
very quickly that the envelopes are blank; this is simply taken for
granted. They also learn that they take responsibility for writing an
address on their respective envelopes. Anyone who asked a child:
'What do you want to be (to become) as a grown-up?' has already
reconfirmed contingency. For this question could never have been
asked of any child prior to the emergence of the modern social
arrangement.

Categories such as the 'significant other', or binary categories such
as 'inner- and outer-directedness'[35] would not make sense in the
pre-modern world, with the exception of periods of cataclysm or
abrupt socio-cultural change. The address on the envelope determined
who the significant others are: those who steer the newborn's life the
way they should, towards the pre-given end. When Jesus said that
you have to hate your father and mother and follow me, he had to
make a strong statement because he became the sole significant other
for his disciples by completely re-writing their addresses. Becoming a
significant other out of the blue was a dangerous venture, even if the
unusual significant other did not undertake to re-write the addresses
of his disciples entirely, as we see in the case of Socrates. At the same
time, Socrates is the most typical and unusual ancient model of
inner-directedness, or of finite subjectivity, to use Hegel's expression.

'Outer' and 'inner' directedness is not differentiated whenever the
envelope is properly addressed. The so-called others, those who direct
a person, *represent* their own address. The representative other (the
significant other in the pre-modern world) is never accidental.

Contingent persons are not determined by the accident of birth; but
their significant others are accidental, and they are not representative.
It is precisely because the envelope is blank that fathers and mothers
are no longer the main representative others. Their name carries no
obligation for their children, neither do the parents' traditions, their
country, their occupation, their political affiliation or their property.
It can take a while for the child to discover that one's significant
others are chosen together with one's destiny and that parents can
become significant others only if one re-chooses them. Those who
never discover this, never become self-destined.

We – modern men and women – are normally influenced by a much
greater number of 'others' than were our pre-modern ancestors, and,
for the most part, for a far shorter time (compared with the duration
of life). We are also dependent on far more others, and far more
others are dependent on us also, through our participation in functionally organized institutions, as required by modern life. Today a

person influences us or we influence him, tomorrow we forget his name and face, or even that he ever existed. Today we are eager to attract the attention of a person (who depends on us, on whom we depend or who appeals to us) but once we enter another institution, or if another appeals to us also, we shall never again be interested in attracting this person's attention, for the person will lose all significance.

We adjust quickly to this situation. Today we love one, tomorrow another. If our friendship is under stress, we do not invest much effort in its restoration. Moderns become increasingly reluctant to 'work on relationships'; it is easier to leave behind one attachment and establish another than to put too much of an effort in the restoration of the old one. Several hundred (or thousand) others interact with us without ever becoming significant.

Other-directedness means to act exclusively under the influence of, or together with, insignificant others, to say what they expect us to say, to adjust. Other-directedness can also be termed conformism. Men and women who conform to the expectations of insignificant others can also be described as one-dimensional.[36] To be one-dimensional means to have no depth, no internal space (*innerliches Raum*), to use Hegel's expression.

Inner-directedness is self-destining, and, as we shall see, it requires that one risk everything. But inner-directedness should not be mistaken for narcissism, self-centredness.[37] Many a thing can be the source of inspiration, but the 'ego' is not one of them. However, there is no inner-directedness without the contribution of significant others. Others become significant for a person insofar as their contribution to the person's life leaves an indelible mark on the very process of this person's 'self-becoming'.

Epicurus said once that to live in necessity is misery, but it is not necessary to live in necessity.[38] A paraphrase of Epicurus's maxim for modern use would read as follows: to live in contingency is misery, but it is not contingent to live in contingency. If contingency is truly the modern condition, then it is also true that to live in contingency is non-contingent. But is it indeed miserable to live in contingency? – not more and not less than living in necessity.[39]

4 From Contingency to Destiny

Contingency is an existential experience; the question of contingency is an existential question. Science cannot raise this question, let alone answer it.

The question of cosmic contingency is eminently speculative and not practical in nature. The issue at stake is the presence or absence of cosmic (universal) telos. Although the question is speculative, the human interest vested in the answer(s) to this question is not. Neither the satisfaction of the desire for more knowledge nor the drive of curiosity spur modern men and women to find an answer to this question. The quest can be described in terms of the subject-object relationship, for it is the subject (the person) who makes a passionate quest for certainty, for truth. But this subject-object relationship is not epistemological in nature, for the answer to this question cannot be squeezed out of the object (whatever that may be). One could say with Kierkegaard[40] that Truth is subjective in a general sense, and that the proposition refers to all kinds of truth. In this case true knowledge (in its interpretation in terms of the correspondence theory of truth) becomes truth if it becomes 'subjective', but it can remain true (or false) knowledge without becoming truth to any individual subject or collectivity. The kind of Truth that cannot be supported by true knowledge of any kind is by definition subjective in the sense that true knowledge is absent from it. But if people in general seek a kind of certainty that cannot be supported by true knowledge of any kind, the motive to seek certainty is not subjective in an epistemological sense, and it cannot be located in the accidental constitution of single individuals. Such a motive is somehow ontological. Kant made a very similar statement when he described the need for metaphysics as ineradicable from the human mind. To seek an answer to the question of cosmic teleology, or the lack thereof, is a metaphysical question of the Kantian sort. The antinomies, however, cannot be resolved by dividing the universe into phenomenon and noumenon. They remain unresolved in the human mind, and if one enters the wager there is nothing else but an 'either-or'. Even to bet against the wager is not, or not necessarily, a Kantian move.

A speculative attitude, a passionate quest for truth, where the subject-object relation has no epistemological value, is existential. The issue at stake, the motivation for the quest, and the quest itself (whatever form it takes) are all existential. At stake in the quest is our own existence: the sense or the meaning of our life, of history, of the universe – our happiness and our freedom.

The existential relationship is thus a subject-object relationship without epistemological value. It is difficult to deny the centrality of this relationship and of the existential experience in general. But one can still relegate this experience to a lower position and deny its claims to ultimacy. That was Hegel's game. In his repeated criticism of Kant and of German Romanticism, Hegel, among others, attributed contingency-experience to a not yet entirely mature modern imagination that had already been overcome. The highest position is taken by the culmination point of the grand narrative where the spirit, returning to itself, discovers not only the historicity, but also the one-sidedness and rigidity of this experience. Although overcome, the contingency experience is not entirely false or lacking in truth. In the Hegelian speculative framework, where cosmic and historical teleology are entirely restored, the initial contingency of the single persons in the modern world is never seriously questioned. The Spirit returns to itself as Absolute Spirit, and not as subjective, not even as objective spirit. But it is difficult to re-transform the subject-object relationship into an onto-epistemological one without denying full recognition to the person's social and historical contingency. Hegel also re-invented man's and woman's destiny as one having been written on the envelope. But this time the whole address was not given, merely the postal code with the name of the post office box where the letter will certainly be dispatched: *Sittlichkeit*.

Neither cosmic nor socio-historical contingency can be wished away.

Cosmic contingency is the existential experience of modernity, because no science, not even the science of philosophy, can produce an answer that would settle the problem of telos positively or negatively for any other person but the philosopher himself. Each person needs to go through the experience of contingency, each of them needs to cope with it on his or her own. Each can bet 'heads' or 'tails' or put all their stakes on betting against the wager. But no prior bet can determine, nor even influence, any single act of successive betting. Every person bets on his or her own. The bet itself results in certitude, and nothing is more certain than certitude. At the same time, one is and remains aware of having been party to a wager. These two elements – certitude or the certitude of uncertainty on the one hand, and the awareness that certitude resulted from the wager and not from objective 'proof' provided by empirical evidence or by rational inference – need to be kept in balance. Both elements have to be present simultaneously and fully. This is how one copes with the experience of cosmic contingency.

The question of socio-historical contingency is eminently practical. There is no knowledge of cosmic contingency, but there is knowledge of social contingency. The soul is filled with horror not because the question of whether blind chance rules the world or whether all things, including human beings, serve some higher purpose, cannot be decided. As far as social contingency is concerned, it is rather the infinitude of our initial possibilities, freedom as nothingness, that makes modern men and women tremble in their boots. With regard to social contingency, there is no 'thing in itself'. One knows that one has been thrown into freedom, that one's life has no pre-set destination, that one is, or is supposed to be, the master of one's own destiny. What one does not know is precisely one's destiny.

Destiny means telos ('the end we should achieve') as well as fate ('the end that visits upon us'). Achilles wept over his destiny to die young; his horse wept along with him. Achilles knew his destiny in both of its interpretations. The moderns, being thrown into freedom, have no prior knowledge of their destiny in either of the two interpretations – not because they are ignorant, but because they do not 'have' a destiny. Born by accident, as all human beings are, they are a number resulting from several unconnected throws of the dice, issued from the *causa efficiens* without a *causa finalis*.

It is widely held that modern men and women are masters of their own destiny. They are supposed to make themselves, to clear their own path in the jungle of infinite possibilities according to their plans. They are supposed to design their goal and to devise their so-called 'life-strategy'. But this is a false picture. Men do not 'create' themselves in the way they manufacture an omnibus. They can daydream about their future self and design futuristic novels with themselves as protagonists of the plot in their phantasy. But they cannot possibly know their telos ahead of time, and without being aware of the goal, no strategy can be devised. The goal of the war is to win, to be victorious; it is the goal that defines the strategy. But to win one's life is not a goal, rather a wish, and no strategy can be designed for wish-fulfilment.

Let us, however, assume for a moment that it is possible to conceive of an end-purpose for one's life in advance. Men and women have to act, they have to choose among a great variety of possibilities every day. Given that the goal of life is fixed in advance, every single choice will become a mere means towards the achievement of that end. But if every step one takes, every decision one makes, remains a means (without becoming an end-in-itself), life will never develop a teleological pattern. The goal will remain extraneous to the actions which are supposed to lead up to it. Internal (non-instrumental, objective) teleology is holistic insofar as it permeates everything, be it spiritual or material, simple or complex. The whole is present in each and every step, for it is omnipresent.

Perceived teleologically, human life, historicity, is a whole. As a consequence, the goal (end-purpose) of a human life cannot be localized or temporalized as something which is bound 'to be there' or to happen 'at the end'. The end must be there all along the path. But if the end is at the end, it is 'not there' all along the path. Along the path, one encounters only means to that end, means which are of equal value insofar as they are evaluated as the means to the end. Under such conditions, men and women could choose themselves only after having arrived at the finish line, for it is only at the end that they become themselves. But can a person ever say (before the moment of his death) that he has already attained the goal of his life? As long as one has not achieved the goal of life, the goal (end) will remain external to oneself, that is, to one's life and to all of one's choices. Moreover, not all means chosen for the end will be the right means to that end – they could just as well be the wrong ones. One or another choice can turn out so disastrous that the actor needs to start from scratch. Disasters or unreasonable choices in general will not be incorporated into the person's life and whole existence; they remain lamentable, but perhaps corrigible, mistakes. To be sure, calculation, right or wrong, is not everything. One can possess the perfect design, nevertheless, the repeated throws of unconnected dice can cross all purposes or bring unexpected fulfilment for some, but not for others. The powers of chance can be brushed aside by life-strategies today as little as they could be yesterday.

The model of life-strategy is supposed to describe what people do if they 'make' (manufacture) themselves, and it lays bare the weaknesses of technological imagination in rendering justice to teleology. Those who 'make' themselves in principle will never actually make themselves whenever the powers of chance cross their calculations. Acting under the delusion of 'making' themselves, modern men and women in fact abandon themselves to the capricious lottery of good or bad luck as well as to their own fragile capacity of prediction. It is entirely illusory that one can calculate well by trying to choose the proper means for the end result of one's life strategy. Since there are always several possibilities to choose from, sometimes even a practically infinite number of combinations, life-choices are, in fact, very much unlike technological choices. So many factors need to be taken into consideration that, should people do what they are supposed to be doing, they could never get to action, for they could never decide what to do first. Moderns are far more engaged in constant reflection than pre-moderns were. This observation is shared by Hegel and Kierkegaard alike. Since there are good arguments for several courses of action, if men ruminate all the time over the strategic or pragmatic viability of a course of action as against the other, they will continue reflection *ad infinitum*. The everyday wisdom that only he who never acts will never make a mistake is banal but true.

Let me rephrase what has been said above in a more direct and blunt fashion: pursuing a life strategy, and thus 'making ourselves' is little more than a stunt of self-delusion. One cannot make choices continuously on the basis of reflection carried out in full, and one does not need to make, nor will one make, exclusively rational choices in the spirit of rational choice theories. If someone were able to 'make oneself' that way and to live according to a consistent life strategy, one would become a perfect computing machine but not a human being.

To be sure, modern men and women are like letters, put or thrown into an unaddressed envelope, possessing an empty freedom of nothingness. In a manner of speaking, the letters will be 'self-addressing' and 'self-addressed', or else the envelopes will remain blank until the dispatcher picks them up from one of the dark street corners to throw them into the rubbish bin. This is the second throw.

And yet the idea that men create themselves, clumsy as it may be, is not that far off the mark. Men and women do not make themselves, but rather they choose themselves. As Kierkegaard once remarked, one does not choose Christianity, one chooses to become a Christian, one chooses oneself as a Christian. The choice of oneself is the gesture that triggers the internal teleology of one's life. Choosing oneself is tantamount to addressing one's own envelope. The hitherto blank envelope will now bear the name of the person (the letter) as that of the being that becomes what he or she is. The letter contains the description of the accidental aggregate of unconnected throws of dice that the naked person is. Calling 'heads' will not cover one's nudity. One can see a divine ordinance in the throw, recognize the writing on the wall or decipher the mysterious hieroglyphs of a cosmic order from it and still fall short of transforming one's contingency into one's destiny.

To address one's own letter to oneself is the fundamental choice that limits the possibilities, as much as it pre-destines the probabilities, of all consecutive choices. The fundamental choice is termed existential choice by Kierkegaard, because it is by this choice that the essence of one's existence becomes determined. Existence is prior to essence. By choosing oneself, a person becomes *causa sui* and *finis sui* and as such, essential.

R. G. Collingwood recollects his existential choice in his autobiography. As a boy, he bumped by chance into Kant's book on the metaphysics of morals; he started to read it and did not understand it.

Disgraceful to confess, here was a book whose words were English and whose sentences were grammatical, but whose meaning baffled me.

Then. . .came the strangest emotion. . .I felt that the contents of this
book, although I could not understand it, were somehow my business:
a matter personal to myself, or rather to some future self of my own.
It was not like the common boyish intention to 'be an engine-driver
when I grow up', for there was no desire in it; I did not, in any natural
sense of the word, 'want' to master the Kantian ethics when I should
be old enough; but I felt as if a veil had been lifted and my destiny
revealed. . . . There came upon me by degrees, after this, a sense of
being burdened with a task whose nature I could not define except by
saying, 'I must think'. What I was to think about I did not know; and
when, obeying this command, I fell silent and absent-minded in
company, or sought solitude in order to think without interruption, I
could not have said, and still cannot say, what it was that I actually
thought. . . . I know now that the problems of my life's work were
taking, deep down inside me, their first embryonic shape.[41]

Choosing oneself (as a philosopher, in the case of Collingwood)
resembles not the choice of a strategic aim ('I want to be an engine-
driver when I grow up'), but it can best be described as becoming
oneself in an 'embryonic shape'. Through the existential choice and
during its course (in experiencing 'the strangest emotion') the person
becomes what he is to become, namely the *dynamis* of his own
energeia/ergon. Dynamis is an active potentiality, not a propensity
that slumbers. If one becomes, through the existential choice, 'burdened with the task' of 'I must think', then one begins to think, one is
in fact already thinking, one cannot help being absorbed by thinking.
Should one stop thinking, one would not simply stop doing something, but also stop being oneself, developing oneself towards one's
own destination. One is carried away by one's destination, one is
sucked towards it by a whirlwind as it were, while one embraces
destiny with existential pathos. One is identical with one's destination
and at the same time non-identical, for one is constantly becoming.
Hegel's World Spirit seems as if it had made an existential choice.

Existential choice is not a choice between two (or more) alternatives. It is neither a rational nor an irrational choice. Had the boy
Collingwood asked himself the question what would be the most
suitable profession for him, once grown up (professor of philosophy,
engine-driver, fiction writer, minister of a local parish etc.), he ought
to have considered many factors, such as his talents, the wishes of his
parents, prospective salary rates, social preferences and much else. He
would have weighed pluses against minuses. He would then have
assessed all such professions by his value preferences such as freedom,
security, adventure, tradition and much else. Finally, in all probability, though not by any compelling necessity, he would have chosen

the profession that promised the optimal combination of spiritual, economic and social benefits. This would have been a rational choice which he could have subsequently regretted, for what seemed advantageous at the time might have turned out to be to his disadvantage.

But Collingwood did nothing of the kind; he did not consider alternatives. Similarly to Marcel Proust of *Remembrance of Things Past*, who, while nibbling at a piece of madeleine-cake, soaked in tea, suddenly chooses to become what he is, the writer of his own life-story,[42] Collingwood, while looking into a book he did not understand, was overcome with the emotion that a task was awaiting him in life, that it was his task, that he was wedded to it, that he was identical with it. A rational choice can be rationally changed, though if it is too frequently changed, contingency will return with a detour. However, an existential choice is not to be changed, which is why it is termed existential. One cannot develop towards anything else but what one already is, what is one's own *dynamis*. Sometimes an existential choice happens to be abandoned, although not changed. By abandoning his existential choice, the person loses himself and is thrown back into freedom-as-nothing.

The gesture of self-choice is the experience of subject-object identity. Trying to interpret the experience that eludes explanation, Kierkegaard introduced the word 'instant', which is the crossing-point of time and eternity. The subject is the gesture of choice and the object is oneself that is to be chosen. But subject and object are not there before the choice; they become subject-object in the 'instant' where they are also sublated. This is an approximate (and perhaps wrong) description given that the instant is the crossing-point of time and eternity. But no better description is available, because there is only approximation.

The object of the choice is the letter in the envelope: the human person is the aggregate of many unrelated throws of the dice. The gesture of existential choice is the gesture of addressing the envelope. The envelope is addressed to oneself. This is, approximately speaking, what happens in the instant. A destiny is chosen; the subject addresses the letter to its own contingency as nothingness; destiny and contingency become one and the same, that is, contingency has been destined. The envelope is not addressed to 'Robin Collingwood', but to 'Robin Collingwood the thinker', whereas at the outset the letter is a young man named 'Robin Collingwood', who can become everything as well as remain nothing; Robin Collingwood the 'throw', the freedom as a bunch of open possibilities, the nothingness. This freedom as nothingness is a complex text or a composite of accidental forces and events (among others, R. G. Collingwood is born with weak blood-vessels, prone to frequent strokes, he is an offspring of parents who respect intellectual achievements, and so on).

By choosing themselves, men and women choose exactly what they are, as they are. They choose their best talents as much as their physical and psychological handicaps, they choose their parents, their childhood, their country, their historical age. They choose their poverty if they happen to be born poor, and their riches if they happen to be born rich. They choose all their accidental features. That which they are by accident they will become by choice. This is how *causa sui* and *finis sui* merge. Their teleology is set. They are no longer contingent. They have transformed their contingency into destiny. It cannot be repeated frequently enough that the person who chooses herself, has chosen herself as the throw *in toto*, although the throw is also negated as an open and empty possibility. Should a single feature of the throw's accident remain unchosen, the person would still be exposed to external determinations, being at the mercy of the powers of chance, never to become its own destiny.

The question of 'who is (the power) that throws' is not being asked here, for it is irrelevant. The choice of ourselves is practical, since we choose our destiny, our destination, our teleology, and not the telos of the cosmos or the end (the final goal) of history.

To assert that existential choice is the only way to overcome historico-social contingency is neither the corroboration nor the refutation of the traditional philosophy of the subject, or of any other kind of epistemological Cartesianism. An existential category is not an epistemological category. The question concerning the sources of our own existence is left wide open, so is the question concerning the content of one's telos and the sources of this content. Whether one subscribes to the intersubjective constitution of the world or to the *ego cogito* as the foundation of knowledge has no bearing on this issue. Collingwood, an idiosyncratic intersubjectivist, marginalized by the English academic philosophical milieu, is a case in point.

There are many kinds of existential choices. I distinguish between two major kinds: existential choice under the category of difference, and existential choice under the category of the universal. Collingwood's choice was an existential choice under the category of difference (he chose himself as a philosopher, just as someone else can choose himself as a politician, yet another again as a lover, etc., but all of them choosing difference). The existential choice under the category of the universal is the moral choice. If one chooses oneself as a good, decent person, one makes an existential choice under the category of the universal. In so choosing, the person becomes what he or she already is, a good and decent person.[43] The choice is universal, for decency is not a particular vocation; anyone can choose themselves as a decent person. This is also the only existential choice that is never revoked or abandoned. Once one becomes what one is (decent and good), one cannot wish to unmake this choice or to regret that it had once been made.

The existential choice is not a bet. Collingwood did not participate in a wager where he could have called heads or tails. He did not bet on philosophy, he chose himself as a philosopher. Conversely, the existential wager is not a choice. One does not choose Providence or the infinitude of the Necropolis when one is calling 'heads' or 'tails'. Furthermore, the party calling 'tails' is making just as much of a bet as the person calling 'heads'; one puts one's stakes on the infinite Necropolis no less than one puts one's stakes on cosmic teleology or on Providence. Conversely, if one chooses existentially (by choosing oneself as such and such), one has already established the inherent telos of one's own life. There is no choice vis-à-vis a telos; avoiding or relinquishing the existential choice is what leaves people in a situation of contingency, living their lives at random, without telos.[44]

There are still striking similarities between the existential wager and the existential choice. Both cut across the 'bad infinity' of reflection. Both can be described with the Kierkegaardian metaphor as the leap. I mention 'the leap' and not 'a leap'. Given that the chain of reflection is practically infinite in the case of every choice, given further that not all arguments and counter-arguments, not all factors that promote or hinder choice can be entirely considered, the person who does not want to postpone decisions *ad calendas Graecas*, hoping that finally all residual counter-arguments will be properly answered (which never happens anyway), must venture, by finally embarking on action, to leap. Every choice is also a kind of leap. One can leap, and then, in an after-thought, one can try to undo the choice, to leap back; one can do this repeatedly. Choices can only retrospectively be entirely confirmed by the person who chooses. If the choice comes off, it is re-confirmed, if it does not, one will come to grief and try something else; or, if it is too late, one will constantly brood over the missed opportunities. On the membrane of remembrance, one's own life will occur as a chain of accidental choices, failed purposes, unused possibilities. Similarly, if many of the choices are prospectively corroborated: although doing well, one feels one could have done much better.

Contingency feeds on the dissatisfaction of modern men and women; constancy in dissatisfaction is the manifestation of contingency. Achilles was sad when he knew that he was going to die young, but not dissatisfied. Avoiding the wager, unless one bets against the wager, shows a similar pattern. One moment one 'believes' in God and His providential dispensations, the other moment one finds far more satisfaction from being the inmate of the infinite Necropolis. One switches from one 'view' to the other 'view'; the bet is replaced by the changing 'point of view' because it is comfortable to remain undecided or because one does not care or does not seem to care. Switching from one 'view' to the other is undoubtedly also a leap, but a pathetic one. In so doing, one does not leap over an abyss, but over a crack in the asphalt.

The fundamental leap (the existential wager or the existential choice) is a leap over an abyss, and this is not a quantitative matter. To leap over the abyss is the metaphor that tries to sensitize the enormity of the risk one takes. One puts the whole of one's life, freedom and happiness at stake.

The participants in the existential wager stake their life, happiness and freedom on the Truth of the Being (or the Non-Being) of that which throws. The participants in the bet against the wager (in the second-order wager) put everything at stake on the primacy of the existential choice against the existential wager, that is, on the primacy of the practical. For historico-social contingency can be sublated only on the practical plain. The antinomies of our socio-historical existence are resolved when we embark on the development of our inherent telos; the antinomies of our cosmic contingence can remain, nevertheless, unresolved. This is what the Kantian 'primacy of practical reason' can mean for the (post-)modern mind.

5 History as Contingency

Whether there is Reason in History or there is none, is yet another of those questions to which the sciences, or philosophy as a science, can offer no answer. The question is primarily existential, and it is epistemological or ontological in a secondary sense only, if at all. Men and women are accidental results of unconnected throws of dice, and they are born as empty possibilities, as nothingness. Their blank envelopes are thrown into various letter boxes. If only they could fathom that all these letter boxes are sub-boxes of one single huge letter box that could be termed History, and that the overarching letter box is properly addressed, they could make sense of their lives even if their own envelopes remained blank. As single entities, they are accidental, dispensable and of no, or of minor, importance. But they are thrown on to the world stage, where the actors follow the script, and where even the minor roles have to be allotted to someone, where, as in all theatres, the understudies have to stand in reserve, in case something happens to the actors. But in order to interpret one's situation like this, the play still must be on, and the end still must be open. This is a paradoxical situation. Had the main letter box been opened in the present, one would know the end, but one would not be edified by this knowledge. For the understudies, or the actors of minor roles, this kind of 'reason in history' is plainly unreason. If the addressee to whom the letter box has to be delivered is a future world, the future script has to be known, and this can only be achieved by being certain that one is the author of this script. This expectation is almost analogous to a representative kind of existential choice. It is assumed in this kind of choice that a group of people, a class or a generation can choose itself, can address its own letter to itself, and it can thus transform its contingency into its destiny.[45] But an existential choice (and the subject-object identity as it appears in the 'instant') is not the gesture of 'recognition' or recollection. The knowledge that shines through is rather vague here, and it is by no means knowledge about the past or the future. It is, to repeat, an experience, and collective actors do not experience collectively. No one can make an existential choice for, or instead of, another person, even if they happen to live in close togetherness. No one can destine another person absolutely, so that she transforms the other person's contingency into the other person's destiny.

Actors on the stage of the present are not authors of a script that will be put on stage in a future theatre, although each actor can be the author of his or her own destiny. This is no novelty. But the hunger for overcoming contingency, growing together with the increasing awareness of contingency, makes old wisdoms look like foolishness. This is why the science that claims to know the script of the future theatre is embraced.

It comes as no surprise that Hegel's 'reason in history' satisfied no one; it is only in philosophy that we accept payment in the currency of tautology. It is equally a small wonder that the interpretation of the Marxian 'laws of history' in terms of 'reason in history', from Lukács through Merleau-Ponty,[46] satisfied many. The Marxian promise satisfied the existential need, the very motivation of those people who raise questions about the reason in history, whereas the Hegelian answer did not. By now, the Marxian answer and all its versions have also become entirely discredited.

But is the proposition 'There is Reason in History' false? Can one assert with certitude that there is no Reason in History? To these questions we do not know the answer. We are thus thrown back into the wager. To shrug our shoulders and say: 'there might be reason in history as well as might not, and who cares?' is the gesture of avoiding the wager.

Lucien Goldmann, a scholar of Pascal, understood this constellation. He knew that he was party to an existential wager, and he put his stakes on the existence of 'reason in history'.[47] But if one bets, one bets absolutely; no croupier in this game will accept a reduced stake. The question is: heads or tails? And one cannot answer: heads in something, tails in another thing. Heads or tails? Either there is telos in (of) the universe, and then there is also Reason in History, or there is none, and then there is no Reason in History either.

The reduced bet, unacceptable for the croupier, is a subtle form of avoiding the wager. Imagine the story: as a result of the accidental combination of accidents in the infinite Necropolis, *homo sapiens* has emerged. Man is rational insofar as s/he acts according to his or her projects (goals). It follows from this that the development – the History – of this race is rational, teleological in character, that the stories of this race unfold according to a hidden pattern, plot or script, and that this plot develops in direction of the End-purpose, towards the fully attained telos of the race. Kant, this most critical of modern minds, was absolutely aware of the invalidity of the alleged 'inference'. He replaced the fraudulent inference with the idea of reason, and later with teleological judgement.[48] Marx's greatest attempt to leap over the theoretical abyss in the *Paris Manuscripts* was a representative fiasco. He bet on the Necropolis, and he conceived of a human race which, by creating itself, created itself as an 'embryo' in a manner of speaking. This embryo cannot develop but by unfolding its own telos. For the young Marx, it was the race that made the existential choice of becoming *in nuce* what it will become in a fully developed state, at the End.[49] But the mythological extension of the existential choice does not work. In Marx (as for many others before and after him) the human race as infinite possibility, as emptiness, as Nothingness, is just the accidental product of the infinite 'throws' of Necropolis. The human race cannot establish its own telos at all. So, there is but Either/Or, heads or tails in general, and not in bits and pieces. One can bet 'heads' or 'tails' absolutely. And one can also be party to the second-order wager, in putting everything at stake for not betting 'heads' or 'tails'. The second-order wager offers the bet for the primacy of the existential choice.

What can a philosopher do if he puts all his stakes against the wager? More specifically, what follows from the existential choice of a person, who, like Collingwood, chose himself as a philosopher? In becoming what he is, a philosopher, must he not bet either heads or tails? It is, perhaps, better suited to the game of philosophy to bet either 'heads' or 'tails', but one can also become a philosopher if one bets against the wager, as best exemplified by Kant's towering figure.

The question of contingency versus teleology may be termed anthropocentric. Only human beings are *existers*.[50] Only existers ask existential questions. Only existers bet. Only existers are thrown (into). I will term the Letter Box, the locus of the throw, History. 'Locus' does not stand for destination. The letter box gathers, but does not sort out or dispatch the letters. Men and women are thrown into History. This History (with capital H) is not to be confused with another History (equally writ large), i.e. the grand narrative termed Universal History, the totalizing teleological rendering of the story of the human race. History, as interpreted here, is not to be confused with histories (writ small), with all stories told about one or another people, their deeds and their fate.[51] This History (writ large) is neither a grand narrative nor a heroic saga nor just a *petit recit*; in fact, it is not a narrative at all, but an existential condition. Men and women are thrown into a World, but only by having been thrown into History do they have a world. Animals are also thrown into the World, but since they are not thrown into History, they do not have a world. 'Being thrown into History' is historicity. Historicity copes with the existential condition of having been thrown into a World.

Although History should not be confused with the grand narrative, the heroic saga or *le petit recit*, all of them equally work upon History. We are thrown into different letter boxes and dispatched from them to different destinations. All narratives, grand or small, make sense out of the throw, the dispatch and the destination. They are the Parcas who spin the threads of accident into strands and weave the strands into the regular patterns of a tapestry.

Philosophy of (our) history is a kind of a narrative, and even if it is not, it relies upon narratives, grand or small. Philosophy of history weaves a tapestry, or plays with mosaics, sometimes with many (different) mosaics, or, alternatively, it employs narratives as a point of reference, as empirical evidence, as interpretandum, or just as the text to be deconstructed. Can a philosopher who does not know the answer as to whether 'heads' or 'tails' will come up, who is engaged in the wager or who bets against the wager, design a tapestry, refer to it, interpret it, or even deconstruct it?

One can tell a meaningful story, or several meaningful stories, even if one puts one's stakes on radical contingency. Actually, as far as sheer story-telling is concerned, the bet can be bracketed. Pascal's example of radical contingency can be easily fitted into an entirely teleological order. After all, Cleopatra's nose could have been shaped by God, in order to serve His higher purpose, the divine blueprint for the fate of Rome. On the other hand, contingency is not the opposite of determination. On the contrary, chance events are believed to be determined by the sheer coincidence of many different, and heterogeneous, chains of determination. The nose of Cleopatra is a coincidence which crosses many other chains of determination; some of these crossings are intended, while others are not. Story-telling explores causes and effects, interprets wills and designs, and this is how it makes both structures and events intelligible. Every story sublates accidents by interpretation and explanation. Story-telling makes sense, it renders meaning – but it does not necessarily sublate contingency. The experience of purposefulness without purpose, attributed by Kant to the perception of beauty, is by no means characteristic of our experience of history. There is no purposefulness in the story of *Iliad*, and what kind of purposefulness can anyone detect in the war of the roses or of the industrial revolution? Most historical narratives depict human (subjective) purposes, frequently crossing others and being crossed themselves. They portray human vices and virtues, explain events by chance determinations and by the operation of institutions. The way in which the potentialities of an institution or a social structure develop towards actuality, without detecting any 'purpose' in the interplay of different and simultaneously operative heterogeneous structures, can also be depicted. A universalistic salvation story (*Heilsgeschichte*) and its counterpart, a universalistic damnation story (*Verfallsgeschichte*), alone are impregnated throughout by teleology.

Petits recits of different kinds can be composed, colourful mosaics can be conjured up from toying with the kaleidoscope and none of them will have anything to do with the preceding or the following pattern. But can philosophy be so self-restricted? A language game that disqualifies all queries about the sense, the meaning, the purpose of existence at the very outset, is not philosophy. Whether one terms the satisfaction of the need for unrestricted speculation philosophy or 'thinking', makes no difference in this context.[52] The satisfaction of this need calls for the kind of speculation that faces precisely the questions of sense, meaning and purpose. But these are foundationalist questions; moreover, they are questions about the ultimate foundation.

All philosophers discuss the ultimate question. Metaphysicians are philosophers who disclose the truth about the ultimate; this is what the phrase 'ultimate foundation' means. Post-metaphysicians are philosophers who are engaged in the wager. Regardless of whether they are calling 'heads' or 'tails' – they remain constantly engaged in nothing but the ultimate. To be constantly engaged in the ultimate without disclosing the truth about the ultimate – this is exactly the wager.

Calling 'heads' or calling 'tails' puts philosophers into a very paradoxical situation. Regardless of their bet, they put all their stakes, their life, their freedom and happiness at stake. If one stakes everything (on either 'heads' or 'tails'), there is a tremendous temptation to arrive at the ultimate foundation. Once one has already staked the whole of one's existence on that wager, one cannot say: 'it is not proven', 'the mind cannot grasp it', 'it is only a bet'. A philosopher who can live and think through this paradox, is the greatest of them all. I would recall for the last time Kierkegaard's remark on Hegel: had Hegel presented his *Science of Logic* as a thought experiment, he would have been the greatest philosopher of all times. He should have said in the preface: in what follows, I am calling 'heads' in the existential wager. If one can only speak so, or do so without speaking, one can still design the complete tapestry of history, of the universe, of the Being of beings – you name it.

Philosophers who bet against the wager do not avoid discussing the ultimate, but they discuss it in negative terms. The ultimate question is not less ultimate for them than for those who are calling 'heads' or 'tails'. But they are aware of the paradox involved in calling 'heads' or 'tails' – the paradox that consists of incessantly discussing something that is inaccessible to human intelligence. One should rather remain silent about the ultimate – this is their choice. And they put their life, happiness and freedom at stake in so betting. Their existential situation is also paradoxical. Since they discuss the Ultimate in negative terms (also in their silences), they have to resist the temptation to design the tapestry of history or of the universe; after all, they did not bet on either 'heads' or 'tails'. But it is difficult to resist the temptation to engage in the grand design for someone who has put all his life, happiness and freedom at stake in a wager. And yet, this temptation has to be resisted, unless one engages in another wager, this time in a primary one (in calling 'heads' or 'tails'). Still, the existential commitment cannot be adandoned – for the existential wager is about the ultimate. The person who forgets this, even for a moment, has already taken back her existential commitment and ceases to be a philosopher, an 'existing thinker' or just a 'thinker' – you name it.[53] Relativism is not an epistemological position, but the philosophical manifestation of avoiding the wager. Relativists are the cowards of thinking.

2
Lived History, Utopia, Apocalypse, Marche Funèbre

1 Spectacle or Lived History; Historical Space; The Close and the Far; The Depth and the Surface; Behind and Ahead

The spectacle is watched from the window, from the rows of the theatre or from a chair in front of the television screen. Something happens, or has happened, or is going to happen out there which does not happen here and now. Something happens or has happened or is going to happen with others which does not happen with us. In a 'live' spectacle, the present is presented; recollection here plays no role. Recollection re-collects past stories, once coherent but now dispersed, and fits them again into an intelligible whole. In the re-collective spectacle, it is the past that is being presented or re-presented. Recollection is not remembrance, for it is not from the traces on the membrane of memory that recollection re-collects its stories. Those who recollect did not live the stories they now recollect – they know about them or they have read about them. They fashion, select and interpret the lived history of others. In a representative spectacle, manoeuvres of this kind have a restricted scope; the originary story (the myth) can only be modified within strict limits.[1]

Thomas Mann remarked that the well of the past is deep.[2] Why the metaphor?

Several spatial metaphors are used to make time, or time-experience, graphic. To refer to the past as to something that has been left 'behind' is a straightforward rendering of a fairly common everyday experience. One says good-bye to the father's house never to return there; one leaves it behind. And indeed, leaving a thing behind or ceasing to do certain things for good is the description of an elementary time experience. Before reflecting on time with the aid of fancy words, our primary time-experience is that of the irreversibility of happenings, events and decisions. Past is, then, 'behind' us, it has left us or we have left it – but why is the well of past deep? 'Deep' is not synonymous with 'very, very long'. A very, very long road is a track on the same horizontal level as a short one. Although we cannot envision the whole length of that road, since only others, living before us, trod on it, we guess that there is no basic difference of altitude between that which has been left behind and that which is still ahead. However, the metaphor of the deep well suggests that we stand on the surface, in contrast to the abyss gaping in front of us. Instead of the 'deep well', a 'deep pit' or a 'deep shaft' could also be mentioned. Associations will change, and yet, we shall still place ourselves (the present) on the surface, on solid ground, looking into the past as if it were deep underneath, inviting us to 'descend' into it.

Thomas Mann wrote: 'deep is the well of the past'. The context – his hero's story – required that he should mention a 'well', and not a pit, a shaft or a subterrestrial labyrinth. But be it a well, a shaft, a subterrestrial labyrinth or anything else, the past is deep; it is deep for us. The past is deep for the moderns.

Time and space are forms of *a priori* imagination.[3] Historical imagination is also *a priori*[4] in a strictly un-Kantian sense. A single person could possibly perceive and think without historical imagination. But a group of people could not survive without it, and thus the person could not survive either. *A priori* historical imagination becomes manifest in a variety of imaginary institutions.[5] Spectacles in general, and spectacle-constituting metaphors in particular, are imaginary institutions. The 'deep' past, or the 'depth of the past' is a modern (modernist) imaginary institution.

We descend to the past as the ancients descended to Hades. But Hades was a limited space, and the Greeks knew only too well whom and what to expect to see there, once descending. The past of the moderns is, however, inexhaustible and infinite, infinite not *in* space and time but just *as* space and time. And we have no idea what to expect to see there, having once embarked on a subterrestrial tour. Moderns have no chthonic deities. Enlightenment fought a no-win-war against God in Heaven, but it carried the day completely in its struggle against the Devil of the underground Hell.[6]

The past is deep. If the past is a well, we see just our own image while trying to look into it. So we send down the bucket. What does it bring up? Dirt? Or pristine water? Moderns let down the bucket in curiosity and terror. And peeking into the bucket that has just recently been brought to the surface of the sublunar region,[7] they see their own distorted image in a bucketful of water. The past is deep, but that which has been brought up from there is on the surface, and it is close. By using our bucket, the most faraway can be made the closest. As Hegel writes: in piety of thinking consciousness arrives at the state of subjectivity 'to non-alienness, as the spirit sinks to the depths that are not afar but absolute closeness, the Present'.[8]

This remains so if we switch from the metaphor of the well to the metaphor of the pit or to that of the underwater iceberg. The voyage into the depth of the past is also a voyage into the depth of the person's own internal spaces. Hegel mentions 'the internal space' of subjectivity. There is, supposedly, a space inside us. This space is certainly not identical with our immortal soul, nor with the mathematical infinite that Pascal said we contain. The 'internal space' does not consist of neutrons and protons – it is a metaphorical space. The 'internal space' can be a well, a pit or a shaft. Yet it is not there at birth, at least not for Hegel. It is created by modern men and women themselves, within themselves. One has a little apartment or a store 'within' oneself. It is within because one does not share it; one can close the door of the apartment. We have privileged access to it, the keys are in our own pocket. We are free to open the door once we so desire that others should see our chambers; we can also keep to ourselves if we so want. We can repose there before we go 'out'. But if the doors remain closed too often, if the windows are never left ajar, the air of the internal space will become foul, even poisonous, and the person will languish, even perish. This danger threatens men if they are not transparent to themselves. But it is hard to imagine that any person with such an 'internal space' will ever be fully transparent to himself or herself. Hegel, the great rationalist as he was, did not suggest that a finite self-consciousness can actually achieve full transparency. The self-created man is the homecoming of self-consciousness, and still, he is not yet the truth. Full transparency (subject-object identity, the sublation of diremption, totality, truth) is achieved by the Absolute Spirit alone.

Modern men are diggers. They sense to have achieved depth in themselves, so they start digging. The past (history) sunk deep in them, thus they keep digging. The person and the race, microcosm and macrocosm go underwater or underground. But for some, all that is just appearance and digging is futile. The underground man. The underground history. Men as archeologists; a hopeful archeologist or a hopeless archeologist.[9]

Imaginary institutions do change. Digging can be stopped; instead, one can start to exhibit. The metaphor of 'depth' can also be dismissed. In exhibiting without digging, finally nothing remains to be exhibited. One exhibits in the external space, but one digs in the internal space of the individual or the race. Close the mine, cover the well and the pit with plaster, and the entrances to the underground labyrinth are firmly sealed. The man who exhibits without digging is the one-dimensional man.

For Walter Benjamin, the past did not resemble a well, rather an immense heap of unconnected ruins, fragments.[10] This, too, is a spatial metaphor but apparently an entirely different one. Thomas Mann could take it for granted that the reader would understand what he meant by saying that the well of the past is deep. However, it was not understanding that Walter Benjamin sought. He wanted to shock us with his metaphor, to challenge head-on the dominant imaginary institution which he shared himself. Therefore, he reversed the original metaphor. He shared the dominant imaginary insofar as he did not see the past as something lying 'behind us' or something that has been left behind. His past (history) is no dwelling, no home, no beginning, not even an open plain. Instead of being hidden in the deep, in the underbelly of the Earth, history is altogether on the surface. The immense heap is nothing else but the immense pit, lifted up and dumped; a convex substituted for a concave.

Archeologists dig deep 'down there'; archeology unearths. Archeologists unearths fragments, and they reconstruct the whole from the fragments. Archeologists believe that from the fragments, the yield of their digging, a text can be deciphered that had once been the text of the whole. Benjamin also mentions fragments. Yet these fragments are not hidden under the Earth and they need not be digged out. History is manifest on the surface; everything we know is a knowledge of ruins. No meaning can be rendered to these ruins by human recollection, for they are entirely void of the kind of sense we could possibly understand. Moreover, recollection, as an attempt to render meaning to the senseless, to bring the speechless to speech, is transgression.

The radical refusal to recollect the past is also the radical negation of history: of past, present and future history simultaneously.[11] Archeological recollection brings forth many a spectacle. The same fragment can tell several stories, and every archeologist comes up with his or her own mise-en-scène. The radical refusal of recollection (qua the negation of recollection) offers a single spectacle; the metaphor of the heap of ruins itself is the spectacle. Since none of the fragments carry meanings which could be deciphered by human archeologists, the same spectacle is re-staged all the time. Catastrophe is repetition and repetition is catastrophe.[12]

Modern historical recollection is archeological, and the spectacle is the rearrangement of the yield of digging. The spectacle may be a story, a scholarly description, a precise imitation of an old city centre, a museum exhibit or anything else. But neither of them is lived history. Nothing those spectacles are all about can be remembered before having been seen. Whatever has been recollected has left no traces on the membrane of the memory of the living. The archeologists assure you that they indeed left such traces on the membrane of the memory of the long dead. But those long dead are not party to the recollection, they do not see the spectacle, and they cannot corroborate the archeologists. The history of the dead is dead history. But Hegel discusses the living Spirit and living (*lebendige*) History.

Only shamelessly teleological history is 'living' (*lebendige*). Hermeneutics, this bashful enterprise, cannot make up the face of the actors of past histories, nor act out, in lieu of them, the role of the puppets pulled by the strings of historical laws and pushed around by causes and effects in the *danse macabre* of contingency.

Nostalgia, and not digging, not even the neat rearrangement of the fragments, inhales life into the dead past. It is nostalgia that resurrects the dead past. It cannot resurrect the dead (only shamelessly teleological history or unbashful messianism can do this), but it makes the dead speak and act as if they were alive. Having been brought to the surface from the well, which mirrors our faces whenever we lean over it, these dead are everything we desire to be. It is in their age and in their habitat that we would like to live. They also do things we are afraid to do, and they go through experiences we are horrified even to dream about.

Nostalgia is not the desire for the other; it is the desire for otherness. The desire for the other is longing. The nostalgic person desires to be elsewhere. He does not want to chat with Socrates in the way Socrates wanted to chat with all those dead 'wise men'; the nostalgic man wants to be Socrates, or at least one of the philosopher's closest disciples. He wants to be present at their conversations and accompany them to the bath and the gymnasium. He wants to be the lover of Alkibiades. The nostalgic man chooses periods and Representative Others for himself and chooses them freely. Nostalgia dreams. The nostalgic man resurrects the dead in his dreams, he resurrects them privately – this is why they remain dead. History lived privately is not lived history. The living does not share it with the living but with the dead. Many a modern man and woman have their moments of nostalgia; among them, also, men and women who have chosen themselves existentially. They enliven the past on the common ground of their lived history. But the nostalgic man is parasitic on the dead.

It is in art, religion and philosophy that the dead can be resurrected, for they unite presentation with re-presentation, re-collection and re-membrance.

Shared myths of people or of religious communities are the forms of pure re-presentation; they do not need to resurrect the dead, since the dead died only physically, but not spiritually. Re-presentation is not the yield of digging; the spectacle is omni-present. Time and eternity, present, past and future merge. The common form of experiencing is also the common form of life. It is not the farthest that becomes the closest. Theseus had never been the farthest who happened to become the closest to the Athenian theatre-goer; Christ has never been the farthest in need to become the closest to the pious Christian. It is only when the past has already been removed from the present, when we start digging and send the bucket down the well that the private experience of nostalgia (and longing) is sought for in turning towards the spectacle. Unless nostalgia and longing are going to be translated into the language of a common form of experiencing, the dead cannot be resurrected to share our forms of life. It is here and now that who was farthest can become the closest.

For modern men and women, the presentation of the past (history) is paramount over re-presentation. The search for 'roots' is just a cheap substitute for re-presentation. Newly fabricated national myths are waning. But can nostalgia (and longing) still be translated into the language of a common form of experiencing? Are life-forms not too fragmented for that? Is nostalgia (or longing) for otherness, as well for the other, still powerful enough a motivation to initiate the venture?

The iceberg is as dead as the ruins; it is only colder. The archeologists of the soul fancy metaphors of the Necropolis. They mention fossils, underground labyrinths, collapsed buildings that had been covered and made untraceable by newer and equally decrepit ones. The goal of digging in spiritual archeology is similar to that of archeological excavation pure and simple: to clear the fossils, to determine their age, to restore the oldest buildings, to fit the ruins into a whole, to bring everything up to the surface. And yet, in spiritual archeology everything happens the other way around. The desire is not on the side of the digger, not even on the side of the audience of the spectacle. It is from under the ruins that the desires spring. The digger does not decipher any sense from the fragmented texts; he assumes that the fragments are fakes and the writings fraudulent testimonies. He reads them with a dictionary of metaphors in hand, looking for the correct translations of the texts. Metaphors are translated here into other metaphors. The key metaphors decipher the 'real meaning' of the original metaphors; the latter are now treated as 'traces'. The metaphors of the dictionary are interrelated: all of them stand for a story in a new mythology. The myth of the past of the soul, of the underground of the soul (remember: the past is deep) is the myth of the private person. In the wording of Adorno's exaggerated but witty pun, the divinities of this (Freudian) myth are the *lares and penates* of the bedroom.

The mythology of the unconscious and the Id dramatizes private life, it enriches private life with a hidden meaning and assigns it a third dimension. Insignificant fathers and mothers are inflated into mythological giants, long-forgotten offences or disturbing experiences assume the dimensions of Greek tragedies. Patricide, incest, fratricide, hatred, despair are no longer privileges of the great. We all have our share in them. The mythology of the private is an attempt to merge re-presentation, instead of presentation, with the imaginary institution of the 'deep past'. The dictionary of the mythology is believed to be re-presentative, given that the Id is timeless, and that it appears in every time as being-in-time of the Timeless. The single person repeats (in the sense of *re-petere*) the representative (and timeless) stories of the race. But he repeats them on his own. Surely, his father and mother, sisters and brothers, protagonists in his story, are actual, not fictitious persons, but in their 'real' lives they do not play in his drama. Everyone is alone with his or her mythological story.

But perhaps not quite. Everyone is together with someone else, with someone who is, by definition, not party to his story: the analyst. Moreover, it is strictly prohibited that the analyst should be party to this story. If he were, they – the digger and the owner of the mine – would live a history in common, but this is not to be. The analyst is the embodiment of the dictionary and the interpreter of the traces in one. But he is a spectator of the spectacle he creates out of the dead traces. Perhaps not even a real spectator. For he resurrects the dead so that they can tell their story once – and no more. The dead are resurrected in order to be forgotten, to be buried for good. Men and women are assigned a third dimension as long as they resist the archeologists. The moment everything comes to the surface in order to cure the patient, what had been dug up will be re-buried, this time for good.

Who is alive and who is dead? What is alive and what is dead? The personal history, that which is actually dug up, is thin; it receives its gigantic dimensions through being deciphered as the re-acting of the non-historical and non-personal. The un-historical, which is void of meaning, injects the thin historical content with meaning. The thin historical content itself is a-teleological. What happens here happens through the coincidence of merely contingent forces. History (of the soul) is a contingent chain of event that gains meaning from the non-event. This is a borrowed meaning.

Lived history remains outside the orbit of private mythology. Lived history can be remembered. In order to remember, one follows the traces left on the membrane of one's own memory and on the memory of others. One remembers together. One does not dig, one re-lives. Yet this is not a spectacle. The kinds of spectacle that belong to lived history are collective re-presentation on the one hand, and presentation of one's own experience in the form of *a priori* experiencing, where the farthest can become the nearest, on the other. The latter kind is modern. Here, too, one remembers together with others, with everyone else whose experiences are re-lived under the spell of the same *a priori* form of historical experiencing (of art, religion and philosophy). However, within the orbit of the un-historical mythology of the private, one merely continues to dig under alien guidance. The living succumbs to the dead; recollection sits in judgement of remembrance.

One remembers together. One experiences together. One lives together. Lived history is shared past. Only shared past is lived history.

When two persons weep together over the ruins of a life they have spent together, their life is not fully in ruins. Whatever one remembers together with others, remains alive; as long as one remembers together with others, one is alive.

In complex social networks, and particularly in modern times, primary and secondary lived histories need to be distinguished. The density (richness) of one's life depends on both.

Having (or sharing) experiences and reflecting on experiences are the two poles of experiencing itself. In the same vein as 'the more one knows, the more one becomes aware of one's ignorance', or 'the purer one is, the more one's sins will become graver',[13] the more one reflects upon one's experiences, the deeper, richer and the more explicit will one's experiences become. People live together if they share experiences in this sense.

Primary lived history is the continuous sharing of experiences. Experiences can be common at the outset or can become common through disclosure. But whatever the source, they are normally kept alive by rehashing or by reflection. Rehashing and reflecting play a different role in the vitality of lived history. Rehashing resembles pulling out the same photograph or film-reel from the archive of our memories (a restaurant, a vacation place, the crying of a child, a ridiculous face and what happened around them). The difference between rehashing and recollection is that the photograph or the film became alienated by having been objectified; the person on the photo is 'really' not us anymore; perhaps it never was.[14] The photograph cannot at any rate be rehashed; rather, it is used, as a rule, as a knot on a kerchief, to serve as triggers for rehashing memories. One soon gets bored by looking at pictures taken of people with whom we never shared life nor do we intend to share any (for there is nothing to be rehashed), unless we switch from memory to recollection, and see in them mere collectible items.

Rehashing in lived history does not concentrate on the object, but on the common experience itself. It is the feelings, the emotions, the affections that we actually rehash. Rehashing is not repetition; one cannot 'bring back' the same feelings one felt once, one does not even know whether they are the same. But when one of us says: 'do you remember X?' and we suddenly collectively burst out into laughter, then rehashing did indeed come off. Rehashing is not reflective. We do not want to find out together what really happened, how one or another of us really felt or understood. Rehashing is unproblematical insofar as it does not endanger lived history but rather confirms it, even when the rehashed experience is painful. A painful experience, which does not call for further reflection, has already been left behind, not because it was forgotten, but because it has been integrated into life.

Rehashing is also topical in secondary lived history. The members of the same generation who were brought up at the same place can also be involved in rehashing. Since everyone knows what the common experiences of one's own generation, or of a certain group within this generation, consist in, rehashing, encapsulated in questions like 'Do you remember X?' is, just as in primary lived history, existentially unproblematic. By this I mean that it does not endanger lived history, but rather re-confirms it. However, if there is too little to rehash (in secondary lived history) or one can rehash one's experiences only together with a few others already at that level, lived history is empty, sporadic and thin.

Reflective interpretation, transformation or the deepening of a common experience is entirely unproblematic existentially, if the experience itself is triggered by the image or the form of *a priori* experiencing (for example, by a painting). Although experiential communication is approximative (except for a poet), the verbalization of this experience, the constant, ongoing and mutual reflection upon the work (in this case: the painting) that has occasioned the aesthetic experience, changes the experience itself. It can deepen experience as well as make it shallower. Actually, aesthetic culture requires ongoing reflection upon works of art, to the same extent as religiousness requires ongoing reflection upon the holy texts. While reflexivity of this kind does not harbour dangers for lived history, it is an entirely different matter whether an escalation of reflexivity endangers art or religion. But this issue remains outside the scope of the present discussion.

It is in primary lived history that reflexivity becomes an absolute must as well as an impending danger.

Every history has a beginning. Lived history (of the primary kind, the only kind I am going to discuss from now on) begins with the initiation of a relationship. My model will be the kind of relationship which is mutually initiated, this being the pure form of lived history. Mutual initiative requires a mutual gesture; the mutual gesture is one of fundamental trust. One cannot know in advance whether the other can indeed be fully trusted – this is why the gesture of total trust is fundamental. It is an existential gesture. One can know about the other person, one can even know him or her. But this knowledge predates lived history. If one starts to reflect upon the trustworthiness of the other party, one can go on *ad infinitum*, for one will always find reasons for trust and mistrust. And the unending chain of reflection would bring the relationship to a halt before it could get started. One can, after all, survive without lived history, not trusting anyone with one's own happiness, freedom and life. Needless to say that, while lending the other absolute trust with a gesture, one simultaneously has to trust oneself with living up to the absolute trust of the Other. And one can similarly go on with reflecting upon one's own trustworthiness *ad infinitum*, and one will find always one 'con' for every 'pro'. One can survive not trusting anyone entirely; 'common wisdom' even holds that withholding trust brings high dividends in life. Whatever those dividends are, lived history is not one of them.

The initial gesture of fundamental trust is the simulacrum of the negative unity of the existential choice and the existential wager. It is a bet, but it is also unlike the existential wager. Lending absolute trust to another person is not the same kind of absolute gesture as calling heads absolutely; one rather creates the optimal conditions for the other person's trustworthiness. The initial gesture of trusting is also a choice of ourselves, but not the absolute existential choice; by choosing ourselves, we also choose the other 'exister' who remains free not to choose himself or us. Had he not remained free, we would have chosen ourselves, not him, and had our gesture been similar to calling heads or tails, we would not have chosen at all. Finally, initial trust is a leap over a wide gap that will be filled only later, but later it has to be filled. Trust can be betrayed, and, as a result, withdrawn. Initial fundamental trust is a risk, as all leaps are. This time, the risk is that one's lived history, the organic part of one's life, will be lost. Lived history is a blood vessel of life's *telos*. The loss of a shared history is the distruption of one vessel of life's *telos* which leaves a painful memory, a sore spot behind.

Although no shared history can begin without mutual fundamental trust being granted, the character and intensity of the relationship defines the content of this trust. Children wisely know that certain kids can be trusted with sharing night-watch in a summer camp, but not with sharing one's confidences with them. The more one shares, the more dense lived history becomes, for it is then that people can remember together, can rehash the past, reflect upon it, keep it alive, within the present.

Everything that lives needs to be cultivated. Once mutual trust has been established, lived history begins. As living and lived, it requires care and circumspection. Living/lived history is teleological, but it has no purpose; one does not cultivate living/lived history from the viewpoint of a required end result. Lived and living history is intersubjectively purposeful without purpose, where the term 'intersubjective' has no epistemological, but an onto-existential status.

One cultivates living/lived history by enriching it and by concretizing its teleological character. A living/lived relationship becomes entirely teleological, once it becomes eternal. In this context eternal does not mean unending as such, but rather unending within finitude. Lived/living history becomes eternal when it becomes timeless insofar as time cannot damage it, for it cannot wither away in duration, only with the cancellation of time. The formula 'till death do us part' is an initiating gesture, and its binding force is only formal. An entirely teleological living/lived history does not need the binding force of the formula, for the latter had already been given content in a concretely purposeful shared life.

Shared history does not require total transparency; not even its most tightly knit kinds do. There are things a person cannot remember; there are things a person does not know about himself; there are things a person can only remember alone, such as old memories, dead leaves of a once lived history. And again, there are certain other things a person wants to keep to himself or herself. But too thick an intransparency endangers shared history. The more one knows that one does not know many an essential thing about the other, the less can the initiating trust be reconfirmed. The risk, involved in the initial leap, increases rather than decreases. Lived history becomes endangered, because one never knows what the other is holding back which makes 'holding back' mutual and lived history inauthentic.

Transparency in *something* is required in each kind of (primary) lived history, transparency in everything is required by none. But since the level of 'intransparency tolerance' is worked out by agreement or accommodation, parties can try to achieve total mutual transparency. Kierkegaard discussed symmetrical-reciprocal love in terms of total transparency.[15] In his mind, without total transparency love remains assymmetrically reciprocal, for the other will be manipulated and used also as a means. In principle, Kierkegaard is right. Lived/living history is not entirely free of power relations. The question is whether attempts at full transparency erase all traces of power-manipulation. The relationship between Simone de Beauvoir and Sartre does not corroborate the assumption. True enough, their common history did not fulfil the conditions set by Kierkegaard. But Kierkegaard's conditions (e.g. first love-only love) are rarely met in modern life.

Intimate attachments (love or certain kinds of friendship) never take off without a greater than average determination for mutual transparency. At the beginning, lovers and friends want to say everything about themselves and they expect the Other to do the same. The practice of mutual disclosure cannot go on unabated once the relationship has been established. Life takes the place of story-telling and the story will become common. But if story-telling stops, the relation between remembrance and recollection will also be cut. It needs to be borne in mind that the dead leaves of past histories can be recollected by one or another party, and not by both of them – they do not belong to the common lived history. If no bridge is erected between recollection and remembrance, no continuity can be maintained in the discontinuity of lived histories.

The multiplicity of attachments is also a source of danger. A person changes in a relationship, and a history in common leaves traces not only on the memory, but also on the body, the attitude, the vocabulary, the taste and much else. One discovers the imprint of an alien presence on just about everything. Without explanation or disclosure, the perception of 'alienness' will extend to the person who envelops himself or herself into obscurity. Lived history will be filled with dead stones. Only reflective interpretation can, if at all, remove those stones.

Reflective interpretation, unlike rehashing, is an ambiguous exercise, but one we cannot dispense with in modern times, because maintaining and cultivating lived history simply requires it. How far one should go and when one should stop in the process of reflective interpretation is to be decided by those who engage themselves in it.

Phronesis, good practical judgement, is required to hit the middle ground between 'too little' and 'too much'. When there are too many dead stones dispersed along the path of lived history, relevant common experiences have to be re-interpreted. Self-disclosure also needs to be intensified, and not for its own sake, not as a kind of exercise in exhibitionism, but in order to enliven the relationship by restoring its initial level of transparency. As a result of reflective interpretation, relations can, although they do not have to, become more transparent than they initially were. The restoration of the initial level of transparency is, however, a must. One need not wait for a crisis in order to engage in reflective interpretation. Doing this from time to time belongs to lived history.

As mentioned, reflective interpretation is an ambiguous kind of practice. If it occupies the centrepoint in shared history, this history will be talked about rather than lived. Lived history, like all history, is past, present and future; overinterpretation of the past (or the present) blocks the movement towards the future. In absence of a constant movement towards the future, the teleological propensity of lived history itself is jeopardized. Instead of making relations more transparent, interpretative reflection obscures them to the point where chaos sets in and people give up hope for setting the relation right forever.

Lived history is not only about remembering, it is also about forgetting. In this context, forgetting is merely the other side of remembering. One remembers and forgets simultaneously. When we remember together, we rehash (or re-interpret) certain experiences frequently, whereas we let others sink into oblivion. In the Freudian lingo, we push them back into the pre-conscious or the upper-level unconscious and keep them that way. Since remembering is not re-collection, we do not remember the lower level of the unconscious (if there is such a 'thing in itself' at all), and no experience that could have been, but was not kept alive by reflection, can be thrown back that deep into the well of the past.

The haste with which unreflected experiences are pushed into the background of forgetting is suspect. Men and women who are in such a haste have no patience required for the cultivation of lived history. Their memory will be sporadic, their lived histories thin or short. But having once undergone serious reflective interpretation, certain experiences – particularly the ones that hurt – need to be pushed into the background and be forgotten if their omnipresence endangers the future, and thus also the life of a relationship, and if forgetting is morally recommendable or at least indifferent. People get hurt in all kinds of relationship; sometime they are right, another time they are wrong. If one keeps alive the wrongs, alleged or real, by constant remembering, one hurts oneself as much as the other. Wrongs that are not of a serious moral order (which should terminate shared history irrespective of personal dimensions), need also be forgotten for moral reasons. In modern times forgiving appears in the form of forgetting.[16]

Fascinated with recollection, with digging into the depth of 'history' and of the 'soul', modern men and women lose their capacity for lived history. And there is no other history that lives. When one cannot remember together with others that which one has experienced together with the same others, onto-existential intersubjecticity is gone. One then remembers on one's own and tries to tell others what one has just remembered. But what one has remembered, they do not remember, they do not even understand, at least not in a way that one would understand it. One remains alone with one's memories, a loner walking amid the dead leaves of alien recollections, becoming old already in its youth.

Modern men avoid the leap of fundamental trust – what if they will be betrayed? They have no patience to cultivate relationships – why repair old hats if one can buy a new one? They are not ready for interpretative reflection – it is too much hassle, and, in addition, it is also embarrassing, while it is much less pain to forget. This is why lived histories become short on thin, perhaps both short and thin. They are thin insofar as mutual expectations are low, and they are short, for they are not 'repaired', but rather thrown into the dustbin of a dead past.

The thirst for novelty – the mere reverse side of the thirst for the old – cannot be quenched by lived history, for the latter is the absolute present, the present that embraces both past and future. Lived history is the unity of temporality and eternity. Modern men and women chase novelty as though by catching novelty, they could capture future as well. Lived history is not an enterprise to catch novelty. Lived history is does not need to capture the future for it contains the future. This is the only living future there is. This is the future that can be remembered and also acted upon.

2 Utopia; Past, Future and Present

Ernst Bloch wrote his *opus magnum* on hope as principle.[17] It is odd to think of hope as *arché*, for commonplace knowledge, *doxa*, suggests that human beings are always hoping for something as well as being afraid of something. But *arché* is the exact opposite of *doxa*. For the ancients, hope was a mere phenomenon of *doxa*; worse than that, it was sometimes regarded as the manifestation of the weakness, or even the baseness, of character. Since then, several rationalists and men of enlightenment echoed the ancient wisdom that hope and fear are negative, unruly passions of the soul.[18] This was a reaction to Judaism and especially Christianity having elevated hope from its lowly status to the highest rank. From then on, there have been two kinds of hope: one invested in the benevolent outcome of the accidental twists and turns of life, and the other invested in the benevolence of God. The first remains *doxa* without the second becoming *nous*. God, the substance, the One, is *arché*. He is *nous*, but hope is not. Instead of becoming *arché*, Hope will rank among the three supreme virtues, together with Faith and Charity.

But future-orientedness, a factor present in the Jewish-Christian 'imaginary institution', yet completely absent from the ancient Greek mind, provides Hope with a special status.[19] Hope is invested in the future. The first (or second) coming of the Messiah, *parousia*, apocalypse, final redemption, Last Judgement and all affiliated images and myths are Expectations. One expects something that 'is not yet here'. Thus understood, the expected Event is bound to occur in the future. This is certainly a misunderstanding, but one which includes understanding. Simulacra of the Kingdom-to-Come are not descriptions of a 'future', because the coming of the Messiah or the Apocalypse are not events in an ordinary sense; they do not happen in time and space. Yet space and time are *a priori* forms of historical imagination. The timeless can be imagined, and normally also thought, only in and by time, that which is to be expected only in future time; without time, there is no timelessness.

The modern consciousness of cosmic contingency seems to provide room for the elevation of hope to the rank of an *arché*. Given that our newly discovered ignorance concerning the very existence of God as substance, *nous*, *telos* and *arché* becomes the condition of the wager, hope could still decide where knowledge is wanting. This is how Kant saw the issue. However, hope remains nothing but the motivation for calling heads, rather than tails, in the cosmic wager. It can only establish a postulate, and even this for practical reason alone. Hope is needed where there is no certainty, yet only certainty can be *arché*, the highest of all certainties.

Due to this impasse, expressed rather than triggered by Kant's philosophy, the term 'principle' itself underwent several semantic transformations. The Kantian regulative and constitutive principles (or ideas), with which philosophy is now replete, do not lay claim to the position of *arché*. The gambit, opening the process of deconstructing metaphysics, ended with the attempt to eliminate all principles completely, a hopeless task from the start, since it was to be accomplished within the framework of a game that permits, even calls for, this gambit. But in everyday life, as well as in empirical social sciences and in politics, 'having principles' means no more than having a firm point of view in seeing, assessing, judging or searching a matter or in doing certain things. Can Hope be called a principle in this vague and general sense? But regardless of whether or not the term makes any sense, no philosophical yield is to be expected from the answer, even one in the affirmative.

Instead of pondering trivialities, one can also associate the 'principle of Hope' with the Jewish-Christian apocalyptic and messianistic imagination. With certain modifications of Bloch's original version, one will then contend that it was the constant drive towards the transcendent future that has become the regulative and constitutive practical principle in European history, where the term 'practical' stands for 'historic-political' and not primarily for 'ethical'. History, then, is made by hope. The ancients had no hope, thus they had no history. Only the vision of the Coming of the Kingdom which is not of this world can make all Kingdoms of this world provisional, that is, historical. The vision of a transcendent history is the imaginary frame or the archetype of immanent history. Hope is a historical principle; moreover, it is the principle of history.

If history comes to an end, there is no longer need for hope. Hegel thus projected hope (as a kind of *Sollen*) on to the future of the past. If one is calling tails, then hoping is nothing but empty talk, or opium for the people who are poor in spirit. As a result, Marx 'inferred' the future from the present 'scientifically'. But Hegel did not abolish history; and future history could not have been foreseen by Marx or anyone else, for history that can be foreseen is no longer history. Marx was quite particularly guided by the principle of Hope that he rejected and ridiculed.[20] The celebrated thesis of secularization simplifies the character of this connection to some extent.[21] The materialist conception of history is not tantamount to the secularized version of Jewish Messianism or the Christian saga of Salvation. But it was indeed formulated under the spell and guidance of the dominant imaginary institution of Judaism and Christianity. Despite all efforts of overt resistance to the principle of hope, future-oriented histories are all guided, if sometimes unconsciously, by this principle.

Utopian imagination predates the vision of the Kingdom in Heaven, and it thrives, where it does, also on its own. Bloch discusses several kinds of utopias, such as the medical, the social, the technical, the architectonic and the geographic, in addition to the Utopia as Kingdom and the Utopia as Art. He does not mention ethical utopia as a separate genre, and for quite good reasons. All utopias, social utopias first and foremost, present a form of life as paradigmatic or exemplary. In them, a form of life is described in terms of its institutions and in those attitudes of the people who keep the institutions going. The model of an exemplary-paradigmatic world is the model of exemplary and paradigmatic institutions. Social utopias can develop an affinity with all other utopias as well. The-place-that-is-not or the-place-that-is-somewhere else is not historically specified. It is not located in time; or if it is, it can be shifted. The golden age or the garden of Eden are thrown back into the past, but images of similar content do not need to be. There is also a non-temporalized garden of Eden, and Eldorado is also like it. The two can merge, as they do in Bosch; they can also be kept apart, as in Breughel's Eldorado.

Utopia is 'somewhere else'; what is here and now is precisely what Utopia is not. That which Utopia is not, is termed 'reality'. It is entirely irrelevant to deconstruct 'reality' here; let us, rather, accept that Reality is that what Utopia is not. If we find out what Utopia is, we shall also come to understand what reality means for all denizens of Here and Now who dream of Nowhere.

> Thus speaks the upright Gonzales:[22]
> I' the commonwealth I would by contraries
> Execute all things; for no kind of traffic
> Would I admit; no name of magistrate;
> Letters should not be known; riches, poverty
> And use of service, none; contract, succession,
> Bourn, bound of land, tilth, vineyard, none;
> No use of metal, corn, or wine, or oil;
> No occupation; all men idle, all;
> And women too, but innocent and pure;
> . . .
> All things in common nature should produce
> Without sweat an endeavour; treason, felony,
> Sword, pike, knife, gun, or need of any engine,
> Would I not have; but nature should bring forth,
> Of its own kind, all foison, all abundance,
> To feed my innocent people.

Utopia is described here in negative terms. Everything that is generally blamed for unmet wants and strife has been eliminated from the picture. The merit and the meaning of all things responsible for unmet wants and strife are annulled. 'Reality' is thus equated with unmet wants and strife. The negation of all things that cause unmet want and strife results in two positive yields: abundance on the one hand, innocence (and purity) of men and women on the other. Abundance takes the place of unmet want, innocence (purity) that of strife. Thus both abundance and innocence are direct results of the total elimination of all factors producing unmet wants and strife. Suffering is caused by these negative factors, and if they are eliminated, suffering itself has also been eliminated. Happiness is defined as the absence of suffering. Utopia is the Kingdom of Happiness, the promise that men and women can be happy and good at the same time.

There are several vulgar and a few extremely refined versions of the story; however, essentially they all are variations on the same theme. The utopia of Eldorado is unrefined but picturesque. There people lay under the tree or on the lawn with open mouths, as one can see on Brueghel's painting, so that the fried pigeon could fly into their mouth. Abundance in food is the utopia of the hungry, idleness that of the overworked. This utopia, which has become the reality of every holiday resort with room service, has always had a light touch of the parody. And yet, this Utopia had once a broader appeal than most of the rest. Actually, we do not know of anyone who expressed his desire to live 'in reality' in one of the most refined utopian states ever conceived, in Plato's republic. But the divine metaphor of Kanaan, the land of milk and honey, can also be taken literally. The image of people lazing around at the bank of a river and living from sucking on the honey stream or the milk stream, can easily be projected. The main issue is not whether the Utopias are attractive, but whether the *thought* at the bottom of them is. Is the unity of goodness and happiness a *desire or a programme*? Is this unity to be linked to abundance on the one hand, harmony on the other?

Before modern times, freedom was not considered a need, except for the freely born once freedom was lost. Hence Utopias of happiness did not have to account for the unmet need for freedom. In a modern Utopia, abundance has to include abundance in freedom as well. This lays a heavy burden on utopian imagination, a burden it cannot carry the same way as it carried the lighter one. The universalization of the value of freedom opens up the avenue for practically an infinite number of interpretations of freedom. There is no satiation with freedom as there is satiation with bread. Moreover, among the many determinants of freedom, those of the free development of human abilities, capacities and skills, occupy an important place. Modern imagination is practically unlimited, from satisfied wants new ones will always spring. Happiness may remain possible in spite of all this, but not the way ancient utopias fathomed happiness to be.

In addition, modern Utopias have to cope with the consciousness of cosmic as well as of social-historical contingency. As a result, Utopias need to be embedded into the stream of an objective purposiveness of historical development, and need to represent the purpose, the Final End of this development. Out of the schema of Final End is born the risk of conflating Utopia with Redemption, with the Coming of the Messiah, and with the Apocalypse, to which its original versions did not bear resemblance.[23] From this unholy alliance many a danger sprang.

The growing complexity of the spirit of utopia can best be exemplified by Kant's efforts to keep as much of the legacy as possible, but not more. Kant's own social utopia of perpetual peace[24] preserves one major element of previous utopias, namely the elimination of suffering caused by strife. As a modern utopia, it is placed into the future; it centres on freedom and not on the satisfaction of needs, although it includes the aspect of need satisfaction also. Wants cannot be fully met, as Kant writes, 'because needs grow much faster than the means of satisfy them'.[25] Apocalypse (in a positive sense) qua End of all things, where End stands for 'telos' and also for final destination is, in Kant's vision, the actual universalization of the Moral Law through the unity of the noumenal and the phenomenal world. This unity itself is the *promesse de bonheur*.

Insofar as the unity of goodness and happiness is a programme, it can be simply dismissed. Kant was sufficiently brave to do so. But if the unity of goodness and happiness is also a desire, it needs to be satisfied one way or another. Kant did not deny the existence of this desire. The contention that good persons are worthy of happiness expresses also *his* desire, but *as a desire* allied with the principle of hope.[26]

Art, religion and philosophy are utopian realities; at least, they are perceived as such by the moderns. They are also perceived as realities which exercise or emanate saving power. Utopia promises happiness, saving power makes no promises, it salvages.

For moderns, art became the foremost source and provider of happiness, utopia incarnate. Art resembles ancient utopias, given that utopia and telos are not conflated.

Utopia is nowhere; it is 'somewhere else'. Time, regardless of whether it is past, present or future, is irrelevant in it. Utopia is the negation of reality, or rather, reality as the negative pole is constituted by utopia as the positive pole. The content of utopia is not necessarily attractive; perhaps no one really wants to live 'there'. Still, utopia promises the satisfaction of all our wants as well as the end of strife.

When someone abandons herself to reading a novel, listening to a piece of music, looking at a painting, she is no longer 'here', but 'there'; one is somewhere else, in another world, in another reality. Time becomes then irrelevant. The work is the negation of reality, and the more it seems to resemble reality, the stronger is the negation.[27] This negation is formal, not substantive. What is negated, and thus constituted as reality, is the contingent matter that lacks meaning or sense. What is posited through negation is exactly meaning and sense: the utopian reality.[28]

Works of art do not merely promise happiness. Contrary to all other utopias, they also deliver what they promise: satisfaction. This is utopian satisfaction, for it is total satisfaction: joy of the sense, erotic pleasure, spiritual elevation – all at once. This kind of total satisfaction is unlike the promise extended by the Utopia, for it is not a lasting state, but a happening, an a-temporal, and also momentary lived, experience (*Erlebnis*). But 'advance felicity' is certain and the promise uncertain. The reconciliation (*Versöhnung*) is also unlike the Hegelian reconciliation with actuality. Works of art do not reconcile men and women with the world they negate; they reconcile them, even if just for a moment, with their own life.

The question is whether works of art have other kinds of happiness in store in addition to the holistic joy one experiences in their reception. Perhaps this 'advance felicity' is all there is to it. For there is only one honest way to speak about an 'advance' and to make allusions to the promise of happiness that is held in store by art: to engage in the cosmic wager of calling heads. Otherwise, allusions made to an alleged *promesse de bonheur* and reconciliation beyond the pale of the this-worldly experience are merely tricks in a foul game of hide and seek. However, those who are calling heads do not need art as warranty of the promise of happiness. They gain the promise of happiness and that of goodness at once, just by calling heads.

If the advance is all that the artwork promises, then all promises are kept and there is no advance. The holistic joy is total happiness and not just a faint echo of another kind of happiness. But then, art work is a utopia which lacks the moral element, that other absolutely necessary constituent of utopia in addition to happiness. The desire for utopia is the desire that the good should also be happy. There are two negative utopias, for there are two aversions. Normally, one desires that the good should not be unhappy as well as that the evil should not be happy. Art, as the Utopian reality, bestows happiness upon good and evil alike. So does love. But Art *can* at least bestow happiness on the good. So can love.

Social-political utopists reject dominant social and political institutions as evil. Some of them are vague about alternatives, like Shakespeare's Gonzago; others are rather explicit insofar as they plan and design an alternative which is good, a set of institutions down to the minutest details, as philosophical utopists did from Plato onwards.

In the best possible world, good persons are also supposed to be happy. They are supposed to be happy either because in such a world only the righteous ones will gain admittance into the Kingdom of eternal happiness, or because perfect earthly institutions there will mould good men and women, promoting goodness and happiness at once. The first idea is apocalyptic, the second utopian.

Modern utopias relate the utopian desire to the principle of hope. The utopian desire (the unity of goodness and happiness) is fixated on history. The principle of hope is, after all, a historical principle. Although the origin of the historical principle is the Kingdom in Heaven, utopias are not concerned with this kingdom. And yet, the principle of hope remains one of transcendence. Guided by the principle of hope, men and women turn their face towards the total transcendence of the present (bad, evil) earthly institutions. Hegel's criticism has its cutting edge: infatuated with all that Ought-To-Be, blinded by the light of Nowhere, men and women become unable to recognize the roses on the cross of the present.

In choosing themselves existentially, men and women choose themselves as they are, together with all their talents and infirmities; they also choose their family, their domicile, their age, briefly, the world into which they have been thrown. The person becomes what he or she is, in and through this choice. Choosing means to attain autonomy: since I chose my world as it is, I cannot blame the world if I fail to become that which I chose myself to be. Thus choosing this world contains the resolve to cope with this world, instead of feigning to be living in a self-styled castle in the air. The rose of the present is first and foremost the rose called life, the accident to be born here and now, rather than not to be born at all. For having been born in another place or in another time is not the alternative of being here and now, but merely a futile castle in the air of an escapist imagination.

Choosing our world is not tantamount to loving it. Political and social institutions are, as a rule, not lovable; but they can be tolerable, at least for some, while being intolerable for others, depending on good luck, bad luck or the person's temperament. They can also be absolutely intolerable. Choosing our world does not exclude the resolve to change it; rather the opposite seems to be true. We are contingent, so is our world. A contingent world exists, but it can just as well not exist. It is such and such, but it can also be different. Contingency-consciousness enhances *utopian imagination.*[29] Contrasting 'good patterns' to 'bad patterns', 'good institutions' to 'bad institutions' became the favorite pastime in the modern age. The question of whether utopias are realized is irrelevant. Some utopian patterns are implemented, others are not, although some of them might have been. The belief that everything that failed to be implemented could not have been implemented is inauthentic throughout. One cannot feed on contingency practically, and deny contingency theoretically, without being guilty of inauthenticity.

Every utopia, even the most modest one, for example, that of a new health system or of a housing project, transcends reality. One proposes a good model, instead of the actually functioning 'bad' one. There is no knowledge concerning its future way of functioning, but educated guesses can be made. This is what lends minor social utopias a technical flavour, for better or for worse. For worse, because in the case of 'minor utopias' neither the principle of hope is forcefully mobilized, nor the desire for utopia is expected to be satisfied, even if all goes according to plan. For better, because utopias of reform are more reversible than others; they do not do much damage. But they remain utopias in the strict sense of the word, for their designers presuppose that people will be better off (happier in a restricted sense) under the future (utopian) conditions. Reform-minded 'minor utopians' also believe that people who are, if marginally, better off, will also become better. This proposition is unambitious, but also solidly grounded, provided that one equates goodness with being a law-abiding citizen.

But the *promesse de bonheur* that men and women are chasing resides in alternative forms of life. Major utopias (in contrast to minor ones) turn imagination towards such forms of life. But we have a problem with the promise of happiness, for we have a problem with happiness. The age of universalization is also the age of individualization. As needs have become individually distinct, so have the dreams of happiness, as well as the images of the political and social conditions that best promote happiness. The greater the differences, the more idiosyncratic utopias become. In pre-modern times, one could present one's own utopia as a panacea since needs were static, values and virtues consensually accepted, and only a few visions of the good life prevailed. In modern times, superimposing one's own utopia on others as their panacea has become an outrage. Utopian imagination, so misused, becomes a weapon against the utopian imagination of others and kills their promise of happiness.

And still, utopian imagination cannot be held back from blooming as long as the well of desire for utopia has not dried out. But instead of designing the best possible world as such, we can envision the best possible world for us, that is, for all those who are like us. Nozick discusses the absolute Utopia which is the simultaneous presence of all utopias.[30] This is, indeed, the utopia which all contingent persons, living in a pluralistic universe, can maintain. Certainly, one envisions only one's own utopia. One is not morally entitled to design dreams qua the promise of other person's happiness, whose conception of happiness and preferred form of life differ from one's own.[31] Utopian imagination may continue to bloom, but there are limits beyond which it cannot be stretched. The limits are ethical. One of them has already been discussed: dreams of other persons' happiness should not be forged without them. The other limit is equally obvious: a utopian form of life, which cannot live together peacefully with all other forms of life, should not be recommended in the form of a socio-political utopia. The model of Absolute Utopia, that is, of the simultaneous existence of all utopias (past, present and future) promises happiness for the decent persons, although, like art and love, it does not deny happiness from the indecent.

Major utopias (of a form of life) differ from the minor ones (of replacing institutions) not solely in their holistic character, but also insofar as they bear no resemblance to the act of modelling or devising a blueprint. In case of a major utopia, utopian imagination and allegiance merge. My major utopia is the promise of *my* happiness (and of the happiness of those who share the utopia with me), as it is also a promise that I (and people like me) can remain decent and be happy simultaneously. The utopian desire drives people to catch as much of this promise as possible. Major utopias are not mere figments of human imagination. They draw their strength from actuality; they exist, insofar as they exist, in the present. Utopia is lived, practised, maintained by men and women as a form of life, to a certain extent, as possibility permits, at least within the confines of a narrow circle of people. The utopian form of life is, for those who live it, the rose on the cross of the present.

In his autobiographical testimony, *Survival in Auschwitz*, Primo Levi writes:

> However little sense there may be in trying to specify why I, rather than thousands of others, managed to survive the test, I believe that it was really due to Lorenzo that I am alive today; and not so much for his material aid, as for having constantly reminded me by his presence,

by his natural and plain manner of being good, that there still existed a just world outside our own, something or someone still pure and whole, not corrupt, not savage, extraneous to hatred and terror; something difficult to define, a remote possibility of good, but for which it was worth surviving.[32]

The good person is utopia *incarnate*.

No utopia can be more real than the utopia that exists and that exists absolutely. No imagination can increase the goodness of a good person or make the original more perfect through embellishment. A good person always stands higher than the image of a good person. Not because actuality always stands higher than imagination, but because the supreme good *and* the ultimate evil cannot be grasped adequately, let alone augmented, by imagination. The good person is absolutely good, although every person is good in his or her way. Primo Levi described the utopian message of the good person succinctly in observing that Lorenzo constantly reminded him of the remote possibility of a good for which it is worth surviving. The possibility is remote and utopian in the sense of transcendence, but survival is worth while for 'the whole' can still make sense somehow. Every good man or woman, utopia incarnate, carries the telos of the world in his or her very being as a single individual.

It is difficult to spot the connection between goodness and happiness. The clumsiest way to do it is to infer that good persons are happy in the sense of the proposition that 'goodness is its own reward'. If this is indeed true, then good people are happy with their goodness in that they enjoy it. But it does not follow from this that they are happy, or entirely happy. The problem can also be approached another way: good persons make others happy, for they care for them, they recognize their needs and they try to satisfy them. Good persons certainly make one happy if happiness requires just the mitigation of suffering, or if it means the exercise of all of our virtues in the consistent fashion of medieval Christians or ancient Greeks. If we are moderns, we can assert without hesitation that good persons give us back the sense of life, that their very existence was received by us as proof of the possibility of the best possible world. But we cannot assert that good persons made us happy. But there is a connection between goodness and happiness that only the past unveils; and this is the strongest connection of them all and also the one which is closest to our (post-)modern world-perception.

All those who were once engaged in a feverish utopian activity, in a family, among friends, in a community, a city, a country, a revolution or otherwise, know well that periods of such activities stand out in our remembrance. We do not remember them only as significant stages of our life. There is a warmth in our remembrance, coupled with the melancholy feeling that something has been lost – the garden of Eden. It does not mitigate the feeling of 'paradise lost' that the goals pursued in old days have already been achieved, that the community went on living since without utopian activities and that life became even better. What made the past a paradise? The circumstance that a feverish utopian atmosphere required from all to act and to behave far *beyond* their usual moral standards. What was, then, better in the past? We were better persons than we are now. As a rule, it happens for just a short period that people exceed their average moral performance. But these periods always retain their utopian flavour in our common memory.

The old Utopia was elsewhere and nowhere, everywhere yet here. The new utopia was hypostatized into the future; spurred by the principle of hope, it transcended past and present. Postmoderns seek their utopia mainly in the present. But the principle of hope still guides them, and their desire is still aroused for felicity coupled with goodness.

Most, although not all, utopias are holistic. So are also most postmodern utopias. Artworks, fragments included, are wholes. The good person is a whole. Major political-social utopias are forms of life, and as such also wholes. The utopian desire for both felicity and goodness has remained, but the incarnation of the utopian reality has become *fragmented*. Art promises felicity without promising goodness, while the utopia incarnate in the very being of the good person promises goodness without promising felicity. Major utopias do not promise either perfect happiness or perfect goodness. Absolute Utopia (the utopia of the simultaneous existence of all utopias) is a regulative theoretical and practical idea. This Absolute Idea exists in the present as a judgement, *Ur/teil*, to express myself in Hegelian terms, but without the possibility of reconciliation. A fragmented world lives with fragmented utopias, and unless the Messiah descends from Heaven (to our fellow creatures who were calling heads), these fragments will remain here unredeemed. Can we ask the fragments whether they want to be redeemed? Are they free to choose their fragmentation instead?

3 Salvation/End/Apocalypse

On the Day of Judgement, so the *Zohar* teaches,[33] the whole of Israel will receive an additional spirit, 'and it will be as on the Sabbath when an extra soul is added to a person'.

For each individual Jew, the additional soul (*nephesh*) descends to him according to his level. If he is a mighty man, fearful of sin, he is given an additional soul (*nephesh*) from the attribute of might. If he is an honest man, he is given an additional soul (*nephesh*) from the attribute of truth (*emet: aleph mem tav*). . . . a person receives from the Sephira of Malkhut according to his character.

If he is a scholar, 'he is given an extra soul (*nephesh*). . . from *Hokmah* (Wisdom). And if he. . . understands one matter from another in the Torah, he is given an extra soul (*nephesh*) from *Binah* (understanding). And if he is completely righteous. . . he is given an extra soul (*nephesh*) from the Righteous One which is *Yesod*. . .'. This is the justest Day of Judgement.

'Were he [man] not in need of reconciliation, so this course (*Gang*) [see also development, walk, story] we discuss here, this Whole [thing] [would be] something superfluous', says Hegel at one stage of his lectures on the philosophy of religion.[34]
Reconciliation (*Versöhnung*) is the sublation of the diremption of the spirit by the spirit. The sublation of the diremption *between* the individual (its purpose, its conscience) and the world is the subject's reconciliation with actuality, objective spirit as world history. The diremption *within* the individual (subject), between spirit and body, between finitude and infinitude is sublated through the absolute spirit, through the recognition that everything is spirit. This is the *absolute* reconciliation, for it is *Versöhnung* through Truth-the-Whole. Absolute *Versöhnung* is the philosophical translation of Salvation (*Erlösung*).
Were man not in need of salvation, this *Gang* (march, walking, course, development, happening) under discussion, this Whole, would have been superfluous. What is this '*Gang*' under discussion? Religion perhaps? But in Hegel, the development of religion is the self-development of Spirit-cum-God itself. Should this *Gang* become superfluous, the development of the Spirit, of the world, becomes superfluous too. If man is not in need of salvation, the world is superfluous. And if 'this Whole' is superfluous, then not just philosophy, but – together with philosophy – Spirit and Truth also would become superfluous. But, of course, man is in need of salvation (*der Versöhnung nötig*). '*Nötig*' is associated with '*Not*' (calamity, torment, suffering). Man is in need of salvation because his life is calamity, torment, suffering. And the internal diremption is the source of all his calamity and suffering. Without man's calamity and suffering (by internal diremption, *Entzweiung*) 'is..this whole course superfluous' (bid.).

Man, then, is in need of salvation. But why? And is that so? One simply presupposes that man is in need of salvation before one begins to discuss salvation. Salvation is the word that stands for the quintessence of everything that man needs. And man needs the quintessence of everything that he needs. Thus man needs salvation.

Diremption of spirit and nature is the source of suffering. Animals are in pain, but they do not suffer; men, however, do. Diremption is the source of anxiety, both of the fear of death and of the fear of life. Diremption is also the source of bad conscience. Tradition promises salvation from suffering and salvation from sin. Suffering and sin together are called Evil. Salvation stands for 'being saved from Evil'. One is saved from evil through the healing of diremption (*Entzweiung*); healing (*heilen*) is associated with grace (*Heil*). Hegel's anaesthetized philosophical teleology does not permit the stage appearance of absolute Negativity, and it forecloses the possibility of the danger to heal diremption through Evil. Hegel's principle of negativity (like that of Goethe, in the figure of Mephisto) is exclusively the master of *Entzweiung* and not of *Heil*.

Traditionally, grace comes from above, and the Saviour's Kingdom is not of this world. One cannot hasten grace, for grace is either granted or not granted. But one can still live an honest life, forgive, repent and hope. In the Christian tradition, salvation is not just that which comes to pass in the timeless future, but also that which came to pass through the suffering of Christ. We need salvation, though we have already been saved; we need salvation, because we have already been saved.

Modern man is also in need of salvation. History, writ large, came into the world by establishing the Kingdom in Heaven; as long as there is History, there remains the need for salvation. The self-perception of man as a being inwardly torn is not specifically Jewish-Christian. And yet, Greeks and early Romans showed no signs of yearning for salvation. First comes the myth, then the yearning. Christians misread the absence of a general vision of salvation. In their reading, a people in no need of salvation must have been cheerful, joyous, merry. We cannot imagine what it would be like to live with unmitigated terror in our soul of everything that is beyond the pale of the city, the only home and shelter they admitted.

Nietzsche was perhaps right in asserting that Jewish-Christian imagination had completely erased Greek (or Roman) imagination.[35] In spite of the free (or at least the freer) 'circulation of letters',[36] the modern world has remained a Jewish-Christian world through and through. Modern men and women return to the Greeks with a grain of artificiality and with much play-acting. Heidegger made the most remarkable effort at resuscitating (allegedly) originary Greek imagination for modern men. Associating *Geschichte* with *Geschick*, lighting of Being with destiny, or speculating about the destiny of the truth of Being point in this direction. But Heidegger's efforts fared like those of Sysiphus. Wittingly, but also unwittingly, this modern pagan[37] has reintroduced the whole paraphernalia of Jewish-Christian imagination into his allegedly archaic Greek philosophical mythology. Destiny comes to pass, we are reminded to harken, we read about awakening, and – lo and behold – salvation returns again in the form of Hölderlin's saving power. And, after all, what is the Heideggerian saga of metaphysics all about if not the Fall and the hope of redemption? The 'end' of philosophy is nothing but the Hegelian telos, *aletheia* resembles more and more revelation, *Andenken* resembles *Andacht*, this act of the piety of thinking where, according to Hegel, the most remote becomes the closest.

To reiterate, modern men and women are also in need of salvation from calamity, torment and suffering. But the perception of calamity, torment and suffering has changed; so has the perception of salvation.

The spiritual torment is no longer the torment of bad conscience.

There were two main sources of spiritual torment stemming from bad conscience: first, uncertainty in matters of faith and second, remorse for the sins committed or anxiety that one might commit sins in the absence of grace.

Modern, sophisticated, reflexive – because contingent – persons do not seek redemption from doubt or sin.

One has no doubts after having called heads or tails in the existential wager. Men and women who put everything at stake for the sake of not being engaged in the first-order wager are in no need of redemption from doubt. This is why they put all their stakes on the second-order wager; as far as spiritual doubt is concerned, their need is to remain unredeemed. They are not in need of salvation, but it is still not certain that this 'March', this 'Whole' is 'something superfluous', for them.

Men and women who choose themselves existentially as good (decent) persons will become what they already are: good, decent persons. They will address the blank envelope to themselves to reach them at the destination called 'decency'. They will not transgress on purpose, for decency is the objective purposefulness of their whole life, although they can still transgress in case of moral conflicts, or due to ignorance.[38] Decent persons regret if they wrong others and they try to rectify this wrong. Sometimes, this is no longer possible. But even then, they are in no need of salvation. The transgression remains external to their character, albeit engraved on their life. They cannot be 'saved' from their 'sins', without losing their character and their life. As far as salvation from sins is concerned, these men and women have no need to be redeemed. But, again, it is not likely that various forms of History, for example, history of the spirit, of a people, of art, of religion and of philosophy, the whole 'Gang', becomes something superfluous for people like them or because of people like them.

Without calling heads in the existential wager, one does not commit sins. Without choosing oneself existentially as a decent person, one will fail to give preference to the good as against the useful, the successful and the pleasant in principle and not solely in practice. In the absence of the divergence between maxim and action, there are no pangs of conscience. There still remains the feeling of unease, the fear of being put to shame, the unpleasant taste of the bitter medicine. But there is no suffering from diremption (*Entzweiung*) and, as a result, no need for salvation from sin.

But there is diremption and there is suffering. Above all, the contingent person, too, suffers from doubt; he may doubt his own abilities to perform, his talents, his power of attraction. He may also distrust the loyalty, truthfulness or fidelity of friends, colleagues, parents, wives or children. He may be uncertain in himself, or diffident in others. Thus he suffers from uncertainty just like the infidel or the sinner who fears the next temptation. The contingent person would also suffer from nostalgia; he would rather live at some other time and in another place than when and where he does; he would escape into the past and the future in his bid for salvation. The contingent person suffers from anxiety – not from anxiety vis-à-vis the evil, but from anxiety vis-à-vis freedom.[39] More precisely, men and women who linger in contingency keep anxiety of evil and anxiety of freedom apart. Moderns are thrown into freedom by the accident of birth. As long as they linger in this accidental state, their existence remains split (*entzweit*). Anxiety of freedom is the existential source of all other anxieties. This split can be healed by the existential choice, although if one chooses oneself existentially under the category of difference,[40] the same split might become rather more pregnant, i.e. conscious. One person's suffering from the split can also enrich others, if the experience gains admittance into the forms of 'absolute spirit'.

Moderns suffer from depression, frustration, inferiority complexes. They suffer from loneliness and also from obligations. They suffer from the unpleasant and the uncanny. They suffer from complications and from uniformity, from excitement and from boredom. They suffer because the world is as it is, and they suffer because things are changing. They suffer from tonal music as well as from atonal music. They suffer because there are too many 'things' on the market out there, and they suffer because they can buy but few of them. They suffer from the very existence of television sets or of washing machines. They are suffering from the monotony of life. They are suffering from emptiness, senselessness, from the loss of meaning or the futility of gaining or regaining meaning. Some yearn for personal salvation, others for the salvation of the modern, contingent, world as it is. They are in need of salvation. They are looking for the 'saving power'. 'But where the danger is, grows the saving power also.'[41]

It is difficult to tell what it now means to be saved. It can mean the elimination of the suffering of the person without the elimination of the cause of that suffering – a kind of low-key reconciliation with oneself, with one's bad fate and with the state of the world. It can also mean the elimination of the cause of suffering, for example that the sick will be healed, the untalented will find their real talents and the impotent will become potent. Attaining peace of mind, making peace with oneself are spiritual states that are traditionally associated with 'being saved'. It can also mean to gain sense, meaning and direction in one's life; making an existential choice is, in this sense, redemptive. To be born for the second time is also traditionally associated with 'being saved'. The promise of an everlasting life, has, however, vanished from modern imagination. Not even calling heads in the cosmic wager brings it back. Without this promise, the salvation of the person loses its cutting edge. Death is final. This is a paradoxical situation. It was Heidegger's merit to spell out that without the acceptance of this finality, the life of modern persons becomes inauthentic. If the existential choice is a kind of salvation (being born for the second time), 'being saved' and the acceptance of the finality of death are linked with one another. But the desire to overcome death is the ultimate need for individual salvation; the immortality of the soul, everlasting life, the resurrection of the dead are only the best-known manifestations of this need. Where the individual does not yet form his or her 'internal space', there is no such need. But the modern person who chooses herself existentially is an individual who is self-endowed with an 'internal space'. The aspect of 'eternity' in salvation returns from the future (after death) to the present (during life). *Memento vivere*, said Nietzsche. Ashes to ashes, and yet you can be saved. Salvation becomes obscure, undefined and undetermined. It is a metaphor that stands for the quintessence of everything that men and women need. Those needs can be authentic or inauthentic. That which men and women need authentically, they can also receive authentically: peace of mind and healing through reconciliation.

Versöhnung is, after all, the philosophical susbstitute for, or rather the equivalent of, religious salvation. The saving power of philosophy rests in *Versöhnung*.

Who (or what) else of the this-worldly actors or props has a 'saving power' in modern imagination?

The 'eternal femininity elevates us' ('Das ewig Weibliche zieht uns hinan').[42] The eternal feminine is supposed to have saving power. This is a theological division of gender roles; man is to be saved and women is the one who saves. Women 'pull' men out of the state of damnation, and they pull them upwards (into Heaven). Women (the repository of saving power) do not need to be saved.

The Victorian idea of *mulier salvatrix* has a comic touch. It had been replaced since with the older, yet also more modern and more general, idea that it is love that has the saving power.

Love, allegedly, 'saves' both sexes – from loneliness, self-doubt, depression, inferiority complexes, addiction, failure and so on. Love as utopia promises happiness, love as saving power promises second birth.

Art is also supposed to be a saving power. Art 'saves' men and women from senselessness, from the fragmentation of their life, from pettiness, from the reconciliation with an unredeemed world. Art as utopia promises happiness, art as redeemer rather saves men and women from succumbing to the temptation of cheap happiness.

Finally, *violence*, too, is supposed to have a saving power. From this saving power, we need to be redeemed.

'Zion shall be redeemed by judgement, and her repentant ones by justice. Rebels and sinners alike shall be crushed, those who desert the LORD shall be consumed.'[43]

Apocalyptic justice is violent. Whatever horror human imagination can project: fire, water, pestilence, darkness, chaos, collapse of mountains, cosmic catastrophies, and above all, rivers and seas full of blood, all these introduce and accompany the final struggle from which the holy Kingdom of the blessed will emerge. Enter the End of all Things, the End of Times, *Dies Irae*, the Day of Universal Violence. The language is matter-of-fact: 'So the four angels were released: this was precisely the hour, the day, the month and the year for which they had been prepared, to kill the third of mankind. . . . By these three plagues – the smoke, the sulphur and fire – . . . a third of mankind was slain.'[44] The watershed between the present and the millenium is bloodshed.

The End is the Goal, the Purpose. The end of all things is the goal as well as the purpose of all things. The end of life is the goal and the purpose of life, the end of the human race is the goal and the purpose of this race, the end of the world is the goal and the purpose of the world. At the end, that which has reached its end ceases to exist.

The end is nothing, the movement is everything. The movement is purposeful; it is the movement which reaches its peak, its perfection at the end. Reaching perfection is death. Whatever does not move or change, is dead. If everything reaches its End, everything dies. God's miracle is not the destruction of the world that has reached its end, but the promise that there is life after the end, that there is a world without end, a world which had been preceeded by the end. One does not need four angels to kill off a third of mankind. Mankind itself can do greater miracles than this; but no phantasy can grasp the Thereafter in other terms than those of Survival. Survival is to live on while turning one's back on Apocalypse, but something must still be ahead. The end of all things is the Mystery. But in the Revelation the end of all things is just the end of all things as they hitherto existed. Many things happen after the end of Time. The Thousand-Year-Kingdom will come. But 'the night shall be no more'.[45]

This grand narrative tells the story of the world (and particularly that of the human race) from the vista of the End. All traditional narratives do likewise. It is not enough to finish a novel; one needs to attach the magic word 'the end' to the end of the last chapter. The reader can start afresh, the characters cannot. They are finished and done with. Sometimes a brief afterword informs us about their further fate; the writer becomes uneasy about having killed the characters she herself created with the magic word 'the end'. At the end of fairy tales, we rest assured that the prince and the princess lived happily ever after. The public likes a happy ending, particularly a wedding; and even more so if the happily wed are finally united after misfortunes, after having been first separated. Wedding is the moment of reconciliation (*Versöhnung*) after the sublation of the diremption and the alienation by cruelty, through luck, collision and misunderstanding. Death is an unhappy ending, particularly in the form of suicide, which is still well-suited for a traditional modern narrative.

Grand narratives are fictions using mainly non-fictitious characters as their protagonists.[46] Hegel writes traditional novels. *The Phenomenology of Spirit* ends, after all, with the consummation of the marriage between the Absolute Spirit and History. Similarly, socialists of the early nineteenth century hypostasize the End into the future as *promesse du bonheur*, as Utopia. There is nothing apocalyptic about them. However, Marx's grand narrative introduces apocalyptic elements into the modern imagination. Sorel, on his part, conjures up the whole paraphernalia of apocalypse as an antidote to Marx's rationalist progressivism.[47] And yet, the two images merge. The radical imagination of twentieth-century Europe, including the radical philosophical imagination, became apocalyptic throughout. In this respect, it makes no difference whether a position is 'for' or 'against', Marxist or anti-Marxist, for or against the grand narrative, rationalist or anti-rationalist, nor whether it is the end of a progression or a regression that is predicted to be consummated in that 'what must happen very soon'.[48] The appointed time is near – says the lord of science or anti-science alike. This struggle will be the last – harken!

'Who will save us from Western civilization?', the young Lukács once asked.[49]

Apocalypse is Western Civilization. Apocalypse should save us from Western Civilization. Western Civilization is to save us from itself, from alienation and from fetishism, from reification and from false consciousness, from the diremption of subject and object and that of the individual and the species, from justice and also from injustice, from domination, from force and from power, from autocracy and democracy, from the market, from selling and buying, from gold and silver, from property and from propertylessness, from equality and inequality, from the burden of work and from the tedium of idleness, from lovelessness and from the family, from nationhood and from solitude, from religion and from paganism, from the division of labour, from – all predicaments of the actual Western civilization. The telos of Western Civilization is the negation of Western Civilization through the apocalyptic vision of the Western Civilization.

But there is something phony about the modern apocalypse. Apocalypse is a religious vision, the modern apocalypse is pagan. The word 'pagan' does not stand here for atheist; the pagan can also be a believer. The real issue is that moderns introduce an alien element into the apocalyptic vision; the pagan-Greek element of *kairos*.

Kairos is the guiding *daimonion* of a free political actor. 'Kairos: moment de décision, occasion critique, conjoncture dans laquelle il importe que quelque chose soit fait ou dit.'[50] The free political actor heeds the hints of *kairos*: now is the time; do not miss the proper time for action. Now you can do it, yesterday it was too early, tomorrow it will be too late. Here is Rhodus, here you jump. And one jumps. One does not expect great things to happen, one makes them happen, one brings them about. One acts upon the matters that are on the agenda, that are 'actual'; the matters of the present matter most.

Nothing is more alien from the mind of the free political actor than the images of apocalypse. Punishment after death, as presented by

Plato in the myth of Er, is un-apocalyptic. The Greek vision of violence and horror was by no means milder than the Jewish-Christian. Parricide, cannibalism, incest, murderous lust on the one hand, pestilence, cosmic catastrophies, indescribable suffering inflicted by gods for the most part as punishment or just out of sheer whim are common occurences in Greek mythology. But neither violence nor horror in its wake had anything to do either with the End (qua telos), or with the purpose and consummation of history. Outbursts of cosmic violence and ensuing horror particularly did not carry with them the meaning of the last happening before the final appearance of Absolute Goodness.

Apocalypse is as alien from *Kairos* as *Kairos* from Apocalypse.[51] But both are Western history. So is their combination in the form of the phony apocalypse. Phony apocalypse is also phony *kairos*. The political actor subtitutes himself for the Angels; it is he who breaks the seals and inflicts the terror. He does the opposite of that which he must do according to the apocalyptic imagination, namely perfect himself and become righteous. The political actor inflicts terror with his glance set on the Kingdom which is not to come. Revelation is not a human affair; only the Lamb and the messenger of the Lamb can reveal. But philosophers are not messengers of the Lamb; neither are political actors. But once he has mounted the Horse of Apocalypse, the actor can no longer heed the voice of *Kairos*. He is in a hurry, for he has received the promise of the Kingdom. The trumpets sound too loud; the heartbeat of the present cannot be heard. The actor pulls out his sword to kill off, if 'it comes to pass', one third of mankind. The time is indeed ripe, the moment has arrived, here is Rhodus, here you jump. . .but into what?

On the apocalyptic tone that became widespread lately in philosophy, by Jacques Derrida.[52] The title is a paraphrasis of Kant.

The (brilliant) booklet is an attempt at the deconstruction of apocalypse through translation(s). In order to give a taste of its character without following it too closely, let me enumerate a few themes of the tonal-atonal composition. Here they are. Apocalypse is the Greek translation of the Hebrew word: *gala*. *Gala* means to unveil (sex, eyes, ear). Jahweh's glory is unveiled for eyes and ears. Circumcision reveals. Uncovering brings danger; see Noah, or the Tetragrammaton. The end is uncovered; it is illuminated by the light of God. Enlightenment. The end of philosophy; the imminence of danger. Nietzsche said that Oedipus was the last man; it is always the last man who speaks. Diversification of eschatological strategies; denouncing oneself in advance. Truth itself is the End; Truth of the Apocalypse is the

Truth of Truth. We are all going to die – it is as if we are already dead. Wake up! Jesus or John speaks? Or rather the messenger? We continue to denounce the impostors, the so-called messengers. Come! There is apocalypse without apocalypse; end without end. Do not seal, do not sign (do not break the seal).

My fake table of contents (that of a mischievous messenger) tried to illuminate (not to reveal) that the deconstruction of apocalypse cannot be carried to its end (end of the end). An entirely ironical and parodistical, i.e. external, presentation of apocalypse – with all its possible translations – runs against the limits of *our* language, against the limits not only of its words and sentences alone, but also of its *tone*, the apocalyptic tone, that remains audible even if it is 'mistuned' (*verstimmt*) or hidden behind atonality. When Derrida quotes 'Come!' – the reader rises. When he quotes 'Wake up!' – the reader prepares for the message. And when he says 'do not seal – do not sign (do not break the seal)!' – the reader hears something in the tone (through the tone) that is not to be found in the text. Behind all the parodies on the theme of signing or not signing, sealing or not sealing, there is an earnestness which is unaccounted for, unless one recalls that it is 'decreed that each of the blessings in the daily prayer be concluded with the name of the Tetragrammaton, which, indeed, *seals* each of the paragraphs' (*Zohar* 569, 64).[53]

Lately, the apocalyptic tune has become very loud and conspicuous in philosophy.

First came the crisis: the crisis of European sciences, of European culture, of rationality, of liberalism, of democracy, and the like. Then came the End: the end of reason, the end of the subject, the end of art, the end of ideology, the end of philosophy – the end of history. The crisis itself came to an end, because it has come to the 'End'.

For sure, the end of reason does not imply that people stop reasoning or telling useful from harmful from this time onward. The end of the subject does not signal the demise of the person, the individual, or even of their self-created 'internal space'. The end of art does not prevent anyone from writing poems or composing music, nor does the end of philosophy prevent us from speculating in a metaphysical style. Finally, the end of history does not exclude the possibility that things of political or social significance may also happen afterwards.

The strong and sometimes shrieking apocalyptic tone makes up for the loss of apocalyptic visions. One is still in a rush; one has to close, to sign, to seal, to break the seal. It is 'the end' that renders meaning in a contingent world. It is from the 'end' that a story can be understood. It is from the end that 'bad infinity' can be overcome. For sure, if we state that the end is here (or in the near future), we are still party to the thing which is now coming to its end: of history, of art, of philosophy, of the subject. We cut ourselves off from the future rather than tie ourselves to the great expectations. The story has both a radical and a liberal version.

As a concise sample of the radical version, let me quote Heidegger: 'The end of philosophy proves to be the triumph of the manipulable arrangement of a scientific-technological world and of the social order proper to this world.'[54] And he continues:

> Thinking must first learn what remains reserved and in store for thinking to get involved in. It prepares its own transformation in its learning. . . . We are thinking of the possibility that the world civilization which is just now beginning might one day overcome the technological-scientific-industrial character as the sole criterion of man's world sojourn. This may happen not of and through itself, but in virtue of the readiness of man for a determination which, whether listened or not, always speaks in the destiny of man which had not yet been decided. It is just as uncertain whether world civilisation will soon be abruptly destroyed or whether it will be stabilized for a long time, in a stabilization, however, which will not rest in something enduring, but rather establish itself in a sequence of changes, each of which presenting the latest fashion.[55]

European culture thus reached its end by carrying its possibilities to the end through the universalization of its technological-manipulative potentials. This part of the story was generally accepted in twentieth-century radicalism. But the expectation is missing. No further reversals of the sign though apocalyptic events is in sight. No longer are infants singing the praise of the Lord. No historical materialism that 'explodes the continuum of history' is in sight.[56] For the later Heidegger, the future is just the flat and monotonous continuation of the present; there is no parousia, no *Jetztzeit*. However, there is still hope, and the possibility of transcendence is not entirely discarded, but transformed from certainty into uncertainty. The element of *kairos* is entirely gone, and the traditional religious attitude returns to its old place: man needs to be prepared for grace, in the awareness that grace can be granted as well as not. And yet, the traditional element is not religious, for the preparation for grace (regardless of whether it is granted or not) does not consist in the practice of goodness (righteousness), but of practising philosophical thinking of a kind, the continuation of the very thinking which has come to its end. But how can one continue after the end or within the end?

There are several variations of the apocalyptic tone which has lately become widespread in philosophy. Some of them are original, others are merely parroting the motif of the 'end of. . .', without meaning too much by it. The weighty word 'End' is taken very lightly.

The assertion 'the end of X' means that the telos of 'X' has been achieved, all of its possibilities developed; nothing more can be expected from it than what has already been revealed; the thing remains as it is, a dead thing, a dead state, a dead metaphor. It can (or might) also disappear, or it might have already disappeared, and become a thing of the past. In asserting 'the end of X' one buries 'X'; one can also bury 'X' alive.[57] One can even kill 'X' in asserting 'the end of X'.

In asserting 'the end of History', one can imply the end of the grand narrative, the end of the principle of hope, the end of European civilization, or the end of all the bad things which have prevented us hitherto from making ourselves comfortable in modern liberal democracies. Since one never knows whether one buries a corpse or declares a living thing dead (since empirical history certainly continues), every utterance about 'the end of X' is an act of murder or a death wish which, in this case, amounts to the same thing, given that a metaphor, an imaginary institution, a belief, a concept, or a language game is effectively killed by the assertion of its end. But, before committing the act of such a ritual philosophical murder, the philosopher should consider whether he wishes the thing really dead, or whether his death wish is but the manifestation of his despair and sorrow because the thing, in which he invested affections, turned out to be different from what he had expected and hoped for.

4 Marche funèbre
1914–89

In our century, the March of History became the funeral march in the wake of the man-inflicted Apocalypse.

Man-inflicted Apocalypse is the parody of apocalypse; as a parody, it is also the final consummation of the most ambitious project of modern man: deification. Men are envious of apocalypse; their ambition is to do it better. Why should angels kill off one third of the human race when the strongest (or the most progressive) human beings are also capable of so doing? And why wait, perhaps forever, for the Messiah to usher in the Millennium, if men-as-Messiah can do it better, and also sooner? The apocalyptic imagination has been preserved, but also given a pagan twist. Modern man identifies with archaic titans like Prometheus, and archaic heroes like Sigfried. Prometheus hated, Sigfried vanquished gods. The potion, concocted of ancient and Jewish-Christian elements, of Kairos and Apocalypse, is lethal. Under its influence, the moderns start to meddle in the work of apocalypse.

The performance of European totalitarianism is the parody of Apocalypse: instead of sense, senselessness, instead of meaning, the lack of meaning. The Angel called Mengele selected those to be saved from those to be doomed; but the saved were also doomed in the unending happening of the bad infinity of violence. In the parodistic Apocalypse there is no difference between Hell and Millennium. As Serenus Zeitblom remarks about the masterwork of his deceased friend, Adrian Leverkühn, *Apocalypsis cum Figuris*: '(T)his hellish laughter at the end of the first part has its pendant in the . . . chorus of children . . . but in the searing, susurrant tones of spheres and angels there is not one note which does not occur, with rigid correspondence, in the hellish laughter.'[58]

Many things that Walter Benjamin divined as signs of this-worldly salvation have actually been realized to the last letter as the funeral march of history passed from stage to stage. Time stoods still in the concentration camps, for there was no 'transition in this present'.[59] In the gas-chambers the continuum of history was certainly exploded,[60] and if there was a place where 'the entire course of history has been preserved and sublated'[61] in its negative totality, it was the Gulag. Everyone turned turned 'towards the sun that rose at the horizon of history',[62] but the rays of this sun did not light up those faces; they burned them. And in the moment of danger people were, indeed, no more tempted to 'tell history as it really happened'.[63]

Walter Benjamin saw in Klee's picture, *Angelus Novus*, the allegory of history as catastrophe. But the man-inflicted apocalypse resists allegorical representation. One cannot invent allegories that would make Auschwitz or the Gulag perceptible. Auschwitz and the Gulag are themselves allegories, and no representation can enlarge and deepen them, or make them more forceful. They are the allegories of Evil. Every age has its own evil. The Evil of the modern age came to pass in the Parody of the Apocalypse.

Evil is not 'bad', it is demonic. The transgression that is the evil and that brings all evils into the world appears in the mantle of the good or the beautiful or the just. The moment evil becomes banal, it has already lost its attraction. At first, evil maxims sound far superior to the laws of common men. They befit to the hero, the overman, the new revolutionary elite, the esoteric seminarist. Evil is temptation.

Whoever is in need for salvation, yearns for a saving power. The moderns, unless they have called heads in the existential wager, turn towards earthly saving powers. Philosophy is said to be a saving power: so is art and love. And so is violence. 'Violence! Who cannot resist Violence?' exclaims Emilia Galotti, the heroine of Lessing, but it is difficult to resist temptation.[64] When violence is presented as a saving power, it tempts, and it becomes demonic. Violence in itself is not evil, but violence invested with saving power is. When Sartre preached the exercise of violence as the therapy against the loss of identity through previous acts of violence, he also coined the apposite term: 'the radicalisation of Evil'.

Force is ubiquitous, so is violence. (The German word used by Benjamin, *Gewalt*, means both.)[65] The assertion that justice and the use of force are merely the two sides of the same coin, can be verified or falsified, depending on the interpretation of justice or (and) of force. For Kant, for example, the modern legal system implies by definition the permission (*Befugnis*) to use force, but there is also a kind of justice, too, (*Billigkeit*) which does not.[66] In agreement with Sorel and other radicals of our century, Benjamin sneers at 'law-preserving, administering force', as well as at the kind of force or violence that clears the way for new institutions, legal orders and concepts of justice. For in both cases, there is a means-end relationship, and force (or violence) is used as a means to achieve an end which remains external to the acts of force or violence, such as the preservation of an existing legal order, or the establishment of a new one. The model of 'pure violence' has to be found, the kind of violence which neither reinforces nor establishes any legal order. Pure violence is not an end, or rather it is an end-in-itself, and as such, non-instrumental. Benjamin identifies the uncorrupted kind of 'pure violence' with divine violence. And divine violence will become the model for revolutionary violence. Hence theology and politics are merged and the struggle between social democracy and communism acquires a theological dimension. This becomes the showdown between 'mythical violence' and 'divine violence', between 'law-establishing violence' and 'law-annihilating violence',[67] just as Sorel associated Jaurez's bid for parliamentary power with all kinds of base cruelties, and hailed Lenin as the Leader who would finally push the world beyond the confines of ugly and petty means-goals calculations.[68]

'Divine violence, which is insignia and seal, and never a means of sacred execution, can be called the violence that reigns.'[69] Divine power is saving power, divine violence redeems. But revolutionary violence is violence inflicted by humans on humans; and no one has special dispensation from the commandment that 'thou shalt not murder'. No human group has the power to sign or to seal (or to break the seal). Universal saving power does not reside in the human race, nor in the best or worst of us. Human groups can only force others, by practising permanent violence, to admit under duress that the other is endowed with the saving power, although it is not, and that it can sign and seal, or break the seal, although it cannot. This is how the permanence of violence comes to pass. The violence of totalitarianism is pure insofar as it is not instrumental in the sense that violence or force generally is. Nothing external to the practice of violence will be achieved by this kind of violence. No holy goal will be justified by it, no new legal order established. Violence will merely go on unabated, breeding new violence, to prove nothing but its own power to save, sign and seal, and to break the seal, by forcing others to believe that this power indeed prevails. This is violence for violence's sake, violence as the parody of Kingdom, for the moment violence ceases, the phony kingdom also disappears.

Violence and force used as means towards goals can be fraudulent, criminal, insufficient or faulty. These kinds of violence can also sometimes precipitate the achievement of certain goals, which, on their part, can be beneficial, ambiguous or criminal. The exercise of force or of violence in order to establish an institution or to achieve a position, that is, as a means to an end, is a typical way of instrumentalizing actions as well as persons. Instrumental force and violence call for critical scrutiny, scorn and anger. But pure violence cannot be criticized. Who would have to courage to 'criticize' Auschwitz? Or, for that matter, the Gulag? Would anyone dare to be 'mad at' Auschwitz? Or, for that matter, at the Gulag? Bloody and lethal is the parody of Apocalypse, and it has no other legacy but corpses.

The cortege slowly proceeds to the cemetery. Six people carry the coffin, men and women who keep pace with the rhythm of the funeral march. Each deceased can have a funeral march from record or disc. The choice is not particularly wide, yet a few suitable funeral marches are always at our disposal, one by Beethoven, another by Chopin and yet another by Wagner. Funeral marches are these days added to religious liturgical music; they are sometimes substitutes for the latter.

A funeral march is composed for heroes. Although Beethoven erased the dedication of his Third Symphony, it is still the military men of the First Consul's army whom we feel are honoured in that famous second movement. And it is Sigfried, the longer, the blond beast, who is being carried to the tune of solemn melodies toward the pyre where the fire will consume the living Brünhilde alongside him, without the accompaniment of a funeral march.

The funeral march honours the modern Liberator. He is the liberator of a brand new myth; not descendant of royal families but one who has risen from humble origins. He is the self-made man; his Self is made by force. He does not restore order but overthrows it, he does not obey gods, but defies them or becomes a demi-god himself. The enthusiastic cult of the grand Liberator fits badly with the prosaic patterns of modern life. This is why the liberating-saving hero remains confined to the operatic stage; attempts at his theatrical resuscitation fails miserably. Yet the appeal of the self-made mythical heros is not entirely lost from modern life; its vestiges gave a natural touch to the unnatural rise of totalitarian dictators. But there are very few common elements between that 'world-spirit on horseback' and the totalitarian dictators. The hero of the bourgeois myth was merely an heroic utilitarian; the violence he practised was the kind of violence Benjamin termed legislative or mythical; it was by no means 'divine'. Mussolini reminds us of this type. But we also know from Goebbels' diary that Mussolini was no match for the genuinely great revolutionaries: Hitler and Stalin. Nothing is less befitting Hitler and Stalin than a funeral march.

And no funeral march surrounds the hearse of the victims of the man-made apocalypse. They have no hearse, not even a coffin or a grave; they did not mount the pyre. They were burned, and starved, and gassed, or shot wholesale. They were not handpicked. Not even the reverse of Judgement day occured to them: neither justice nor injustice. For there is no justice or injustice without yardsticks; and pure violence is not familiar with them. The victims never knew why precisely they had been selected. They were robbed, not only of their lives, but also of their deaths; of the meaning of life, of the meaning of death. The *Eroica* does not sound for them. Only after the rare moments when resistance, with a visible face and with a name we know, brought pure violence to a temporary stop, when the victim, robbed of his life, could not at least be robbed of the meaning of his death, do we lend our ears to the mourning sound of the trumpets of the *Eroica*. For a funeral march befits the victim who was handpicked and yet who resisted. But it is not for them that we are mourning.

We are mourning in silence, for the unknown, for the nameless, for those who were not handpicked. We seek comfort, but not for ourselves. Rather, we are intent on finding out what comfort they can have for whom no trumpet sounds.

I skim through the volumes of Walter Benjamin again, in order to seek an answer. Benjamin is the right author, for he, as so many others, was tempted by the beauty of the recipe concocted and mixed from theology and politics; for a while, he has even flirted with the demon. he was also one of the numberless victims of that Parodistic Apocalypse.

I take some samples from his notebooks containing unfinished thoughts on the philosophy of history.

'Should critique and prophecy be the categories which merge in "salvaging" the past?'[70] Rather not. We are mourning the victims of an age which is beneath criticism, and no prophecied future can attach sense to their fate, however luminous that future may be.

'The subject of history: the oppressed, not humankind'.[71] The dignity of the 'subject of history' can make the slave's slavery more bearable and the drudgery of the (Marxian) proletariat easier – for their respective historians. But the victims of the parodistic Apocalypse were not subjects of history. They were not 'humankind', nor were they treated as humans. They were not the 'oppressed', who, as the slaves in Hegel, stand in reciprocal relationship to those who dominate them. They were swept away by violence, useless even to occupy the place of the oppressed.

'Every epoque dreams about the next' ('Chaque epoque reve la suivante').[72] But the mourners dream about the previous epoque – this is their nightmare.

'The eternal lamp is an image with a genuine historical existence. It is the image of the redeemed mankind – the flame, lighted on Judgment Day, will be nourished by everything that had ever existed among humans.'[73] Men and women, who were calling heads in the cosmic wager, might find consolation in these thoughts. But there are many amongst the mourners who were calling tails, and some of them put everything they had, their freedom, life and happiness, at risk to resist betting in this wager. For them, the eternal lamp is just an allegory. But, on second thoughts, had I called heads in the cosmic wager, I do think I still would not find comfort in the expectation of this final judgement. The divine flame is too great an equalizer; it is not just. The suffering of the victims of the man-made apocalypse cannot be equalized with other sufferers. They should have a special place, not because of the greater quantity of their suffering but because of the special quality of their plight. After all, Apocalypse itself is co-responsible for its own parody.

'But from what can something be salvaged which had already happened?. . . From a certain manner of its being passed on.'[74] As a very modest endeavour, this can indeed be in the mourner's reach; in addition, the mourners can do this without lying. Neither saving power nor prophetic vision is required to rescue the silences of the victims from the outrage of cheap sentimentality, from academic hair-splitting, from political machinations, and from too noisy a lamentation. The mourners can, further, unearth the ruins of the man-inflicted apocalypse from under the new debris which has already been piled upon them. Perhaps the children of the mourners will also join the labour, while listening to the rhythm of the soundless funeral march.

3

Introducing Reason, Will and Other Characters

1 The Philosophical Characters In Order of Appearance

Philosophers call their characters ideas, categories, speculative concepts and the like; students of philosophy refer to all of them as 'categories'. Philosophers write plays and stage them; categories are the actors of these plays. The dramatic composition of philosophy was still explicit in Plato, particularly in the young one. But already Plato, and even more so Aristotle, came to realize that categories are characters in their own right. This is why they decided to abandon the ancient set of real-life characters in order to compose their plays with the new set alone. The new actors do not need mouthpieces, they attack the others on their own and they are their own lawyers.

In order to discuss philosophical characters, one needs to speak philosophically, that is, one has to introduce a few philosophical characters. Here is an example:

Socrates: Tell, me, Theaitetos, is there one single philosophical play or are there many?

Theaitetos: It seems to me that there is only one.

Socrates: So you maintain that philosophy participates only in the One and not also in the Many?

Theaitetos: There are many philosophies, indeed, and so it appears as if philosophy would also participate in the Many. But there is only one true philosophy, that is, truly, there is only one.

Socrates: Is the One in motion?

Theaitetos: Certainly not.

Socrates: If not in motion, it is always in the state of Rest.

Theaitetos: So it seems to me.

Socrates: Didn't we agree previously[1] that thinking is the conversation the soul conducts with itself?

Theaitetos: We did.
Socrates: Does a conversation take place in time, or is it timeless?
Theaitetos: It needs time.
Socrates: Listen, Theaitetos. You said that philosophy participates only in the One and by no means in the Many. But we also agreed that the One in itself is eternal, timeless, motionless.
Theaitetos: So we did.
Socrates: But philosophy is a kind of thinking, isn't it?
Theaitetos: How could I deny this!
Socrates: And since thinking goes on in time, it participates in Motion and also in the Many. Can you still maintain that philosophy does not participate in the Many?
Theaitetos: I realize now how great a fool I was . . . and so on . . .

In this brief and imaginary dialogue many philosophical characters have already been introduced, such as the One and the Many, the True and (at least by implication) the False, the Motion and the Rest, the Eternal and the Temporal. It is thus that one stages the philosophical play that plays itself.

To speak a slightly archaic language, philosophy is One and it is also Many. However, the relation between philosophy as One and philosophies as Many is more complex than that between a species and its specimen or between the General on the one hand, and the Particular and Singular which this General encompasses on the other. For example, the genre of the novel is a species, whereas single novels are specimens of this species. The same holds true about philosophy. And yet, a work of philosophy does not relate to the genre called Philosophy in the same way as a novel relates to Novel. In each novel the story is new and so are the characters. Although Balzac re-stages many of his characters in his gigantic cycle, no one dreamt after Balzac of using them again. A character is somehow the private property of a novelist. But a philosophical Character is not the private property of a philosopher in the above sense, or, put more cautiously, this has not been the usage up until recently. The Oneness of philosophy as a genre requires that philosophers draw their characters from a common pool.

Philosophers borrow their characters from this pool but they do not take them exactly as they find them. They reshape them, they re-write the roles those characters play, they modify the cast, and thus the relation of the characters changes also. They can also make many characters out of a single one or, the other way around, they can fuse several characters into a single one. As Hegel put it,[2] Art falls apart into the single works of Art, whereas philosophy does not split at all, rather, it becomes more and more synthesized. Viewed in retrospect, so Hegel believes, philosophy turned out to be a single One that has developed in and through its Many shapes. Hegel's successors do not share his vision. For them, Hegel's philosophy, just like all other outstanding specimens of the species, is one philosophy out of many.

Philosophy is One, but also Many, Identity as well as Difference. But neither Many nor Difference are mere determinations (*Bestimmungen*) of the One or of Identity. They could be understood as such if philosophy were an ongoing attempt at problem-solving or an ongoing hermeneutical (interpretative) exercise practised on the self-same text.

Assume that there is a problem to solved (for example, the problem of Being) and from Thales to Heidegger all philosophers addressed themselves to the solution of this problem. Were this the case, we could argue that all attempts at the solution of this problem added something to the final, satisfactory, true, perfect and complete answer. But this assumption is misconceived in several respects. First, there are no 'perennial' problems that every generation from Thales onwards tried to solve, if in different ways. The questions that philosophers ask from their world create the philosophical problems to be addressed.[3] However, if philosophers do not make attempts at the solution of the same perennial problems, but create their problems by the questions they put, it is then hardly possible to regard philosophical solutions as cumulative determinations (*Bestimmungen*) of the same Universal (for example, Being). Further, although philosophy mobilizes 'problem-solving' thinking also, the latter plays the second fiddle in philosophical speculations. Finally, problem-solving thinking is spurious for the most part, as it serves as a facade to legitimize the philosopher's intuition that has grasped the result of the problem-solving operation before it had been embarked upon.

A similar difficulty arises if one assumes that there is *one* meaning (text) to interpret (for example, the meaning of Being) and that from Thales to Heidegger all philosophers interpreted and reinterpreted the meaning of Being. If this were the case, it could be maintained that all interpretations of Being contributed to the determination (*Bestimmung*) of Being, that the Many has already filled the One just as Difference has filled Identity. An open philosophy would add that the philosophical-interpretative labour is still, or permanently, going on. The futuristic extension is of no help, for the assumption that the same text is continuously interpreted is also difficult to maintain. A perennial interpretandum is like a 'perennial problem'. Philosophy (as the One) is not an exercise where the same interpretandum(s) are to be interpreted. New *interpretanda* are introduced, old ones are – sometimes – abandoned. If interpretations change the interpretandum(s) themselves, and, in fact, every interpretation changes its interpretandum, the interpretandum itself ceases to be the Same. Something similar, but not quite the same, happens in all kinds of interpretation. Every Hamlet-interpretation changes Hamlet, every interpretation of Being changes Being, but whereas the interpreters of Hamlet have access to the original text that has been changed by its interpretations, there is no original text of Being other than interpretations of Being itself, either someone else's or our own. Despite Whitehead's witty remark,[4] philosophy is not an ongoing Plato-interpretation. It is hard to imagine philosophy as a Universal, or a One that contains all its interpretations. And it is equally hard to understand philosophy as an exclusively interpretive exercise, for if one does so, one also rejects all the traditional claims raised by time-honoured philosophies, first of all their claims to the Knowledge of Truth, as self-delusory. But self-interpretation too belongs to interpretation. If Socrates were familiar with some branches of contemporary philosophy, he would allow himself the remark that a merely hermeneutical understanding of philosophy is self-contradictory. Moderns, on their part, might warn him that the law of contradiction does not apply here. After all, a thousand stories can be told about the same thing, all of them remaining different, many of them becoming incompatible, while all will still be relevant and philosophically sound. Yet our Socrates might still ask whether people who declare his playful argumentation, and especially the way in which he manoeuvres his interlocutors into self-contradiction, alien to the spirit of philosophy, are authorized to declare themselves his exclusive successors.

But if philosophy is neither an exercise in solving perennial problems, nor the ongoing interpretation of primordial texts, the supposition that all philosophies are just the determinations (*Bestimmungen*) of the One and the Same philosophy does not rest on solid ground. Let us suppose rather that the relationship between Philosophy and philosophies is unlike the relation between the One and the Many or between Identity and Difference. I would propose to describe it rather as the relation between the *Common* and the *Idiosyncratic*, where Common does not stand for One or for Identity, but Idiosyncratic does stand for Many as well as for Difference.

Logos is not simply the opposite of *Mythos*, as philosophers used to believe. Neither is Logos merely a kind of Mythos or a friendly relation of Mythos as some of our contemporaries begin to believe.[5] Philosophy qua Logos was conceived as the opposite of Mythos, by substituting its own Characters for the Characters of Myth. Philosophy was and remains authentically the radical Other of Myth, precisely in the sense that was claimed by the first philosophers.

One can hardly witness a *Turn* (*Kehre*) as radical as the gesture of substituting philosophy for myth. The transformation of Mythos into Logos entails that the visible characters are replaced by invisible characters, and, more importantly, that the combination of the characters and their staging becomes free from pre-philosophical tradition; as a consequence, speculative imagination becomes unbound. Zeus can take the most phantastic and varied shapes, he can even become temporarily invisible; metamorphosis belongs to the world of myths. But when Okeanos becomes Water, or Athena Wisdom,[6] this is no longer metamorphosis but transfiguration. There is a leap between Mythos and Logos. Logos (as philosophy) can be sympathetic to Mythos and can also make plentiful use of it as Plato did (thereby earning Hegel's disapproval). It can also allow mythological characters to enter the territory of philosophical speculation (as Christian myths were used from medieval philosophers through Hegel and beyond); the leap remains a leap and the abyss cannot be bridged.

It is misleading to identify Mythos with Imagination and Logos (as philosophy) with problem-solving, cognition or argumentation. One can also tell the story the other way around. Mythical imagination flourishes best in oral cultures; literacy fossilizes it. Greek democracies, as cultures of widespread literacy, hardly inspired the free play of imagination within the narrower territory of myths. So the mythical characters became re-cast in tragedies. Philosophy (Logos) did something else: by creating entirely new characters, it established a new world-drama, or rather *the* world-drama as such. Logos liberated Imagination. No tradition limited it, no old rules applied to it – here everything was still possible. Reason flies like Phaedrus who re-gained the wings of his soul. One can also distinguish between that which philosophy (sometimes) asserts and what it (mostly) does. Philosophers abuse the imagination of the visible, whereas they release speculative imagination, imagination in the kingdom of the invisible.[7]

World-drama is not a metaphor that stands for Philosophy. Neither are the main Philosophical Characters metaphors,[8] although sometimes philosophers enliven their narratives with metaphors. Still, philosophy does not stage its characters exactly in the same way as does drama, and certainly not the way modern drama has staged them from the Elizabethan times onwards.

In a literary genre, the appearance needs to be maintained that the dramatis personae move and act on their own without the intervention of the author. In the philosophical drama, however, at least the main Characters (who happen to be also the main Actors) are mostly introduced by the author (the philosopher) himself. Sometimes this happens in a very direct way. For example, Spinoza introduces all his major characters personally before the curtain is raised, beginning with *Causa Sui*. 'By Causa Sui I understand . . .'[9] means: look, here is my chief character, called Causa Sui. Such and such are its major character traits. Now, please, Causa Sui, bow to the audience and then step aside. And Spinoza continues: here is another chief character of the world drama, termed Substance. Please, Substance, come forward, and bow to the audience, so that they can learn the main thing about you and about your Fellow Characters, called Attribute and Modi, in a proper way before the performance begins, and so forth. And even while the performance is already on, and the Characters began to play their assigned roles, Spinoza re-appears several times in order to correct something on the shape of his main Characters, to re-combine them, or to make them repeat some of their old scenes. Not all philosophers are as straightforward as Spinoza, yet all of them introduce their Characters, and all of them distinguish, and make the audience distinguish, between main characters on the one hand, and mere supporting actors and actresses on the other hand.

Philosophy is the world-drama – but so is myth.

Logos turned out to be the authentic Other of Mythos via the introduction of an entirely new set of characters (mainly of the invisible kind) so that the internal vision of the soul, that is *theoria*, could replace the external vision of the retina, that major source of the phantasy of fraudulent appearances. Yet, insofar as they both perform the world-drama, or rather the Cosmic Drama, Myth and Philosophy have also much in common. Both handle their own characters in very similar ways, both talk about the Whole (of the Universe) and both share the quasi-natural convinction that this Universe, and everything it essentially entails, can be presented on their stages, and can be truly delivered by their characters. It merely follows from the peculiarity of philosophical imagination that a mythological story is normally very detailed, whereas in philosophy stories are rather short and less complicated, since the philosopher prefers to reserve complexity for the underpinning argument. Since philosophical characters, unlike mythical characters, were invented together with philosophy, and thereby established their own tradition, philosophy was not, and was never going to be, so closely related to, or inspired by, local traditions than mythical narratives are. This is how philosophy could be *authentically* universal.

Philosophy can very easily incorporate large blocks of myths, provided that these myths have a universal message or can thus be interpreted. All myths dealing with universal concerns such as the beginning and the end, Cosmos (Universe), death, afterlife, suffering, work, love, the origins of political institutions, of justice and injustice and the like, are welcome by philosophies, and they are duly inserted into philosophical speculations. But philosophy cannot do a thing with more concrete, time-and-culture-bound aspects of myths other than pulling those myths out of their context in order to universalize them, and this is true not only of ancient, traditional myths, but also of modern ones.[10] The characters of philosophy must be transcontextual first, in order to be re-contexualized within each and every original philosophy. This is why philosophy is not only more universal than myth, but also more idiosyncratic.

Not all philosophical Characters are shaped in the same way, but they are mostly (originally) created from the words of ordinary language. Only translation alienates these characters from their original birthplace and transforms them into free-floating categories; this is true also about the Characters that had been termed categories by Aristotle. A thing *is, hence it participates in Being, hence Being is.* So there is also Non-Being (or is there not?) And since we reason, there is Reason, and since we will, there is Will, and since we imagine, there is Imagination. We discuss all things or some things or many things – so there are All, Some, Many and their companions. Similarly, there is Difference, Number, Knowledge, Now, Limit, Time, Space, also Freedom, Justice and Injustice, and, certainly, Truth and Falsity. Reason reasons, Imagination imagines, Will wills, and Language speaks (*die Sprache spricht*).[11] This is how characters became actors in their own right. They come into existence. They live independently from their creators, but they can also die. They can be resurrected, too.

Metamorphosis, as the miraculous transformation of the external shape, is a mythological figure. No metamorphosis takes place between mythological figures on the one hand and philosophical figures on the other. But with some caution, one can re-introduce the term 'metamorphosis' in order to describe the miraculous transformations of philosophical characters. That which is called Being in one philosophy can differ as much from that which is also called Being in another as a woman differs from a swan, both called Leda. This is not simply a matter of reinterpretation. The swan is not the interpretation of the woman, nor is the woman of the swan, and still, both are Leda, because in saying 'Leda', we understand both the woman and the swan. So when we say Reason we understand many a thing, entirely different characters which happened to play their role in one or another philosophy under this name. The metamorphosis lasts until a philosopher discovers that a woman, indeed, differs from a swan and that it is misleading to call both of them Leda. So either none of them is actually Leda, or there exists no Leda, or only one of them is Leda, or both of them are, yet in an entirely different fashion. We will then distinguish between the first and the second Leda, between the earthly and the divine Leda and so on.

Original philosophies mostly present their 'who is who'-registers. A relatively new beginning in philosophy makes the design of such a 'who is who'-register almost obligatory. At such junctures, but also at minor ones, the set of philosophical Characters gets drastically re-organized. Previously insignificant Characters become protagonists of many a new world-drama, whereas old stars are reduced to insignificance. New Characters are also introduced. Several old ones are fused into one, while former chief Characters are subdivided into a few chief Characters on the one hand, and some supporting ones on the other.

Although the plot played by the whole cast is idiosyncratic, and, as a result, each Character can be combined practically with each other, there are typical Character configurations also which are taken up as such with slight modifications by many generations of philosophers. This typical character-configurations are mistakenly called 'perennial problems'. Perennial they are not, for nothing is perennial which began in time, as did so-called philosophical configurations. In addition, what has been asserted about single Characters, can also be stated about typical character configurations of the philosophical tradition. The tradition suggests in such a case that 'this goes with this and with this', and for a longer time, the configuration of these Characters constitutes a 'problem' which is almost taken for granted. Character configurations are the fundamental themes, the philosophical scenes, the elementary plots of a period, a culture, or of subsequent periods and cultures. The fate of these elementary plots resembles the fate of the single Characters – they appear, re-appear or disappear, they rise from a secondary status to the uppermost rank, as they can also sink from an exalted place to the bottom of insignificance. Character-configurations are *'master narratives'* as long as they occupy a dominant position that endows them with a universal, or at least a wide, explanatory or meaning-rendering power.

Such a typical character-configuration is the philosophical plot that was crystallized around the Biblical story of Genesis, and especially around that of the expulsion from the Paradise. This configuration occupied the position of a master narrative for one and a half thousand years of philosophy. The decay of the configuration began first when philosophers started to take it as a metaphor, as is the case with original (non-borrowed) philosophical Characters in general.

Their metaphorical use normally indicates their 'imminent decay.[12] In the last hundred years even the metaphorical and playful, that is the modern, version of the original Fall/Sin plot is rarely staged.

It would be ridiculous to say that 'original sin' is a 'problem' and that one and a half thousand years of philosophy solved this problem, so that the 'problem' could now be regarded as being solved and, as such, it can disappear. It would be equally ridiculous to maintain that the philosophical character-configuration that grew out from the myth of original Sin is but one interpretation of the Main Single Interpretandum, and that it has been abandoned for reasons of hermeneutical exhaustion alone. But there is nothing ridiculous or mysterious about the fate of the master narrative if one speaks about philosophical Characters and Character-Configurations. When Manicheism threatened the Catholic-Christian creed and world order, philosophers took up some of their time-honoured Characters and made them co-players in the myth-begotten plot. Moreover, the characters of the Myth were assimilated into philosophy and paired with already traditional philosophical characters. The scene, or the scenario, has been perfected by Augustine. From then on, it became the main or the 'master' plot in the *theatrum mundi*. The stock of characters remained unchanged, but many a new character appeared later, whereas others disappeared. The plot is not yet the play. Moreover: one can create quite different plays out of the same plot; not only the atmosphere but also the 'aura' of the drama varies, so does the message, the meaning that it conveys. Lorenzo Valla, Luther and Erasmus belong to the universe of a roughly common cultural imagination. But Erasmus polemicized against the later Luther's dark drama about man's servitude in order to re-confirm human freedom, and Valla's previous treatment of the Character-Configuration is already, if only to a slight degree, metaphorical.[13]

Let me enumerate only the main Characters of the configuration: The First Couple (Man and Woman), Will, Antecedent Will, After-Will, Freedom, Choice, Deliberation, (Pre)destination, Good, Evil (Devil), Cause, Reason, Determination, Actorship (Authorship) – full or partial, Responsibility (positive and by deficit), Punishment, Reward, Justice, Injustice, Knowledge (also divine), Foreknowledge (divine), Love (also divine), Wisdom (divine too), Worlds, Possible, Probable, Necessary, Contingent, and – on the summit – God, The Saviour, Trinity, Omnipotency, Omniscience. Most of these Characters are absolutely needed for the staging of this plot; no theatre director could do without them. The relation between the characters cannot be changed at will either, although it can be shifted and re-interpreted. Yet the plot can be staged in the absence of a few above enumerated characters. For example, our theatre-director could stage the plot quite successfully with one single Character called Will, and he would not need two – the Antecedent Will and the After-Will. The roles of Choice and Deliberation can be played by one actor. One of the Characters from among the Possible, the Probable and the Necessary could also be omitted in case of shortage of actors or if the cast becomes too numerous. One need not relate the Character called World to the Characters called All and Possible – unless the director wants to stage the Leibniz-version of our story.[14]

Let us return to the starting-point.

Logos is the opposite of Mythos, Philosophy is the Other of Myth. Myth suggests something that is universal just by staging the images of one particular culture, and it points to the invisible (to a greater or lesser extent) through its colourful and very much visible characters. Philosophy does, indeed, the opposite. Yet philosophy is also very much like Myth; the two are as close to one another as only twin sisters can be. Both share the resolve to participate in the grandest spiritual adventure; they write for, perform on, the stage of the world-theatre. This common ambition appears in the way they deal with their own respective Characters which are dressed up to play their roles on the stage of *Theatrum Mundi*.

Both philosophy and myth take their players from their own pool of characters and character-configurations, even if they sometimes borrow from other pools as well. The emphasis is put on the word *pool*. Myth and philosophy are both a kind of a spiritual republic; their Characters are communal – *rei publicae*. The pool of the Characters and the pool of the Character-configurations warrant that the enterprise is not private. Although philosophy, for reasons already discussed, is more universal and at the same time more idiosyncratic than myth, private it is not. At least, up until now, philosophy had never been private.

Philosophy and myth are literary genres, for language is their medium, as for tragedy, comedy and epic poetry. Among the latter, tragedy behaved for a long time very much like philosophy, insofar as all tragic Characters and Character-configurations were borrowed from a common pool. This was a recurring phenomenon also in non-literary genres (especially in sculpture and painting) until the ascendancy of modernity. However, in modern times, it is philosophy, and philosophy alone, that sticks to the old habit. Early moderns – from Bacon to Descartes – have declared that the old Characters need to be replaced. But they have not accomplished this self-professed task. Certainly, they re-shaped some old characters, created a few new scripts and character-configurations, allocated former protagonists to subordinate roles, and elevated inferior Characters out of the same pool, although with some misgivings and amidst loud protest. As a matter of fact, Logos, the most adamant enemy of Mythos, remained in the modern world a lonely rear-guard, the Last Mohican of a once flourishing spiritual enterprise. Sharing the pool of characters that is spiritual republicanism is, after all, the *arche* of human imagination.

The genesis of tragedy and philosophy was intertwined. The birth of Tragedy might also be linked to the revolt of creative imagination against the too narrow limitations put on free phantasy by traditional-mythical narratives at a juncture when the latter mobilized only the reproductive kind of imagination. Yet tragic and philosophical imagination are both creative in different ways. Contrary to philosophy, tragedy directly 'works on myth', to use Blumenberg's expression,[15] to aquire its Characters, its Character-configurations and its main plots. But not all Characters of this pool can be borrowed and actually only few of them are. Mythological characters can fit the new bill only under the condition that they can (re)-present freedom of a kind, and the protagonists must be finite (human) beings. (Prometheus of Aischylos is also a suffering, and free, human being.) Like philosophy, tragedy, too, is more universal and more idiosyncratic than myth. Yet the genre called tragedy presents finite characters; moreover, it puts emphasis on their finitude. After all, the protagonists of a drama are going to die, and so are the actors. If the main Characters of tragedies were not mortals, they could not remain (or become) tragic. Just the opposite happens in philosophy. Here, all main characters are supposed to be Eternal, Timeless, or, in the worse case, Immortal, this is why (and how) they occupy the position of chief characters. Philosophy speaks about our finitude, addresses it; one can even say that philosophy is obsessed by the theme of our mortality, perhaps more than tragedy ever was. But the Characters themselves, the puppets of the World Theatre called philosophy, remain in all these occupations and through all those obsessions still eternal/immortal/perpetual. They are pulled out of the common pool, where they were put by virtue of their (supposed) Eternity.

Tragedy is the world theatre of finitude, because the tragic characters are finite. This is so, even if they are supposed to play for Gods. The attempt to fuse metaphysics and tragedy remained a philosophical exercise. In drama, it turned out to be a disaster.[16] In drama, characters must remain just what they are – it is finite beings alone who put everything at stake. On the other hand, the characters of philosophy are ambiguous, since they are playing for an audience of finite beings, yet without sharing their finitude. If tragic heroes are mortals in communication with the divine, philosophical characters are like ancient Gods who communicate with mortals.

It is worth concentrating on this puzzle: why and how has philosophy carried an archaic tradition right into the heart of modernity? No other genre did so. Tragedy made the last attempt at it in *tragédie classique*, and even then, there was much misgiving about the limitation put on creative fantasy by merely re-shaping characters taken from a common pool. Lukács rightly observed that in tragedy history is just a substitute for myth.[17] Historical drama, particularly that of Shakespeare, represents a unique, and uniquely successful, artistic balance between the ancient and the modern. The characters come from a common pool, yet there are no traditionally pre-set character-configurations in this pool. Besides, no tragedies of significance use the same histories for their own plot. This circumstance offers greater freedom for idiosyncratic imagination. The manneristic and affected staging of historical characters from the nineteenth century onwards indicates the general trend. Originality now requires that character presentations have to start from scratch, since each and every character is expected to be self-explanatory, to stand on its own (in all its relations with other characters who on their part have to stand on their own, too), without being enriched by all the associations stemming from their previous performances in antecedent plays. There is a similar shift in fine arts and in epic poetry.[18]

By now, philosophy is really on its own. Only Logos has remained true to Mythos. Whether philosophy's oversensitivity to its own problems of genre, or rather those serious problems themselves, have anything to do with the rearguard position of philosophy remains still to be seen.

There is painting, and there are paintings, although painters no longer rely on the common (mythical) pool of characters; there is the novel (there are novels); there is drama (there are dramas) long after the ancient practice of re-staging traditional-mythical characters is gone. Is philosophy, then, the only genre of individual authorship that can survive only as long as the common pool of characters last?[19] Can a philosopher remain a philosopher without speaking about Being, All, Many, Reason, Knowledge, Freedom, Beautiful, Good, Appearances, Truth, and a handful of other archaic characters? There were times when no one could conceive that tragedies can be written without staging characters like Oedipus, Electra, Achilles or other mythical heroes. Why not, then, philosophy without its own mythical heroes?

As the story of all the other genres suggests, modernity is not too sympathetic to the common pool of Characters. It is primarily due to the special propensity of its Characters, particularily to their invisibility, that Philosophy has survived amidst all those changes as an archaic memento.

Perhaps more new philosophical characters were created and put on the world-stage in the last fifty years than in the last five centuries altogether. A drive towards the personalization of philosophy seems to be in full swing. We to talk about ek/sistence, language games, différance, differend, and frequently, the philosophical newborn dies with the author or lingers on exclusively in the works of epigons. Philosophies begin to resemble more and more other literary genres, yet not because the genre of 'philosophy' is in a state of disolution or because its genre boundaries became elusive. One still asks questions of a different kind from a philosophical text than from a literary fiction simply because their respective characters are staged in as different a way as ever before. Philosophy resembles literature in general more and more, because it is now going through a development similar to that which other literary genres – for example tragedy – had already gone through many centuries ago.

Contemporary philosophies have added many new Characters to the old ones. Originality requires the invention of a few new Character-configurations also. The ambition to enrich the *common* pool of Characters with the Creations of personal imagination is still strong, and Heidegger is still the most typical case in point. A tension can be perceived here. Philosophical tradition is for the most part abandoned, yet the will to originate a new one is still there. There is a limit: in tragedy, where mortal Characters are supposed to play before God, the set of Characters can become a variable. But where immortal, or rather eternal, Characters are supposed to play their role before a mortal audience, it is difficult to see how a similar change can be effected. Actually, the Heideggerian narrative of the 'end of metaphysics', and all the modifications of the philosophical imagination that it entails, do not put the traditional pool out of use. Common Characters can be privatized to a degree that the readers need to learn an entirely new 'who is who' separately in the case of each and every philosophy. Yet the common pool is far from being abandoned, because without plundering the old Characters no one is able to speak philosophically. The old Characters of philosophy were always reshaped and re-cast, and a few new Characters have also always been added to the inherited cast of Character-configurations. Only the proportion between the two manifestations of creative imagination has changed, though drastically. Yet certain old Characters have to stay, even if between quotation marks, for they are the fixed stars, whereas the new Characters are being illuminated by borrowed light. The host of new Characters can be attractive, meaning-providing and mysterious, even if their life-span is as short as the productive life of a single philosopher. The mortal Characters of philosophical imagination can speak to the mortal audience just as the Eternal One did, as long as they still bask in the light of the ancient gods of the philosophical Pantheon. Just as the mythical characters once re-appeared as metaphors in the republic of philosophy, so are the old philosophical Characters recast as metaphors in an increasingly privatized philosophy.[20]

The term 'personalization' refers only to the uniqueness of the Characters. For as far as meaning (message), appeal, enquiry is concerned, no philosophy is personal.[21] In *Hamlet* the tragic plot unfolds, without relying on a single mythological resting-point, just by the immanent power of its self-explanatory characters and character-constellations, and it is thus that the drama acquires metaphysical dimensions. Likewise, philosophy does not appeal to the separate problems of each member of its audience or to their private headaches, but to their shared need for meaning, which is what still can be called the need for metaphysics.

2 On the Character(s) That Are Called Reason

Men feel themselves betrayed.

One is betrayed when promises are not kept, expectations remain unfulfilled, when things or people turn out to be just the opposite of what they seemed to be, when the end does not fit the purpose or the result the intention.

To begin with: Life itself is Betrayal since men are going to die. And the good life is a betrayal also, for one expects health and falls ill, one expects wealth and becomes poor, one foresees victory, yet will be defeated. Supposedly less frequently, but gloomy expectations, too, can be betrayed. Nothing can be known for sure; whimsical fate rules the world.

What is Life that betrays? Several philosophical Characters called Life have made their appearance on the stage of the *theatrum mundi*, but none of them fits exactly the bill of Life, the Betrayer. Life, contrasted to the Good Life, stands for survival. The Life/Death character pair can stand for many different things also. Life can refer only to humans, encompass the animal kingdom too, or even the whole cosmos (the universe), it can evoke this world, yet also the heavenly other world (afterlife). Life can stand for activity in general, or for certain activities (for example, for metabolism, or for any motion with the exception of sheer locomotion). In particular, it can stand for the presence of Spirit or of Consciousness or of the Soul and much else.[22] The kind of Life that one calls Sacred is different from the kind one calls Good.

Life is an important, although by no means a main, Character in the philosophical world theatre. The character was reshaped and recast in several versions and combinations, yet the kind of Life that plays such an outstanding role in the works of moralists, tragedy writers and also in the wisdom of everyday language users, the kind of Life that constantly betrays us mortals, remains steadily and conspicuously absent from the philosophical Cast of Characters. The expression that Life betrays is dismissed as banausic or banal, a homespun wisdom at best, yet one entirely unworthy of philosophical attention. This great silence is extremely telling. For it is philosophy's major mission to attack this 'banality' head on, to ridicule it and to defeat it.

Myth subscribes to the banal utterance that Life betrays us mortals, yet it de-banalizes the feeling of having been betrayed through the presentation of the stories of betrayal, where gods, demi-gods and men can all show their worth. In myth, it is the Other that betrays man: gods, devils, all kinds of phantastic creatures, and, certainly, other men and women, too. The other betrays us on purpose, for the sake of a good joke, in revenge or as a punishment. The God of Israel becomes fit to occupy the position of the Chief philosophical Character insofar as he becomes entirely invisible. From then on, his tricks become tests, and the deceived ones, if they turn out to be worthy, are all finally rescued from deception.[23,24]

What myth accepts, philosophy rejects. Philosophy is about undeceiving the deceived. Practising philosophy is the process of undeceiving. Unconcealment is undeceiving. The philosopher cannot be betrayed, for he has learned how to see through all deceptions. No evil demiurge can outsmart philosophy, for philosophy knows that there is no such a demiurge. In Philosophy, betrayal is, in the last instance, always self-betrayal.[25] There is no remedy against being deceived by whimsical, alien and therefore uncontrollable powers.[26] Yet there is a remedy against self-betrayal. It is the finest medicine coming from the shelves of the cosmic pharmacy.[27] The name of this finest Medicine that cures, which perhaps prevents even Deception and Betrayal, is *Reason*. Reason is the power that never betrays, cheats or lies. It does not play tricks; we can rely upon it unconditionally.

What is Reason?

Reason is the remedy against self-deception. Put another way, all remedies that have ever been recommended by all doctors of philosophy against self-deception (and deception), belong to, or are composed of, Reason. Reason is like a book of herbs; quite different remedies are to be found there. There are similar herbs and also entirely different ones. Sometimes there is almost nothing common in them, save that they are all remedies against deception – self/deception. Not all medicines are equally powerful. The doctors of philosophy will tell you which have the poorest, which ones the strongest effect. For example, true opinion has a less strong effect than true knowledge. Not all philosophical herbs serve the same purpose. One only purges, the other strengthens, the third opens the eye, the fourth reinvigorates or makes us resistant. The most precious herb is to be taken against death; not necessarily against the fear of death, for this sickness can be taken care of by less forceful pills, but against Death as such, against the very Existence of the Other. The all-powerful herb, recommended by Christian philosophers, did not have exactly the same composition as the old (for example, the Platonic) medicine. To those who refuse to take a medicine against the Other, Being-Toward-Death is perhaps one of the the best herbs to be recommended from the book of herbs called Reason. Needless to say, no two books of herbs are completely alike, no two original philosophies actually agree in all their therapeutic recommendations. One learned doctor may discourage you from using the herb that another has warmly recommended. Doctors of philosophy can recommend long-forgotten medicines also without knowing exactly how they were once used, as Heidegger did with the herb of *aletheia*.

Reason is an institution of philosophical imagination.[28] Or rather, philosophy became an independent genre and also a transcultural tradition-builder by invoking and creating the imaginary entity called Reason. The whole *theatrum mundi* of philosophy rests on this creative gesture.

By no means are the acts, the structures, the conditions, the situations, the procedures, the relations, the modification, or any of the remedies recommended by any book of herbs called Reason mere products of philosophical imagination. Men had solved problems and built houses before the invention of Characters such as *Phronesis* or *Techné*, they answered when called by name and normally also recognized their mothers without being familiar with the principle of identity. Yet it was philosophical imagination that brought these and all the other heterogeneous phenomena together under the heading of Reason, that shaped them and groomed them so that they could play their roles as chief actors in the *theatrum mundi* of immortals.

It is always miserable to be betrayed and deceived. One is undeceived when one becomes aware of the betrayal, when one knows all about it and begins to reflect upon it. There are people who prefer to stay in ignorance; they would rather remain deceived about the betrayal than to become undeceived. Aristotle opened his book on first philosophy with the sentence: 'all men by nature desire to know'.[29] If one takes the verb 'to know' in general terms, the assertion is obviously true. All children are curious – they desire to know this or that. But how about desiring to know everything? Is it truly so that every man (or woman) by nature desires to know? Experience teaches us that most men and women are rather afraid of being undeceived even about minor issues whenever knowledge hurts. How can one, then, seriously maintain that they desire to know everything about even the most momentous issue, when both deceiving and undeceiving attack the very heart of human existence?

Aristotle said in the first sentence of his first philosophy that every man by nature desires to know. But only people who turn towards the first philosophy are spurred by the desire to know, not only this or that, but everything, whatever it turns out to be. Philosophy was meant to be the literary genre for the mentally courageous, for the spiritual explorers. Courage is a virtue, courage is rewarded, if nowhere else, at least in philosophy. The Reason of the philosophers may lead the wanderer through narrow passages above the abyss, but finally it will provide a certainty that cannot hurt; the wanderer will come home or return home. Exceptionally, he chooses to make himself comfortable in one of the suites of the Grand Hotel Abyss.[30]

What is encompassed by Reason?

Language, argumentation (the so-called identity logic), true knowledge itself or the best means to achieve it, thinking, cognition in general, prudence, cleverness in general, Truth, God, the Order of Beauty, the immortal part of the soul, Spirit in general, science or scientific thinking, the natural 'light', (*lumiere*) and so on. 'To act according to reason', that is, to be rational, includes virtuous activity, the successful accomplishment of one's business, to hit the proper means/end relationship in technological procedures, to follow the internal procedures of single sciences, to obey the law, to sit in counsel in order to establish new laws, to listen to the arguments of others, to apply rules properly, in the proper time and place, and so on. When many concepts of Reason co-exist in the same philosophy, they have sometimes separate names, and play the roles of independent character-units, like units of the same, and always victorious, army. The names vary; they can be *phronesis* (of different kinds), *techné, episthemé, sophia, nous (pathetikos nous, poietikos nous)*, or *Ratio* and *Intellectus, Verstand* and *Vernunft*. None of these kinds of reason or rationality are philosophical inventions, but they are dressed up and brought together in the *theatrum mundi* of philosophy.

Since Reason is the remedy against betrayal, deception and incertitude, all herbs in the Book of Herbs called Reason are of this kind.

Language is home. When in a foreign country, we can easily separate our mother tongue from the incoherent chorus of alien voices as a frame within which mutual understanding is at least possible. Logos (language) fortifies against the terror of total irrationality, the tower of Babel. Loqos (logic) presents three principles. A thing is identical with itself; a certain quality and its opposite cannot be attributed to the same substance at the same time. The principles simply describe what people anyway do, how people anyway speak, communicate and labour. One could not survive if some expectations were not constantly and continuously met, if signs did not signify roughly the same thing or event within a considerable time-span. Identity-logic is the human way to stabilize expectations via repetition; it is a substitute for the loss of animal instincts. Without identity logic, there is no human survival. If man is a rational being, human rationality is founded in part (or perhaps primarily) on an approximate identity logic of basic mental-pragmatic-practical operations. But in philosophy, the principles (or laws) of identity, contradiction and the exclusion of the third are not only descriptive, but also prescriptive. For philosophers, they prescribe the proper (rational) conduct for argumentation. The principle of identity does not primarily challenge the everyday language-users, but the competitors of philosophy, such as myth and rhetoric, which are always suspect of concocting betrayal and deception. One can minimize deception and self-deception provided that one rigidly sticks to the laws of logic.

God (that is the Christian God) is Reason, for He is Certitude Incarnate. The 'natural' light is reason, for it is planted by the Creator into the soul of all humans. Knowledge is rational precisely because it is certain or insofar as it is certain. This is why Leibniz, who felt particularly strongly about this issue, excluded probable knowledge, even of the scientific kind, from the cluster of the 'truths of Reason'. Reason (as true knowledge) is, contrary to Logos, juxtaposed to probability-based everyday thinking which is sometimes entirely dismissed as the mixture of unfounded opinions. Reason is said to be methodical thinking (this was the case for Descartes, among others,[31] who made it entirely clear that he recommends reason as the remedy against the fear from having been betrayed by the evil demiurge). *Ratio* can stand for the kind of Reason that provides certitude on a lower level, whereas Intellect stands for Reason on the highest level. The Characters can also be swapped, or rather cross-baptized, but one of them invariably stands for scientific and another for spiritual knowledge.

Although all herbs of the Book of Herbs termed Reason can be taken as medicine against deception and betrayal, there are different kinds of deception and betrayal and not each of the herbs cures all pains. Some of them can work as poison if taken at an improper time or in the wrong dosage. Without the guidance of a good doctor of philosophy, a particular medicine can also turn out to be lethal – a Deceiver Incarnate. Kant's critique of reason is the critique of the misuse of reason by traditional metaphysics. The proper use of reason leads to the restoration of Reason's ancient dignity and meaning. The (critical) philosopher shapes the great Undeceiver in such a fashion that none of its elements could deceive anymore.

So what is then in common between God and proper moral deliberation-decision, between the immortal spirit and a logical argumentation? Security, certainty, undeceiving, prevention against betrayal, rationality, that is Reason. And this is how all of them represent (or at least have a share in) eternity, and this is why all of them are contrasted to sensation, perception and to sensual imagination.

Love and Faith are the sole experiences of the soul that have received entrance into the philosophical paradise. They alone appeal to infinitude and deserve immortality. But the light of immortality is lit by that which is experienced, and not by experiencing. 'The finite nature tries to remain for eternity and to become immortal – according to possibility'[32] says Diotima as she speaks about Eros as the desire for immortality.[33] Eros satisfies its desire in the visual contemplation of immortal things, such as virtue and beauty. Similarily, faith in God links men and women with Eternity. Beauty is Order and Order is Reason, and God is all Beauty and Order and Reason. Thus Love and Faith are divine insofar as they are vested in Reason; they render sense to life because of this. Diotima, in her Socratic presentation, says: 'Only if humans arrive at the visual contemplation of the in-itself existing Beauty, then is life worth living.'[34]

No other sensual experience, be it sensation, perception, feeling or imagination, gets its share in immortality. So-called empiricists do not differ here from so-called rationalists. The certainty that rests in sensual experience is fluid, temporal and, for the most part also personal. Furthermore, even if sensual experience is the source of all knowledge, the source stands lower than the result. The result, which does deceive, is now called Science. One character mask of Reason occupies then the supreme position of all-encompassing Reason. And if reason turns out to be just the slave of passions, and not to be deceived by reason the gravest of all deceptions, then the standpoint of scepticism will appear in the the supreme position of the Great Undeceiver, Reason, in yet another character-mask.[35]

Reason is the Republic: It is that which we share, the common thing. We understand, we can make ourselves understood, we live in a world together with others. Our gestures make sense for others; other's gestures make sense for us also. In the Republic of Reason we are at home just as in our mother tongue. But perception is personal; sensation (provided that we distinguish it from perception) is strong, vivid, intensive, and it strikes us as absolute and sure. But it is just our sensation, and we cannot be sure whether it is sure; so absolute it cannot be. We do not share another person's eyesight, so the colour of the sky may be different for all of us, although we all refer to it as 'blue'. The private is sweet, strong, sensuous – everything that which the common thing is not. But if we come to think about it, the same sweetness turns sour, and the strong becomes weak. For we never arrive at certainty through our senses; this way, we shall never know the world. The ever-changing impressions and sensuous experiences are imprisoned in our finite body and soul, and neither the pleasant nor the unpleasant prisoners know anything about the world that stretches outside the prison walls, the world, the steady thing, the thing one builds, in what one dwells, together with others, not only with human beings, but also with animals, cosmic powers, gods, artifacts and states.

The world which is not shared remains the constantly changing product of private imagination, a kind of dream. Indeed, how do we know that our life is not a dream and that which we are dreaming is not instead our 'real' life? In our dreams, so philosophy maintains since Heraclitus, we are entirely abandoned to ourselves. And the name of a totally unshared world is *Madness*.

Without having a share in the Republic of Reason, men and women cannot have a world. We do things others understand, and others do things we understand; the expectations, at least the banal ones, are – to a certain extent and for the most part – fulfilled. There are rules to be applied, there are norms to be followed, at least to some extent. Members of a particular group share the way one tells good from bad, useful from harmful, sacred from profane etc., or can explain the difference to others who do not share their way.[36] One communicates with one's fellow creatures in the expectation of mutual understanding.[37] It is only in a catatonic state that men fail to have a world in this sense.

The question is how common does the common world need to be? Common to whom? All that is shared by a group, by men and women of a particular culture, is already common, it is reason of a kind, and not the offspring of madness or deceit. And yet, that which is shared by a group or by a culture alone is mortal, and whatever is mortal can still deceive. The common world is the world of reason, but this sort of reason is of a very low status. It is true opinion, but still a mere opinion, it is an idea, but still a confused or inadequate idea, an 'idol' of kind, not the kind of certainty that comes from god alone. Reason of the supreme kind is the knowledge that is shared by every human creature, or rather, that which should be shared by all of them. It is also the divine light that illuminates the world's otherwise inscrutable darkness and reveals all its colours.

The world that people normally share can be called 'rational' also in traditional philosophical terms. For one is best protected against deception and betrayal while one continues to dwell within this world. Still, philosophers see little merit in this (everyday) rationality. And, paradoxically, the Reason of philosophers is not shared but unshared. Philosophers bring forth something that is supposed to be universal, absolute and certain. But in the eye of the beholder, of men and women of all ages, philosophy, together with its Reason, is a game of abstractions, a combination of pale or entirely invisible ghosts, a dream, a kind of madness, a private, because isolating play of mere personal phantasy. The Tracian slave-woman's laughter is rational.[38] Philosophers have to silence this laughter first, abuse rational people as slaves of their senses and opinions, and create uncertainty in their souls. They must arouse anxiety through doubt, insecurity, bewilderment. The seed of the dark suspicion of betrayal has to grow and to multiply in the mind of previously level-headed and no-nonsense creatures, in order to make them ready for the sacred journey towards Eternal Certainty while carrying them away on the wings of philosophical imagination. In an empirical sense the Reason of philosophers is not rational at all, for it is unshared, and yet it is also rational (namely normatively rational) for it can be made plausible for everyone who catches its message. The distinction between empirical and normative universality, between *doxa* and *epistheme*, between unclear and indistinct knowledge on the one hand, and clear and distinct knowledge on the other, are steady props in the philosophical *theatrum mundi* for reasons of self-justification. Philosophical imagination creates *Poietikos Nous*, and *Poietikos Nous* (creative Reason as such) constitutes, or conjures up, or thinks, philosophy. Thinking, indeed, thinks itself. Self-conscious circularity is the insignium of sacredness.

Men and women were supposed to live in two worlds, one private and the other common, in the sensuous world of perception, dreams and affects on the one hand, and in the world of reason(s) on the other hand. But this onto-epistemological game is too neat to be appealing. After closer scrutiny, philosophers no longer deny the relevance of the everyday observation that the sensuous is not merely private, and that the rational is not exhausted by what is commonly shared. Actually, one becomes a human person when the two worlds intertwine,[39] even if their unity can never entirely sublate their contradictions and tensions. This is so regardless of Hegel's effort to develop his story towards a happy ending of this kind, under the guidance of all-encompassing Reason,[40] which, perhaps, would not be ultimately all that happy.

If there are two worlds, it is Creative Imagination that unites them. Creative Imagination gives birth to everything that endures, to the world we have, share and unshare. Creative Imagination is both public and private, both rational and sensuous, and it is so on all levels: on the level of the creators, on the level of objectivation, and on the level of the recipients. After all, Love and Beauty (characters of sensuous origin) are attributes of the Reason of philosophers.

Language, Logos, is the backbone of the world that we share. Creative imagination returns to it, for it remains the warranty of the solidity of all that which is shared. We touch base: the countries of new exploits can become one's home as long as one can return home. Madness is the loss of home.

Numberless accounts can be given of creative imagination. There is the tale of Castoriadis who sees it being rooted in the magma of the unconscious psyche.[41] Other narrators would compare it rather to the act of weaving a tapestry, others again to the act of reading the eternal text. In our times, when the old *theatrum mundi* of philosophy is more and more privately staged, and several character-configurations appear only in one single drama, one can anticipate numberless and different accounts. It happens not in spite of this, but rather because of this new development that the philosophical Character called Imagination, a fairly neglected supporting actor in modern philosophy (with the exception of Kant), now begins to get bigger roles, sometimes even leading ones, in (post-)modern plays.

The kind of Imagination that brings forth something that had never ever existed before, that will exist from now on (forever?) and will be generally and commonly shared, the kind of imagination that objectifies and that has been objectified, is named in traditional philosophy *poietikos nous*, reason of the supreme kind. Hegel's Reason that encompasses all other – lower – forms of reason, is of this kind. The scope of productive imagination is broader than that of *poietikos nous*. Thinking, with the exception of sheer repetitive thinking, proceeds with the support of imagination which explores the horizon of further possibilities for thinking and also synthetizes thoughts within the flow.[42] Recollection, the imagination of the past, is also of the productive sort, provided that the combination of diverse and loosely associated memory traces are pulled together in a new and relatively coherent image. Productive imagination can remain private in a broader and a narrower sense. But creative imagination as *poietikos nous* cannot remain so. It is the most sublime kind of *nous*, because it gives birth to an image, a product, a text, a narrative, a configuration of consciousness that is accessible to others (the term depends on the paradigm one chooses). One can discuss it, sit in judgement over it, be delighted by it, and also re-imagine, re-transform and subvert it; it presents itself as an interpretandum, a puzzle, a significant metaphor for many successive generations. In this sense, *the creature of poietikos nous* acquires certain mythical propensities.[43]

Philosophy is the yield of *poietikos nous*; the creature of creative Reason that thinks Reason, the being that thinks itself – the god of Aristotle. Circularity is built in to this way of thinking. Reason is thought as thinking, logos, prudence etc., so that it should clearly manifest itself as the Supreme Kind of Creative Imagination. This is how Mythos – yet another creature of *poietikos nous* – will be juxtaposed to philosophy as the Alien, the Other, because of its lack in Logos, and to Sophism (Rhetorics) also, because of its lack in the creative power of Imagination.

Dreams and, in another way, also daydreams and phantasies, cast suspicion on sensuousness, perceptions and the image. They seem to be private, unshared experiences. They threaten with insecurity, anxiety, unease and terror. They tear us away from our city, habitat, or home. They make us alien to ourselves, inflict wounds that hurt more than any others. They bring joy, but of an unsteady kind which is always mixed with fear. Dreams are the offspring of productive phantasy, they always bring forth something new. But they are not the offspring of creative phantasy. Others have no access to them save through the dreamers' own reports; but dreamers rarely have access to their own dreams either, or if they do, only to a very limited degree. Dreams are not objectified in beings that will stand here for eternity. Of all beings, they are the most fluid, they cannot be caught (*begreifen*).

Worse still, dreams deceive, they cheat. Yet only beings that carry a message can cheat. Dreams cheat because they are supposed to carry such a message. They cheat, because, although they tell us something vitally important, the message cannot be read and understood, or, rather, it is always misunderstood, as if an alien and hostile power would send those dreams upon us, in order to deceive us. Yet if all dreams were untrue, no dream could deceive. But there is, or there can always be, a degree of truth hidden in them, a distorted message of a kind that should be deciphered. Then in turn, certain dreams simply tell the truth, and nothing but the truth, about ourselves, our past or our future. They can be revelations; they can be sent by benevolent as well as by malevolent powers. One needs to harken to dreams and find out what they are telling us, without ever being certain that the message meant what it was supposed to mean. Whenever dreams are read as predictions (about the future or the future understanding of a past) they are understood retrospectively, after the event they were supposed to foretell has already set in.

Descartes said that dreams are unreliable, because they follow no rules at all.[44] If 'rule' meant the rules of reason (as established in the *Regulae*) or the rules of identity logic alone, the statement would be certainly true. But if dreams cheat (and Descartes maintained that dreams are deceptive), there must be still certain rules (or regularities) in dreams, just that they must differ from those valid for the thinking of a fully awake rational being. Interpretation of dreams, perhaps the most ancient branch of hermeneutics, proceeds on the assumption that there are such regularities in dreams. Moreover, they decipher dreams on the assumption that the seemingly utterly private kind of phantastic imagination is not as private as it looks. For example, dreams can hide foreknowledge of momentous events that will shatter the throne or of a disaster that will befall the whole city. By deciphering dreams, one can also prevent the worse from happening.

Dream-interpretation has been a kind of translation since times immemorial. There is a dream-world which speaks its own sign-language perfectly, but the grammar and dictionary of this language cannot be understood by the wide-awake human mind. A special interpreter, a professional of good intuition and great experience in dream-reading, can acquire the ability to translate dream-language into the language of wide-awake consciousness. Moreover, everyone has access to a few cues, there is a general grammar and dictionary of the basic dream-language. Certain images or tropes are known as having a well-circumscribed meaning (good or bad luck, birth of children, disaster, war, death and so on).[45] One deciphers dreams in the same way as one has deciphered Maya writing: without knowing the language but hoping that one discovers its basic message while deciphering the script.

Nowadays, psychoanalysis takes over the second (or first?) most ancient profession. It has its own grammar and dictionary of dreams.

The basic assumptions about dreams and the fundamental require-ments for deciphering them have not changed. It is presupposed that a complete translation is impossible, for dream language is entirely different from wide-awake language, and it is also presupposed that there are reliable cues which refer to the same (or similar) meaning in the dreams of every private dreamer, but that intuition and special-ized skill are required to do a good job in deciphering them. That dreams cheat is taken for granted in psychoanalysis to the same degree as it has always been in the art of magicians and soothsayers. The danger of misreading dreams always loomed large, as it does now. Dreams continue to deceive, to play tricks and cheat in the process of deciphering. And yet, psychoanalysis is not just a streamlined book of dreams applied by well-versed and skilled modern soothsayers. The content of this book has not been passed down from old magic and mythical traditions. Freud's (and his successors') interpretation of dreams, as the life of the soul in general, is performed in the fashion of philosophy. Characters appear, mostly new or remodelled ones, sometimes taken from the vocabulary of myths such as Trans-ference, the Super-Ego, Libido. They begin to play their acts in the *theatrum mundi* of microcosm/macrocosm. And the great soul Healer – knowledge, light, understanding, science, you name it – makes its appearance again. Finally it is Reason the invisible that guides us back from our private hallucinations, phantasies and fears into the republic of the shared world.

Freud, like Marx or Max Weber, introduced so many new Charac-ters into philosophy that they were able, for a time, to mystify their enterprise. They were believed to have established a new science, although, in fact, they staged a few new dramas in the *theatrum mundi*, while mobilizing all their new actors. Nowadays, their Char-acters are involved in many a philosophical plot in just the same way as the most archaic philosophical Characters are.[46]

Freud dismissed the teleological explanations of dream phantasies. Born under the sun of the age of science, he vested his faith in causality alone. But can't we re-read all dreams again with the help of a new dictionary and grammar book, this time inspired by teleology?

The 'end of reason' is an apocalyptic slogan.[47] It has the advantage that it can be easily repeated without having been understood. For there is nothing to understand, unless one knows (identity logic, alas!) what reason is (means). If one knew only that, reason would still be with us. And since those who spread the slogan about the end of reason expect us to understand, at least roughly, what they mean in referring to the 'the end of reason', we can rest assured that reason is still around. My objection is not that the claim is self-contradictory; to this objection they could easily retort that their apocalyptic slogan is not the conclusion of an argument, thus self-contradictory it cannot be. They have told a tale. My objection is, however, that one cannot tell a tale without making the characters ready for doing their parts in the tale. No story comes off if I do not know whether I speak about the wolf or the lamb. Certainly, in a dream, the wolf and the lamb can be the same figures subsequently, also simultaneously. One can say, then, that life is a dream, but this is hardly a philosophical statement, since, as mentioned before, the kind of Life that betrays us is the only Character which is entirely dismissed from philosophical speculations. But the slogan about the 'end of reason' can also be read as follows: 'down with reason – life better be a dream' – whatever the term 'dream' stands for. To wish that life better be a dream is the death-wish of philosophy, so it is only consistent (identity logic, alas!) to couple the slogan of 'the end of reason' with the slogan of the 'end of philosophy'. The desire that 'life better be a dream' is anti-republican insofar as it denigrates and, by implication, also abuses, all common things, all that which is shared. A wish cannot be refuted or dismissed, one is not even entitled to accuse it of inauthenticity. But I have the feeling that the apocalyptic slogans has been repeated so frequently and so easily because men and women have failed to mobilize their imagination to explore the horizons of the possibilities involved by this innocent-sounding slogan. Before attacking reason on the one hand, 'irrationalism' on the other, it is better to ask first the ironical questions of Silone's novel *Fontamaras*,[48] 'Long live – who?', 'Down with – whom?'.

Asking such questions does not call for any specific justification as long as one continues to play the philosophical drama in the *theatrum mundi*, in other words, as long as one remains within the broad and elastic confines, which are nonetheless confines, of a philosophical genre. Here, I continue to speak about philosophical Characters.

'Down with – whom?' 'Long live – who?'

The end of reason cannot mean the end of all things that had been encompassed as remedies in the Book of Herbs called Reason. One will not address bearded magistrates as Lady (even if, as an exception, they can be hermaphrodites or women too); one will continue to install the computer according to the instructions for use (though innovation can result from misuse); one will wait for the bus at the stop as usual (though, incidentally, it can take another route); and one will continue to listen to another person's self-justification, accept it or reject it, or remain sceptical, while still relying upon the criteria of verisimilitude.[49] One will still expect one's friends to arrive roughly at the time they promised they would, not a year later nor a day earlier or never, and one will still expect that this friend will remain roughly the same person, instead of taking the shape of an elephant or a tablecloth instead. This is a caricature, as a new and understandably offended Callicles could say, because the word reason (in the exclamation 'down with reason') does not stand for rational behaviour, expectation or action in everyday life, institutions, sciences, technology or communication. Reason, he would continue, needs to meet its end, because it is a criminal character, guilty of many bad things. Firstly, kinds of rationality enumerated above are misused by Reason; they are expanded far beyond their proper boundaries, they became imperialists, and so on. All these have to go. In addition, the deification of reason became intolerable. Reason terrorizes all of us. It has marginalized and suppressed the sensuous, playful, dreamlike delights of the human body and mind. Further on, Reason is the universal, the general – but the individual desires stand higher than the general. Finally, modernity, history, industry, and – first and foremost – philosophy, are responsible for all disasters that befell our century. Reason destroys the world.

The new Callicles' first accusation against reason is an old philosophical trick taken from the repertoire of the philosophical *theatrum mundi*. One or another kind of rationality has always been blamed for many ills, and the misuse of reason has always been censured. Even the contemporary defenders of reason are doing the same.[50] The 'this reason good, that reason bad' game does not justify the other game whose catchword is 'down with reason'. They are rather antagonistic and agonistic.

Yet the new Callicles' second and the third accusations strike at the heart of philosophy. The 'what' in the question of 'Down with *what?*' appears now not as a kind of reason (as logic, technique, ordinary language, ethics), not even as their unlawful extension, to use Kant's expression, that could be dismissed also from the standpoint of this or that philosophy, and incidentally also by everyday common sense, but Reason *as such*, the imaginary institution of philosophy which thinks philosophy that had imagined it, the book of Herbs in the pharmacy that keeps alive the invisible dramatis personae in the universal *theatrum mundi*. In the slogan 'down with reason', reason stands for the philosophical Character Reason and for Reason who directs the play behind the curtain – yet they are the same Reason.

Callicles' fourth accusation reads: 'Down with the God of philosophy, because this is the God that failed.' It is the Undeceiver that deceives. Does it really?

The man-made Apocalypse is the offspring of two parents: the rational Imagination of the mind and the irrational Desires and devices of the unconscious soul; they did the bloody work together.[51] The finger of the accuser can point everywhere. Nothing lends here full credence to any of the agonistic standpoints. If one says: 'Down with reason!', one needs to add immediately: 'long live. . .' – but what? Whatever is going to replace Reason, *petit recit*, difference, play, literature, thinking or else, whatever occupies the position of the Healer – becomes the substitute for Reason, Reason in disguise, the new god. Alternatively, the place of reason can be left empty – there may still remain something that one can wish to live long or to remain with us, for long or forever, but this something can be something else for me and for you. If this is so, then 'Down with Reason' ceases to be a slogan or a battle cry, and it becomes a subdued, an almost inaudible stuttering, or a mere sigh. A sigh of farewell to the invisible powers of eternity, to knowledge which promises full protection against betrayal, to the great and always reliable undeceiver, to the Herb that cures all of our Ills. In this sense, and in this sense alone, it is also a farewell bid to universality, to the kind of Reason that is Absolute for us all, to the Absoluteness that can be proven, or at least presented, for everyone, men and gods alike, for all eternity and absolutely. Farewell, my lovely – let us make peace with our finitude.

3 Exit Will

A drama can be played as long as there are characters and actors (who can be the same persons), writers and stage-directors (who can also be the same persons), conceiving and staging a plot among themselves, and as long as there is an audience, big or small, but passionately interested in the characters and the plot. Whenever a character or an actor meets with the disapproval of the audience, or if the audience gets deadly bored by his handstands or finds the plots where this character plays the leading role utterly unconvincing, the play must be taken off the programme. Something similar happens to the philosophical Character termed Will, together with the plot that required his greatest stunt. Given the total disinterest of the audience for the staging of the well-known character-configuration Sin-Freedom-Necessity-God-Justice-Will, together with all supporting actors, a roughly thousand-and-six-hundred-years-old star of the philosophical *theatrum mundi* will be, in all probability, taken off the stage. Small consolation that his theological status will still remain high.

Reason is far from being taken off the stage. In the story about 'the end of reason', the Character termed Reason plays the role of *Prügelknabe*, a well-known leading part in several comedies. Yet no slogan has been coined to declare 'the End of Will', for no one cares for Will at all (except historically), not even to abuse it. Will is already off stage.

Ancient philosophy did not yet need this character.[52] Aristotle's *prohairesis* can be translated (or rather interpreted) as free choice or decision, because the mental event *prohairesis* mediates between *boulesis* (deliberation) on the one hand, and action on the other hand.[53] The presence of *prohairesis* indicates that the person is the author of his deed and that he must assume full responsibility for his action. *Prohairesis* is not a power that does something on its own. The person, not the decision, decides. *Prohairesis* is the mental act of the person that includes the *causa finalis* and becomes the *causa efficiens* of his action. Freedom stands here for accountability, and accountability for authorship.

The theoretical clarification of the character of decision is but the necessary stepping-stone along the way that leads to the most sublime issue about the conditions and the essence of the right (virtuous, good, proper) decision. This is true for Aristotle, and, with a few exceptions, for philosophers in general. Aristotle holds that men who do the wrong things are authors of their own acts to the same degree as men who do everything in the right way. Commitment to virtues (a rational commitment), good habits that are acquired by right ethical and mental training, and, finally, sound practical judgement (*phronesis*), all warrant the goodness of all of man's choices. The practice of ethical virtues is the manifestation, as much as the result, of ethical rationality which includes stabilized good habits. The issue at stake is reliability versus unreliability, frankness (openness) versus deception, Logos versus non-rationality (*alogon*). If a person is decent, one knows what to expect from him, traits such as decency, reliability, loyalty. If a person is indecent, he is also unreliable, non-rational, and perhaps deceptive and disloyal.

Although Willing assumed the status of a philosophical character earlier, the staging of Will as a major Character of the philosophical *theatrum mundi* had not been canonized before Augustine. Augustine deemed it crucial to establish a good philosophical pedigree for this new, and theologically already well-entrenched, Character. In *De libero Arbitrio*, Augustine still hesitates. It is only under the heavy theological pressure to prove the following line of argument: 'It would not be just to punish evil deeds if they were not done wilfully';[54] God 'is not the author of sin',[55] that the conclusion: 'we have freedom of the will' and with it, the independent actor called Will is forged. Actually, even in the first conclusion (quoted above), *Voluntas* is merely something that we have. But Augustine realizes that in order to fit Will into his drama so that it becomes the crucial element of the whole Character-configuration, he needs to elevate Will to the status of an entirely independent Character. It is not man that wills; Will will is the source of Willing; it is Will that wills; Will wills (or can will) itself. Augustine claims, with faultless logic, that he has attributed the same kind of actorship to volition as did traditional philosophy to Logos, Knowledge, Thinking, Science, and in exactly the same fashion:

> In the same way as we know by reason everything that we know, nevertheless even reason itself is numbered among the things we know by reason. Have you forgotten that when we asked what is known by reason, you admitted that reason is known by reason? Do not wonder then that we can use the free will by means of itself, if we use other things through our free will. As reason, knowing other things, also knows itself, so free will, which makes use of other things, also makes use of itself et cetera.[56]

Before making his exit, the Character Will celebrated a Pyrrhic victory in his short-lived alliance with Power.[57] Regardless of whether it was a metaphysical device or not, the combination 'Will-to-Power' has retained its fascination for the interpreters, but the Character-configuration was, nonetheless, re-staged no more, not even in a second drama. For Foucault, for example, only Power remained. The configuration 'Will-to-Power' anticipated the new age with its 'privatization' of the philosophical Characters. The appeal can be general, immense and lasting, but the character itself remains confined to a single story. The early privatization of Will (in the above sense) made it perhaps even more plausible that the traditional configuration has lost its magic.

But why did Will lose its magic, at least for the present? Certainly not because it plays the role of an independent Character. For as Augustine said, Will became an independent creature in exactly the same way as did Reason, or one could add, as did Perception or Imagination or Being or Appearance and the like. There must have been something wrong with the performance of this Character, or perhaps the kind of play for the sake of which it had been invented is no longer welcome on the stage.

As a spectator of *theatrum mundi*, I have enjoyed the Great Drama where Will was one of the most magnificent actors; I still do. But now

I want Will to be off-stage for, with the sole exception of the Drama, where he made his debut and also his unforgettably brilliant performance, he just spoils the play and makes it foul.

Reverence for tradition kept the Character Will alive in a modern world that no longer needed it. In Kant, pure Will is identical with (practical) Reason, only a seemingly independent Character, actually a mere nickname or an alter-ego. But since Kant has contrasted determination by freedom and determination by nature absolutely, the nickname Will is telling as so many nicknames are. In Hegel, where the two determinations are no longer absolutely contrasted, Will as an independent Character is maintained as a matter of convenience (especially in the sphere of the objective spirit), and it begins to retreat till it indicates a mental act like *prohairesis* (it is man, not Will, that wills).

I want Will, qua an independent Character, off-stage, because fundamental moral questions remain sidetracked through the intervention of Will and all of his supporting actors. To avoid misunderstandings, I do not will that Will leave the stage because the problems, for whose solution's sake Will was invented, were never solved. Philosophy is not about problem-solving. Being preoccupied with keeping the danger of Manicheism at bay is not a so-called 'problem', so it cannot be solved even by the best of metaphysical devices. Sin was not a 'problem', but the central imaginary institution of morals for more than thousand years, and as long as sin (against God) remained the centrepoint of moral imagination for all people and not just for philosophers, Will continued to occupy the royal place that had been allocated to him by Augustine. But this is no longer the case. Philosophy was in the position to sense, as a good seismograph, the tremblings and foreshocks of a new world, far more and far earlier than theology proper.

It is obvious that for now Sin has entirely lost its central position amongst our moral imaginary institutions. The Social Contract (among men) is already a strong and alternative tale. Whether modern political concepts are theological in their origin and whether their charisma is a borrowed one or not, is of secondary importance in this respect. In modern political philosophy only pagan radical intellectuals use the term Sin, although with reversed signs.[58] To the degree that they become contingent, men and women arrive at the point where the existential choice of goodness alone can establish decency. Sometimes the paradoxical statement is made about the new constellation that one can commit a sin only against oneself. The paradoxical position of Sin in this statement indicates more than anything else that it is not the fear of Sin (in the original sense of the term, coupled with all of its imaginary connotations) that modern decency is all about.[59]

Yet with Sin having been buried, its hair and nails continue to grow, and one carries on the hocus-pocus with them in moral philosophy. The issues of moral freedom and of responsibility still remain under the spell of the other question of whether men are 'determined' or not (this time not by God, but by nature or by 'milieu'). If one assumes that one cannot act but in the way one does in each moment while the action is 'on', because thousand heterogeneous factors have determined the decision (Will) itself, and all those heterogeneous factors, on their part, had been previously determined in the same way by many a thousand other factors, and so on, following the chain of infinite regression, our decision (will) is never free; as a consequence, no man is responsible for his or her acts, thus morals is just a fancy, a myth, an (unscientific) ideology, or, alternatively, a clever social institution of convenience which is pragmatically maintained without the slightest ontological justification. The only refutation of this argument could be the Kantian one. In its terms, all our decisions and volitions are indeed determined, either by nature or by freedom. We are moral creatures to the degree that our volition is determined by Will, that is, by (practical) Reason, that is by Freedom. Trying to answer the question of whether our decision (Will) is determined or not, and if so, by whom, one still continues to groom the evergrowing nails and hair of the corpse called Sin diligently, in order to carry on with the hocus-pocus. So the whole plot, the whole story, had better be sent off-stage by the (post-)modern directors of *theatrum mundi*.

By returning, via recollection, to Aristotle's times, the whole dilemma will be dismissed. One will arrive at the insight that the question concerning the freedom or unfreedom of decisions or choices, and of the human responsibility and accountability for such choices, as well as for the actions resulting therefrom, have absolutely nothing to do with the other question of whether or not effects have their causes. Philosophical imagination alone has tied the two issues together in a representative dramatic plot. The plot has lost its significance, why should we not uncouple them? Provided that philosophical imagination uncouples that which had once been tied together, the so-called 'ontological link' between the two questions will also disappear. But the ontological foundation of human freedom, responsibility, accountability will not equally disappear together with the now already missing connection, for it is again a matter of philosophical imagination whether there will be again such an ontological foundation or there will be none. If one makes the objection that providing a solid ontological foundation for free decision or choice, for responsibility and accountability, without touching upon the issue of determinacy or indeterminacy, is a task that can never be solved, I would answer that the old task of grounding free decision in (in)determinacy has never been solved either, but both versions of presenting the problem can be made plausible by alternative stories. Finally, one can ask questions about the character of an ontological foundation. A contingent person's existential choice can also be understood as a kind of ontological foundation. It can be mantained that autonomy rests on self-choice in principle, 'for all eternity', and not only historically, and so does our being as autonomous moral agents. Only that which was implicit hitherto becomes explicit in the state of contingency. Certainly, one can also make a case for the existential choice and deny its ontological status.

But whether or not one ascribes an ontological status to the existential choice, the moral scenario has already been shifted. *Not determination versus indeterminacy, but authorship versus the absence of authorship is now the decisive issue in ethics.* If one mentions authorship, one also implies the responsibility and accountability of the actor, and thus one discusses morality. One can deny authorship, and say in the same breath that the person is neither responsible nor accountable for his or her deeds, and that the distinction between permitted and unpermitted is a matter of sheer convenience. Alternatively, one can continue to tell the tale of morals in a mystical manner, pointing to a deeply disguised God as to the sole author and judge, but merely metaphorically.

Moral authorship is a simple issue.

A person assumes responsibility when he responds to the question of 'Did you do it?' truly. When God asked Cain: 'Where is your brother, Abel?', and Cain responded: 'Am I my brother's keeper?', this was the wrong answer. The moral precision of the Book of Genesis surpasses that which can be found in all books of philosophy. Cain did not answer, for example, that 'Abel is hiding in the bush', he did not tell an outspoken lie, he, instead, pleaded ignorance and substituted a fake question for an outright lie. Telling the truth is only one aspect of taking responsibility; one tells the truth because one takes responsibility and does not try to avoid it. The only adequate answer to the question of 'Where is your brother, Abel?' is: 'He is dead, because I killed him.' One thus establishes a causal relation between the person and the deed, in order to acknowledge the deed as one's own, to recognize oneself as the author of the deed. The Book of Genesis hints at the motivations for the murder. Cain was envious, jealous, because his brother was more favoured by God. Cain could have answered this way: 'I killed my brother, because I was jealous, because you have favoured him for no reason', but that, *too*, would have been a wrong answer. Hundreds of thousands of motivations or 'causes' would not have changed the basic thing, namely authorship – he was the one who had murdered. Certainly, external or internal reasons qualify the act itself. Killing is not always murder, and there are many cases of justified homicide. But the moral re-qualification of the deed does not annul authorship. If the deed was not murder, but justified homicide, or even a heroic act (for example, in war), the person who did it still remains its author. Not only the qualification, but also the amount of responsibility or accountability, can be modified in the presence of certain internal or external circumstances, but not authorship itself.[60]

But are there authors at all?

We are complex beings, multiple selves, and tomorrow we can differ from our self of yesteryear. This is why we now have become reluctant (with a few representative exceptions) to refer to a person as, for example, a murderer. Yet this has again nothing to do with authorship. One can take responsibility, while responding truly: 'I did it, I was the one who did it', without identifying oneself with the deed. The interpretation (or self- interpretation) of the deed always oscillates, and not only in the aftermath of the deed but every time from then on, but this circumstance does not touch upon the issue of authorship. One can say 'I did it', proudly, tormented by pangs of conscience, impudently, with sorrow or with glee – as long as he or she states: 'I did it' (provided that he or she did or has reasons to believe so), the person has established his/her authorship for the good as much as for the bad things.

That there are deeds which can be attributed to multiple actors, to each in the same or to each in different degrees, is true. Misusing the reference to multiple authorship for the purposes of a bashful re-introduction of the old argument of determination is, however, foul play. Yet there is a difference between Cain and a person who murders now. Cain brought murder into the world where there had been none. He was an absolute author of his deed. Nowadays, many murder, but the murderers do not invent murder, they do a thing that others do as well, it is in the 'air', they receive orders and so on. Still, each member of Murder Incorporated does what *he* does, he remains the author of his deed whatever others do. And if the divine question of 'Where is your brother, Abel?' has been asked, he should answer: 'I have killed him', or 'I was party to his murder'.

The acknowledgement of authorship is *the attitude of authenticity*. Authentic people attribute moral weight to one single chain of causality, namely to the link between their own actions and the act they see resulting therefrom. Authenticity is not a humble virtue, rather the resolve to acquire moral autonomy, the sole kind of autonomy a person can achieve on his or her own, that is, autonomously. The existential choice of oneself is the leap towards all kinds of autonomy. Moral autonomy can be acquired through the existential choice of oneself as a decent person.[61]

All paths lead back to the question of contingency.

A person who chooses him or herself as good, chooses all of his or her determinations also. As a result, they cease to be determinations. A person like this be comes the author of all of his/her deeds, and it is thus that he or she transforms contingency into destiny.

Existential Choice and Authenticity are quite new (modern) philosophical Characters.

I did what philosophers normally do. I took these two major Characters (and a few supporting actors in addition) and combined them with traditional protagonists, such as Freedom, Authorship, Goodness and others, and devised a plot for this Character-configuration. I understand if other philosophers dismiss this plot because they play with other Characters or devise and stage an entirely different drama. Their works appeal to me, if only the characters are interesting and the drama is good. But the group of the Characters of my drama assumes an agonistic stance against certain other Character-configurations which play the game of burying practical reason, morals, responsibility and moral authorship, without giving a damn for their resurrection. The good person is the Absolute Utopia. Without good persons, life is simply not worth living. As far as this is concerned, nothing has changed since the text of Genesis and the Voice of Socrates' daemonion.

4

The Question of Truth

1 Aporias of Truth

The question of Truth is historical, since each and every Truth makes its appearance in time. But, more often than not, Truth itself was associated with a-temporality, with eternity. Providing an answer to the questions 'What is Truth?' (a question concerning the concept of truth) and 'What is the Truth' (a question concerning the content of truth-related sentences) usually involved a tortuous journey whose final destination was *adequatio* and *certitudo*. Truth, by definition, was not supposed to undergo changes; Truth was Truth, once and for all.

The question of Truth comes into being through the concept of Truth. The concept of Truth is dialectical both in the Socratic-Platonic and the Hegelian sense; it results from negation. All the mere 'opinions', that is inherited knowledge, traditional meaning, are put under reflective-critical scrutiny in forms such as: 'not this is true, but that is true', 'not this is beautiful but that is beautiful', 'not this is right, but that is right'. What is recognized, deciphered, demonstrated to be the really, the finally, as well as the absolutely true and right (perhaps also beautiful) is termed the truth.

Philosophy is bound to answer both questions concerning Truth ('What is Truth?' and 'What is the Truth?'). This is why philosophical Truth cannot be entirely epiphanic. When Jesus said:[1] 'The reason I was born, the reason why I came into the world, is to testify the truth', he *revealed* 'what' Truth is, so he did not need to enter into speculations about the essence of Truth. Pilate's question, or rather rejoinder to this, 'Truth! What does that mean?' is strictly philosophical, and by no means necessarily also sceptical. In philosophy, one has to clarify the issue of the essence of Truth in order to reveal Truth. 'I came to testify the Truth' is not an answer to the philosophical question of what Truth is. Conversely, when one learns that the essence of Truth (the answer to the question what Truth is) is *certitudo et adequatio*, one does not at once learn thereby what Truth is. Many things, several kinds of knowledge, carved images and much else, can compete for the place of the highest adequacy and certitude.

The knowledge of good and bad (evil), right and wrong, true and untrue precedes the emergence of the question concerning Truth. Several human groups and cultures have been born, grown and vanished without ever having asked this question. But no human group and culture can exist without making the distinction between good and bad, true and untrue, right and wrong as well as a few similar distinctions. Men and women normally accept the stories, judgements and images of their own tradition or group as true, and the customs, rules and behavioural patterns of their own tradition or group as right. Diverging stories, creeds and customs, those of other groups, are therefore, as a rule, regarded as false, untrue, wrong and the like. Everyone is supposed to know how to discriminate between true and false, right and wrong.[2] Stories change, so do customs; hence what is right and what is true changes also.

The historical question, the question concerning Truth, is the question of enlightenment. Or, put differently, cultures undergo the stage of enlightenment whenever or wherever the question concerning Truth is raised. Enlightenment is the consistent or continuous questioning of opinions within the selfsame world or community where those opinions are still held. It is common practice that the victor's deities are embraced as the true gods by the vanquished. It is rather uncommon to believe that the stories and the creeds of the vanquished stand higher than those of the victors. And it is equally uncommon to reject opinions as untrue or wrong as long as they remain effective.[3] The question concerning Truth appears as the uncommon and uncanny intruder into the world, for it makes the world perpetually problematic by 'intellectualizing' it.

The original scenario or 'the primal scene' of Truth was set roughly two and a half thousand years ago. But the two aporias of Truth were not made explicit and elaborated upon in the original scenario.

The negation 'this is not the right thing, this is merely an opinion', etc., is invariably the second step in religious imagination; first comes the revelation of Truth. In actual fact, this is what happened also in the primal scene of philosophy. The conceptualization of the essence of Truth and the revelation or the demonstration of what Truth really is, happened in just one stroke, so that the second position (on the content of Truth) preceded the mode of questioning (the negation). This is the procedure of traditional metaphysics. Plato wanted to avoid this pitfall by letting Socrates do the talking in the mask of questioning. At least in the early dialogues of Plato, Socrates conducted an open-ended discourse. Negation here played the role of deconstruction; Truth was supposed to be the result of re-arrangement and of de-centring. But in the main, philosophical Truth was presented in the categories of eternity (unchangeability), absoluteness, one-ness, unity and all that constitutes the dignity of things pre-modern. As a result, sceptics, who denied certainty and absoluteness, had to question truth as a whole, the concept (essence) of truth included.

The aporias of Truth were discovered by the moderns; the concept of truth became pregnant with twin aporias in the last century. Out of this pregnancy new visions of truth were expected to be born. In what follows, I shall concentrate on these expectations.

The first aporia was formulated by Kierkegaard. In discussing Christianity, he pondered the following puzzle: 'How can eternal Truth emerge historically?'[4] He termed the historical emergence of eternal Truth a paradoxical event, which, being absurd, cannot be rationally comprehended. Since he discussed a Truth which appeared in history almost two thousand years ago, Kierkegaard had no use for the smokescreen of his philosophical predecessors, Kant or Hegel. Hegel in particular seemed to step beyond the paradox. In his vision, History was at once the self-development of Truth, and at the end of History the Absolute Spirit grasped Truth as the Whole. In this scenario, the historical finally coincided with the eternal, the contextual with the absolute, the conditional with the unconditional. Kierkegaard utterly disliked this traditional metaphysical gimmick, and he thus ushered in a new philosophical vision.

Wittgenstein[5] speaks about placing a new picture before the eye of the other, so that the other finally acknowledges: 'this is true', 'this, too, can be thought', so that he compares all things from now on with this new picture. Post-classical philosophers, including Wittgenstein, held out a new image to the denizens of the twentieth century so that more and more of us could think about Truth in a different way.

It is through this different vision that the aporias of Truth present themselves. It is also through this new vision that we make the strict distinction between the two questions concerning Truth ('What is Truth?', 'What is the truth?'). Religion does not raise the first question at all; what has become philosophically absurd can still be thought as religious Truth. We can think that eternal Truth has emerged historically, provided that we abolish History (Time, that is) in the reception of this Truth. Kierkegaard discusses 'the Instant', Walter Benjamin refers to the *Jetztzeit* in order to describe this mystical way of seeing and experiencing.[6]

The concept of Truth (the answer to the question of what Truth is) needs to encompass religious Truth also. We cannot thus exclude from the concept of Truth the claim that Eternal Truth emerges historically. But the (previous) concept of Truth itself became historicized after having been presented by a new 'picture' concerning Truth. It has by now become absurd to claim that the Truth that emerges historically (in philosophy or in any other kind of discursive thinking), is of an 'eternal' character. As long as we were sure that there is only one answer to the first question, albeit several different ones to the second (this being the main reason for not noticing the difference between the two questions), we could be satisfied with the Hegelian solution of the aporia. But our age turns towards another solution: to the pluralization of Truth(s), not simply according to their contents, but also according to their concepts.

I mentioned the two aporias of (metaphysical) Truth but discussed only one of them (eternal truth emerging historically). The second aporia is methodological. Truth is a dialectical concept born of negation. Yet the metaphysical answers to the question of Truth exclude all further negations absolutely. This is, of course, not a historical but a methodological kind of exclusion. New and new kinds of Truth emerge all the time, each of them being conceived *sub specie aeternitatis*. As bodies of meaning, the philosophies of (absolute, eternal) Truth execute the task of Enlightenment while negating it simultaneously. Whether the pluralization of Truth does a better or a worse job, remains to be seen.

2 Spheres of Truth

Paul Veyne answers the question of whether the Greeks believed in their myths[7] with both 'yes' and 'no'. Greeks had two realities at their disposal, the mythical and the everyday, and they lived in both. I would add to this that human groups in general live at least in two realities, and sometimes in more than two. In stepping into one reality, one 'believes' in one set of things, stories, etc., and in stepping into another, one believes in another set. What is accepted as true in one of the realities, appears as false in the other, and vice versa. And not only the 'content' of truth changes in shifting from one reality to another; so do the criteria of truth, the ways of challenging the truth of a statement, of a story or a theory, which are all different in kind. One can also tell a lie within different realities. If there is Truth in painting, there must be also falsity and lie. But one tells a lie in a different way in painting than in daily life.

To divide multiple realities into 'real reality' on the one hand, and 'fictitious realities' on the other, is grossly misleading. Although everyday life feeds other realities with contents and concrete meanings, this – fundamental – reality is not a truth-provider, but rather a truth-receiver. I term the everyday sphere of customs, language use and technology the sphere of 'objectivation in itself', and all the subspheres of the truth (meaning) providing reality lumped together, the sphere of 'objectivation for itself'.[8] The third major sphere, termed by Hegel 'objective spirit', and by me the sphere of 'objectivation for and in itself', need not be discussed separately in this context, for it is normally regarded as a kind of 'reality' to the same extent as is daily life, and as such, it is juxtaposed to 'mere fiction'.

Everyday-life reality is more real than others, for it is the world of possible (personal) experiencing and thus, the world of action and work. Kant's 'phenomena' is the extension of the everyday perception of reality. Things are 'real' in everyday terms if everyone can experience them, react upon them, manipulate them (although in fact not everyone does all that), and if the result(s) of action(s) depends on human agent(s). A story is 'real' in everyday terms if it recounts what has happened in the world of this reality. Whatever is real, can be true here, because in this context, 'the true' is connected to the possibility of (past, present, and future experiencing). Whatever is real, is equally real; whatever is true, is equally true.

Things are more real in the world of non-everyday realities than in the everyday world, for they are meaningful on a higher and more dense level. Although certain non-everyday realities can be experienced by everyone (e.g. everyone can look at paintings), not everything belonging to this reality is equally meaningful on that more dense and higher level. It is the density, the height and the complexity of meaning, not the mere possibility of experiencing, that can make them true. Furthermore, experiencing itself is not real to the same extent in all cases, since the reality-value of a particular experience depends on the quality and depth of one's understanding the '*what*' of experiencing.

Everyday reality and non-everyday reality together make a world (any world). Non-everyday (metaphysical, suprasensible, superintensive) reality is woven into the fibres of everyday life; still, the two kinds of reality are distinguished. No sacrifice is a substitute for the preparation for battle, nor is care taken to avoid the evil eye for planting crops in the proper way, at the proper time, and in the proper soil. It is not the appearance of the suprasensible or metaphysical and its interference with human affairs that is called 'a miracle', but the fictitious annulment of the expectations of everyday reality (for example, turning stones into bread). Everyday actors become suspect if they tell miraculous stories about themselves. Christianity penalizes them as heretics, moderns put them into mental asylums. What is truth in one sphere, is fraud, diabolic delusion or madness in the other. The tendency to keep certain spheres of truth apart is required by everyday rationality, but it is usually overdetermined by the institutions of the dominating meaning-providing reality, religious or scientific.

It would be too bold (and for my purpose unnecessary) to suggest that the distinction between two levels of reality is somehow innate. Freud's distinction between the Id and the Ego can be used in support of this hypothesis. What we can at any rate observe is the attempt of young children to get a sense of proper orientation by separating the spheres of reality. When one tells an unusual story about one's own life or the life of another 'real' person, the child will be eager to inquire whether the story has really happened the way it was told. If it turns out that a father has invented a story (for example a war adventure) about himself, the child will be disappointed. Her trust in her father will decrease, and, simultaneously, she will lose interest in the story. Nothing similar can happen with the story of Little Red Riding Hood. The child accepts the story as true and she will believe in it, but in an entirely different way from her belief in her father's personal account. She believes in a fairy tale just as much and in the same way as the Greeks believed in their myths. Fairy tales have their own truth, as have real life-stories. A down-to-earth, uneventful fairy tale is not 'the real stuff'; at the same time, children would not normally expect little girls and grandmothers to jump out of the wolf's belly when they see one in the zoo. Keen on distinguishing between multiple realities in the stories of others, children nonetheless frequently 'mix up' realities in telling stories about themselves. Phantasy lies may be regarded as the rejection of entering into a relation of symmetric reciprocity with those other persons who occupy a very asymmetrical position (of power) in comparison to children; as such, they can be considered a strategy of self-defence.

The emergence of the question concerning Truth contributes to the multiplication of meaning-providing realities. First, philosophy establishes itself as the one and only reality providing an answer to the question of what Truth is. The Truth of philosophy (both as the Truth of Being and the Truth of beings),[9] is revealed by philosophy alone. Second, philosophy distinguishes between different kinds of Truth and Untruth (for example, the truth or untruth of myth, the truth or untruth of the Homeric epic poetry, the truth or untruth of tragedy, or the truth or untruth of *Historia*.[10] Meaning-providing Truths (in the plural) are ranked. They have been constantly re-ranked for two and a half thousand years. It happens now, in the post-modern era, for the first time that ranking the meaning-providing spheres (of truth) becomes suspect.

Two interconnected tendencies gather momentum in modernity. Several meaning-providing spheres are elevated far beyond the scope of everyday reality, and the division of truth along the various sub-spheres results in an ever increasing professionalization of 'truth production'. Culture writ large is soon divided into 'high' and 'low' cultures, and truth-providing is projected on to high culture alone.

Truth fell into disrepute in the ranks of the eminent thinkers of the nineteenth and twentieth centuries – the more so, the more the corres-pondence theory of truth, which has been taken for granted during many centuries of philosophical speculation, has become suspect. For example Foucault, following the tradition of Nietzsche, saw truth as a weapon manufactured by power. In terms of this understanding, every discourse produces its own truth which in turn becomes deeply entrenched in the power-position of that particular discourse.[11] This is, in my mind, a correct (and in this sense true) description of certain, but not all, kinds of truth. When I assumed that the multiplicity of realities is the precondition of the plurality of Truth, I have also accepted the contention that the increasing multiplication of the spheres of reality results in an increasing pluralization of truth, and also that truth and power are related. But I did not simultaneously subscribe to the most simplistic kind of identity logic, which is content with the assertion that *A est A*, that is, Truth is Truth, or *A est B*, that is, Truth is Power, whatever kind of truth one may have in mind.

Heidegger has to be credited for coming to the rescue of the good reputation of Truth. He had made several slightly different but equally courageous attempts at understanding Truth as a thoroughly historical concept, without resigning completely the task of offering an overarching vision of the essence of Truth. The correspondence theory of truth is not unmasked by him as plain Untruth, but under-stood as the Truth of the Western Culture, as the manifestation of the modern, metaphysical and technological 'opening of Being', or rather, as one of its manifestations. Heidegger merged radical philo-sophy and cultural traditionalism, as did the young Lukács. For them, Truth presents itself in the great works of art. And the Truth of Art is truth not by virtue of its correspondence to some other kind of 'reality' but rather by virtue of its non-correspondence. In terms of the Lukácsian paradox, the more a work of art 'resembles' everyday reality, the more unlike this reality it actually becomes. In Heidegger's formulation, every ordinary and hitherto existing being becomes an unbeing in the light of the work. Both Lukács and Heidegger render the uniqueness of the Truth of the artwork perceptible by using the Kierkegaardian metaphor of the leap. An abyss separates the Work from the author, the recipient, and life, as well as from the other spheres of Truth.[12]

The question concerning the Truth in the artwork was raised to create an unconquerable bastion against the imperialism of the correspondence theory of truth. In the last decades, Kuhn and Feyerabend carried the campaign over to the territory of the philosophy of science, the heartland of the correspondence theory. They have contributed to the post-modern understanding of the diversity of the kinds of Truth (an issue I shall presently address), whereas the question concerning the 'Truth in Art' also contributes to the post-modern speculations concerning the spheres of Truth.

Realistic (figurative) representation best served Lukács and Heidegger to make their point that Truth in the work of art is the world of the work which, by its very existence, unmasks the other worlds (of daily life, politics, etc.) as untrue, fraudulent and banal. For example, Heidegger shows that things of use, like peasant shoes, the perishable things of our modern 'technological' universe, are presented in the world of the artwork as things that they are not; the imperishable symbols of a way of life. The total rejection of the 'world of ultimate sinfulness', or, in Heidegger's paraphrasis, 'the world of ultimate mataphysics' is a wilfully apocalyptic gesture which, for the time being, does not appeal to our post-modern consciousness. When Derrida, in his *Truth in Painting*, radicalizes Heidegger by having recourse to Kant,[13] he also abandons the latter's extreme apocalyptic thrust. Let me tell in my own way what I believe to be an important aspect of Derrida's story.

Insofar as one speculates on 'truth in art' one speaks the language of philosophy.[14] The question about the essence of Truth (in art) is philosophical in nature, so the answer will be as well. Whatever philosophy has to say about 'Truth-in-Art' will not be truth *in* art: the latter can be presented by art alone, and never by philosophy. Yet it is philosophy, not art, that ponders 'Truth-in-Art'; art cannot reflect upon the Truth it presents (though the artist can reflect upon the Truth of her own work). Philosophy asserts 'the Truth-in-Art', and tries to comprehend and to illuminate that Truth.

Parergon, the frame of the painting, does not belong to the work it enframes. It is not in the work, nor is it entirely outside the work (as the wall of a gallery is). Philosophical speculations about the Truth-in-Art are *parerga*. They enframe this truth in a dual sense. They make this Truth stand out, they isolate it from the wall (everyday reality) by pointing at its intrinsic quality; but they enframe the same Truth by limiting, cutting, and thus attempting to determine it through philosophical speculations.

Similarly, a philosophy of religion is a *parergon* to religion with a difference.[15] Art is enframed (by philosophy) as a sphere which presents Truth. It is the self-appointed task of philosophies of art to tell us what 'truth-in-art' is, as it is the self-appointed task of art criticism to tell us whether Truth or Untruth has been presented in one or another concrete work or artistic style. Yet religions, unlike works of art, provide answers to the question of what Truth is. As *parergon*, philosophy speculates solely upon Truth in religion, not upon the Truth of (one or another) religion. When philosophers express their personal preferences, they step outside the *parergon*. Certainly, philosophy can brush aside the sphere of religion as the manifestation of Untruth in general, a practice common to so many men of the Enlightnment. Or, alternatively, they can attribute a merely historical Truth to religion, in contrast to the alleged a-temporal Truth of scientific inquiry (as did Freud).[16] But there is no 'religion criticism' analogous to art criticism.

Among the many kinds of truths distributed along, or manufactured by, the spheres of reality, 'truth in art' can best be enframed by modern philosophy precisely because 'truth in art' does not enframe art itself. The theory of gravitation belongs to the description (the perception) of gravitation, but the theory of painting does not belong to painting. This frame has also served as a fence; it has fenced off the total domination of the 'scientific', i.e. correspondence, concept of Truth with all its variants. Once 'scientific truth' resigned its title to domination and slowly withdrew, philosophy, too, could relax. More attention can now be paid to the question of what the Truth (in art) is. Here, too, universalism has lost its cutting edge; so has normativity. When the apocalyptic passion, which has enframed art with a claim to higher Truth in order to contrast this Truth to the baseness and depravity of life, has been deflated, this much abused life also becomes worthy of philosophical speculation.

3 The Kinds of Truth

At the beginning of the first section, I mentioned in passing that the categories of value-orientation, 'true and false', are, together with some other value-orientative categories, empirical human universals; they operate as sheer formal *a prioris*. Their content is given by the descriptive and normative knowledge of a way of life, and by the personal experience of the actors as crystallized within and around this common knowledge. What is called Truth is always a content given to the True. But not every kind of content given to the True can become Truth. We confidently refer to certain things, affairs or stories as 'true' without associating them with 'truth'. But one can hardly speak about something as 'true' if this thing could never become truth (under specific circumstances, within the framework of a particular vision, in a particular institution, for someone).

In what follows, I will present an almost random sample of the proper use of the orientative categories 'true and false', where in some cases true/false can be related to Truth, and in some others cannot. The sample is not entirely random, for I do not exemplify the same kind of truth more than once. But it is random inasmuch as not all kinds of truth will be discussed here. Readers can extend the list many times over.

Case 1 X. remarks: 'It is raining.' The sentence is true if it corresponds to the fact of raining; our senses are the most reliable source of true information (we look out of the window). The sentence can also be false. No knowledge is conveyed, no complex intellectual process is involved here. The person who remarks: 'Indeed, it is raining', will normally not burst out in an exclamation such as 'It is raining! I see the truth, I now know the truth.' But if a discourse of domination disallows people to trust the testimony of their senses, then an exclamation similar to the above can be proper and meaningful.

Case 2 A group of people plays the game 'blind man's bluff'. The blindfolded person catches someone and says: 'This is Peter!'. The others applaud: 'Right, right' – it is true. Here, too, there is correspondence. The correspondence is achieved by a guess, not by observation; sometimes by a 'learned guess'. Such a guess can be the starting-point for further exploration. If the participants of a more complex game accept the results, then they also accept the guess as the source of true statement. It is (mostly) such that groups start to accumulate new knowledge, and also new techniques. The original gambit (the guess) is soon forgotten, and the participants in the complex game accept the rules thus confirmed; they take the knowledge acquired by those rules for granted. True knowledge of this sort is pragmatic (it is true insofar as it works in the given community). And it is, normally, 'true knowledge', not Truth or Untruth. Very exceptionally, e.g. when a new guess, and the knowledge attained by it, comes to the support of a not-yet-accepted paradigm or becomes inspired by it, exclamations like 'this is the Truth' do make sense.[17]

Case 3 A student solves a mathematical equation. He exclaims: 'I got it right!' This case (and that of a correct logical inference) can be termed, by paraphrasing Leibniz, 'Rational Truth' and contrasted to 'Factual Truth'. Here, the use of the term Truth may sound extremely odd to our (post-modern) ears. 'I got it right' or 'A is A' cannot be meaningfully replaced with the exclamation 'This is the Truth'. Similarly to the cases of correspondence, right solutions or non-self-contradictory propositions cannot be referred to as 'the Truth' without further qualifications.

The idea of 'Rational Truth', as well as, although to a lesser extent, the idea of 'Factual Truth', is responsible for an extraordinary statement, which has assumed an almost axiomatic status for a long time, namely that 'truth compels'. Assume that the axiom is entirely acceptable in mathematics and in logic (with the exception of borderline models), for example in the BARBARA form of syllogism. The acceptance of the propositions major and minor compels the acceptance of the conclusion rationally and universally. This means that a logically correct inference compels. But nothing compels us rationally, even less universally, to identify correct inference with Truth. Correct inference indeed compels, but Truth cannot be inferred from that which is True. Similarly, the evidence of 'mere facts' (whatever that means) can compel me to accept e.g. the existence of a thing ('there are cable cars in San-Francisco – look!') or the use of that thing. I might be compelled to say that 'this is, indeed, the case', but I am not, as a result, also compelled to accept the axiom that whatever is the case, it equals Truth.[18]

'Truth compels' is not a true statement about Truth unless it compels. As long as Truth is defined as something that compels, compulsion of a kind and Truth are closely related. In answering the question what Truth is, philosophers of yesteryear defined Truth after the model of true (correct) inference or the true (correct) recording of what a single case is. Thus, wittingly or unwittingly, they authorized the coercive mechanism of a dominating discourse. The question concerning the essence of Truth and the question concerning the content of Truth are certainly different. But what is considered to be true in a dominating discourse is compulsory truth; their alternatives are outlawed, and those who seek them are rejected by communities as heretics, dilettantes or madmen. What seems to be an axiom (truth compels) is just an interpretation of truth. The announcement of a new Truth: 'what you believe to be true is Untruth, something else is

Truth', gets a peculiar twist if truth compels. For it reads as follows: 'not this should compel you, but rather something else should compel you'.

Post-modern men and women, and among them post-modern philosophers, seek the kinds of Truth which do not universally compel. On the one hand, they do not believe that whatever has such power to compel is superior to anything that has no such power. On the other hand, they do not believe in the traditional claim to universality in terms of which whatever compels certain persons, participants in a particular way of life, should also compel other persons, participants in other ways of life. A correct mathematical solution compels everyone; in this sense, it universally compels; but to associate Truth with such a solution, or with any kind of 'solution', is a historically conditioned and personal (not universally valid) decision. Some will find Truth rather in the Puzzle, the Insoluble, in art or in religion.[19]

To these questions I shall return in the following section. But first I continue with my random sample and discuss a few additional cases. This time such kinds of truth will be on the agenda which are neither 'rational' nor 'factual' in a strict sense, yet still acknowledged as relevant, that is, decisive kinds of Truth since times immemorial, or recognized as such by modern philosophy and sciences.

Case 4 According to Ranke, historians should narrate past events as they have really happened. Each historian narrates those events differently. Every historical epoch has its own past.[20] There are many true accounts of the same story, and none of them compels us to total assent. A historical account, be it an everyday story or a history book, is accepted as more or less true provided that it offers a plausible interpretation and explanation of the events without overturning the consensually accepted core-knowledge about the event, unless reasons are given or additional information provided as to why the core-knowledge needs to be overturned. True narratives are always also false, insofar as they include elements of falsity (implausibility) for subsequent narrators. At least a level or an aspect of verisimilitude in the works of previous narrators has to be considered to have been true by subsequent narrators if they use them as sources or as testimonies. But in recounting their new story truly *and* in withdrawing the acknowledgement of verisimilitude from a narrative text of the past, the new narrators falsify this text, sometimes for a while, sometimes forever. Historical narratives never pretend to provide conditions for any other but the historical kind of Truth.

The traditional criteria of Truth, *adequatio* and *certitudo*, have a very restricted sense here. True (plausible) narratives weave interpretation, explanation and information into a kind of true, that is, meaningful (meaning-providing), knowledge. Although historical narratives do not 'contain' Truths, any one of them, not only the representative ones, can be Truth for someone. Everyday stories may serve as the Truth for one or for a few persons; representative stories may serve as such for many, sometimes for the duration of a whole historical period.

Case 5 We discuss true and false theories as well as true and false theoretical ideas. Nowadays, true and false paradigms have joined the distinguished list. The greatest and the most spectacular theoretical upheavals in modernity occurred around these fundamental questions, because it is here that the issue of possibility and impossibility, as well as that of the conditions of true knowledge in the sciences, are raised. Looking back to the story of true scientific knowledge with postmodern eyes, the claim of modern science to certitude and adequacy[21] seems unwarranted, even perverse. There is no 'final' theory about the criteria of True in scientific (or any other) theory. Everyday actors who theorize everyday matters, can, for example, easily be followers of Popper. In this sphere, the best (truest) theory is still that which enables everyday actors to fit together interpreted everyday facts and mini-narratives relatively consistently, in order to illuminate and explain one, or several (recurring), everyday problems or occurences. In other spheres, this kind of criteria will not suffice. But whether Kantians, Popperians, Kuhnians, Davidsonians, or merely well-informed 'eclectic' citizens, post-modern men and women do not believe in the idea of a 'world picture', in the one, absolute, and incontestable theory which mirrors 'reality' out there, and provides us with a clue to the 'riddles of nature'.

And still, the dominating power of science as ideology holds its sway even in its suicidal gestures, exaggerated as they are. Several more recent theorists, although concerned about the new criteria of truth and falsity in science, do not take into consideration different concepts of Truth, particularly those which have remained outside the orbit of sciences and continue to forge general concepts of truth and falsity.[22] Lip-service is frequently paid to the multi-faceted character of Truth. However, the proper appraisal of realities requires that the general (universal), all-encompassing understanding (definition) of true knowledge, of Truth, or of the procedures through which something is accepted as True, be abandoned.

It is still possible to make assertions about true knowledge in general, to come up with a 'definition' which includes all kinds and types. Several theorists are interested in forging such definitions; I am not. Still, for the reader's sake, I present my own (pragmatic) version: true knowledge is the kind of 'know-what' and 'know-how' that serves as the most reliable crutch in world-orientation, and which guides denizens of this world in their attempt to expand the scope of their action and thinking with the least amount of risk of relapsing into chaos. But the criteria of the reliability of that crutch are so different, depending on the sphere, the kind, or the type of true knowledge, that the generalized sentence (my own 'definition') can barely hide its own emptiness.

Case 6 Who is a true, who is a false prophet? Who is a true, who is a false friend? Who is a true, who is an untrue human being? Pondering the meaning of the term 'true' in the context of these and similar questions raises a host of issues at the outset which have remained untouched in all former reflections. The true prophet speaks with authority, his moral judgements are right and true, he lives as he teaches, in other words, he is authentic. A true prophet can be trusted; so can a true friend or a true person. Trustworthiness is a common feature of all men and women who are 'true'. Another is truthfulness. One expects a true friend to be loyal, and a true man as good as his word. The term 'true' is filled here with ethical content. The model Greeks could not imagine a man being good otherwise than in the possession of knowledge of the Good. But in their mind, true knowledge about anything else but of the Good does not make a man good (true).

This understanding of the 'true' seems to be intimately related to Truth. A prophet partakes of Truth and tells the Truth. This is so even if his prophecy does not come true (as in the case of Jonah). We expect true friends to tell us the truth 'face to face', even if truth pains them or us. Let me note that the ethically informed concept of the true underwent far smaller changes in the last two and a half thousand years than the ones associated with knowledge or any other kind of subject-object relationship.[23]

Case 7 'I tell the Truth, nothing but the Truth, so help me God!' Telling the truth is here contrasted to lying, not to erring or giving a piece of false (erroneous) knowledge. The injunction 'tell the Truth!' is an obligation to disclose one's knowledge, information about a thing, one's experiences, all that is on one's mind or in one's feelings about a particular issue, person or anything else. Anyone who tells the Truth on a witness-stand recounts matters truthfully, but this truthfulness is not identical with the truthfulness of a 'true' person, even less with that of a 'true' prophet. Furthermore, if one tells exactly what is on one's mind about a concrete issue or a first-hand experience, one rarely tells 'the Truth', only something that is true, correct. It would be odd to say that the teacher who instructs students in a foreign language and corrects their grammatical mistakes, 'tells the Truth'. The dialectical character of the concept of Truth is tacitly presupposed in ordinary language use. The expression 'telling the Truth' implies a negation, the overcoming of an obstacle such as fear, self-interest, inhibition, or the eventual commitment not to disclose this particular thing. This kind of obligation to disclose 'the truth of the matter' is a primary moral category, so is the injunction to tell the Truth. As such, the norm did not change since times immemorial, although its interpretation and application did.

4 The True Is the Whole; Truth Is Subjective

Kierkegaard's dictum that Truth is subjective sounds at first philosophically absurd, irrational and subjective. Whether we conceive of Truth as absolute or as historical, whether we believe that Truth is the mirror of the Universe or a mere convention, we normally associate Truth with the term 'objective' and not 'subjective'. Objectivity, like the power to compel, has traditionally acquired a much higher dignity than anything termed 'subjective'. Subjective is 'only' subjective, it is merely personal, contingent. Provided that it is more than a chimera, it is there only to be overcome. This is the main message of Descartes' story. The philosophy of the cogito and an entire branch of modern philosophy termed 'epistemology' relentlessly pursued an offensive to conquer a purely objective territory of Truth, and each of them fought with different weapons.

The subject, as the single person, the single mind, the atom of societal world, has gained recognition and this is how it became the methodological starting-point of inquiry. But everything that a single person really *is* was downgraded as secondary reality and untruth. This stands to reason if one bears in mind that the person was conceptualized as a *mind at point zero* before embarking on its climb towards Truth, while Truth was identified with true knowledge, and particularly with true scientific knowledge as it was then understood. Everything that happened in philosophy during modern times has become topsy-turvy in our (post-modern) mind.

There are exceptions though. Kant stood in the tradition, hostile to subjectivity, which he thoroughly upset in matters of knowledge and morals, but not in his reflections on the beautiful. This is the main reason for the recent upsurge of interest in Kant's third Critique.

Judgement of taste is characterized by a subjective purposiveness without purpose, by the absence of the concept (knowledge), but nevertheless contains necessity and universality, the two constituents of Truth according to Kant. And in a further, significant episode, Kierkegaard's polemics against Hegel's dictum, 'the True is the Whole', should be noted. In Kierkegaard's mind, and here he is on the same wavelength as Feuerbach, Hegel is the ultimate metaphysician. In a sense, Hegel indeed is, but in another sense, he is the bringer of new tidings.

Hegel's concept of Truth is outside the framework of this discussion; I want to sidestep all concrete issues of history of philosophy. I have conjured up these celebrated spirits only as sources of inspiration. For in a post-modern vision of Truth the two, seemingly entirely contradictory, assertions, 'the True is the whole' and 'Truth is subjective', can be reconciled.

The last sentence of Kierkegaard's *Either/Or* reads: 'Only the Truth which edifies is Truth for you.'[24] In *Concluding Unscientific Postcript* he formulates the same in a more elaborate way: 'An objective uncertainty held fast in an appropriation process of the most passionate inwardness is the truth, the highest truth attainable for an existing individual.'[25] Truth is subjective precisely in this sense.

Only the Truth which edifies someone is Truth for this or that individual. The idea presupposes that there are several different kinds of Truth; some of them are 'truth for you' (insofar as they edify you), some others are not, yet they are still 'truth for others' (for those whom they edify). A truth which edified certain persons in certain times may by now have ceased to edify anyone; if so, it will no longer be Truth. The assertion 'Truth is subjective' implies that Truth is historical and that in our historical present there are many Truths.

Only the truth that edifies *you* can be Truth for *you*, but by no means necessarily the Truth for you *alone*. The same Truth can edify few, many, and even all men and women. But as far as truth-value is concerned, it remains completely irrelevant whether one, a few, many or all are edified by this Truth. Since in Kierkegaard's teaching the individual is the universal, one cannot 'increase' universality by adding numbers.

The assertion that truth is subjective is an epistemologically open one. Whether Truth is constituted by individual minds, revealed by God, achieved by the application of scientific standards, gained via the contemplation of an artwork, is of no relevance for the status of this assertion. Truth is certainly not identified in it with 'true knowledge', 'correspondence', 'correct information' and the like; but if a kind of true knowledge edifies you, this true knowledge will be 'truth for you', and insofar as the correspondence theory of Truth edifies you, it will remain Truth for you.

The idea of the subjective quality of Truth is entirely unrelated to the question (of quite meagre substance) whether Truth is absolute or relative. But it helps us (post-moderns) to set aside this question, and together with it, the unrewarding task of defending new concepts of truth against the accusations of relativism. As if everything that does not compel, that is freely choosen, received, or merely contemplated, would be guilty of relativism! The Truth which edifies me is Truth for me, but not for others; yet this Truth can still shine in the light of the Absolute for me, although I am aware that it does not do so for (certain) others. Absolute may have the meaning of unconditional, total, as well as that of certitude. Although Truth-for-me can be absolute, it does not need to be. Agnosticism is the Truth for the agnostics, if they are edified by agnosticism. Certitude is a possible, but by no means necessary, aspect of the knowledge about the Absolute Truth, be it discursive, intuitive or epiphanic. The universe, the world of numbers and signs, the ways of God Almighty can be Truths for men and women just because they are incomprehensible, enshrined in mysteries, and not because one comes to understand or know them with certitude. Kant, who identified Truth entirely with true knowledge, would have described all previous questions as ones pertaining to hope alone, and the answers to those questions as unauthorized (by reason) to raise truth-claims. It seems as if I had relapsed into a pre-critical stage. In fact, together with my many contemporaries, I reject the pre-Kantian epistemological and ontological positions altogether, and the Kantian proposition only insofar as it resembles the former. The modified Kierkegaardian idea of Truth makes complete sense within the framework of a post-epistemological theory of knowledge. There are many competing theories of this kind today, most of them being committed to one or another version of the language paradigm. The contention that true knowledge and its criteria are historical and as such, diverse and changing, is common to them all, some a-prioristic theories of speech included.[26]

Why 'reality', the so-called objective world, is essentially the same for all single minds, ceases to be a puzzle for philosophies since the intersubjective constitution of the world has become the credo of our time. How we can bring our mind to the point that it corresponds to the objects is an issue we do not ponder, for we assume that such a correspondence does not normally occur. To sum up a very complex story in a much too simple way, true knowledge appears for us as something socially produced. The stark juxtaposition between true knowledge and mere opinion cannot be upheld, especially not when true knowledge is comprehended as *adequatio* to a kind of essence.

Certainly, the great philosophers of the early modern age were not less clever than we are. They knew, as much as we do, that the newborn is thrown into a network of socially produced and upheld conventions, norms, and bodies of science, and that language is the main carrier of, and mediator between, these constituents of the network. Only they did not accept this existential condition as the untranscendable condition of human (social) life. They charged those limits in the full confidence that a breakthrough is possible. This confidence or naivety was also their strength. Historically speaking, they had to do what they were doing. They were busy with clearing the ground for modernity, for the modern way of thinking. As long as everyday life and thinking, convention and tradition, was through-and-through pre-modern, as long as everything that had been 'inter-subjectively constituted' had to appear therefore to the newcomers as the cognitive system of domination, the mirror image of a world of assymetric reciprocity, and thus a world of sheer appearances, philosophers had to make a clean sweep and start with a purported *tabula rasa*. Since only the single mind (and the senses of the single person) can be elevated to the height of an absolute starting point in the philosophical laboratory, the *cogito* or the senses must provide the ultimate evidence, although very rarely also the ultimate reality. To commence world-construction with *more geometrico* axioms is exactly the same game played with other means. Contract theories proceed in similar fashion, and for the same historical reason. It can be pointed out without an excessive degree of sociologizing that, with the sole exception of Vico, the 'clean sweep' method was abandoned only at the moment when the new (modern) way of life began to establish itself.[27] Since our 'intersubjective reality', our conventions, our perceptions of the world and of the criteria of true knowledge became increasingly 'modernized', no 'clean sweep' was needed anymore. However, it still remained general practice for a while, simply because it has already established itself as our own tradition.

The post-modern position is the reconciliation with the historical condition as the 'human' condition. As far as true knowledge is concerned, we shut the door of historicity upon ourselves. Truth is not identical with true knowledge, but true knowledge can also be Truth (if it edifies). Yet once true knowledge edifies and becomes Truth, it does not necessarily remain historical in its quality as Truth. Or rather, the historicity of true knowledge in general does not matter whenever a piece of true knowledge becomes Truth for one person, for a few or for many. One can envision Truth through a scientific paradigm, through a historical explanation, in the awareness that, perhaps tomorrow, they might be replaced by others. One can also wager that they will never be replaced. True knowledge about a single case – an ephemeral phenomenon altogether – can also be Truth for the person whose life it concerns.

The spheres of truth produce their own criteria of true knowledge, belief, right way of thinking, acting and the like. Whenever a person enters one sphere or the other, she has to take certain truth claims for granted, she has to play the language game she has chosen to play. Men and women are normally participant members of many a language game, and, under certain conditions and in certain ways, they can criticize, reject, or even over-rule, a few norms of a particular language game from the vantage-point of another language game. One can safely navigate in the medium of a sphere even if one does not subscribe to all criteria of 'truth' accepted by the mainstream, but never if one does not subscribe to a single one.[28] Total consensus is neither the criterion of truth, nor the result of true knowledge.[29] Not just the content, but also the criteria of the True are different in different spheres, and they are changing. What is changing is, first, the determination of Truth ('this or that is true'), second, the procedure to attain it, and third, the criteria for its acceptance. (For example, is 'low' art true or false art; are there criteria for distinguishing between true and false art, and if so, what are they?)

To cut a long story short, it has become deeply problematic for us, post-moderns, to forge a single overarching concept of Truth. As far as we can see, no new general answer to the question of what Truth is can be offered, not, at least, one that would outlast the year of its conception. Heidegger made a go at it, and he kept banging on the door of the prisonhouse of historicity. But finally, he too came to admit that his overarching concept of Truth (*aletheia*) cannot be equated with Truth, but rather with what grants truth (the opening of Being).[30] Yet the conclusion to be drawn from the above need not result in the abandonment of the question of Truth.

The assertion 'Truth is subjective' is not the definition of Truth. The formula 'Only that which edifies you is Truth for you' leaves the door open for the plurality of truths as well as for the plurality of the concepts of truth. It does not tell you what Truth is, nor does it reveal what Truth is. It is an *idea* of Truth.

The idea of Truth has been arrived at in the same way as the concept of Truth, namely dialectically, via negation. The idea of Truth does not negate the possibility or the relevance of the concept of Truth. But it does negate the validity of the universal claim that Truth is solely about true knowledge; furthermore, it negates the claim that it is true knowledge that should (universally) decide on what Truth is. It negates the right (the authority) of metaphysics and of the sciences to tell us once and for all what Truth (for us) is or can be. It negates the imperialism of the concept of Truth.

The idea of Truth is the (dialectical) sublation of the concept of Truth and that of its negation. The idea of Truth provides knowledge: it informs you whether a kind of Truth is truth for you. It also informs you about whether a kind of truth is 'truth for others' (it is, if this Truth edifies others). If something is not Truth for you, it can still be Truth for others. Even if a kind of Truth is absolute and ultimate for you, you can still recognize that the same Truth is not Truth for others. *The idea of Truth enjoins us mutually to recognize each other's Truth*. It is the highest form of the recognition of the Other.

The idea that Truth is subjective has nothing to say about the source of Truth (any Truth that is). It has nothing to do with solipsism, with the subjective constitution of the world. By no means does it suggest that Truth is Truth about the Subject. One can see in the Heideggerian *aletheia* (qua opening of Being) the condition of all Truth and stick to the idea of Truth in terms of which Truth is subjective. For it is, after all, *Ex/istenz* (standing in the lighting of Being) that asserts that Truth is subjective in the above sense. 'Lighting of Being' is the presence; it is (to remain in Heidegger's jargon) 'presencing'. The idea that Truth is subjective is historical; it is historical Truth that pertains to the present. But it does not define the content of any single Truth. The idea that Truth is subjective is historical in nature but the Truth that edifies us and becomes 'truth for us' is not necessarily to be comprehended as historical. This idea of Truth allows us to believe in eternal Truth.

At the end of the dialogue conducted with himself about the Truth in Van Gogh's painting (in *Truth in Painting*), Derrida remarks: 'All these shoes remain there, in a sale, so you can compare them, pair them up, unpair them, bet or not bet on the pair. The trap is the inevitability of betting. The logic of the disparate . . .'[31] Positing Truth as subjective entails the inevitability of betting. Truth for me is my bet as that of a contingent person, but the *object* (the stake) of my wager can be thought as non-contingent. I termed the stake of the wager the object of the bet to make it clearer what is at stake here: a kind of subject-object relation, or even subject-object identity (in a Hegelian sense), with or without correspondence.

To paraphrase Derrida further: betting on the shoes is the interpretation of those shoes. My bet is the Truth that is truth for me; the shoes are the stake of my bet, the shoes become the shoes according to my bet (interpretation). This is, indeed, subject-object identity. But I will never *possess* those shoes. 'Truth for me' is not identical with 'my

Truth'. No one possesses Truth. One is edified by Truth. But what does it mean to be edified?

One can be edified in different ways. Yet whatever appears in a sphere of truth as true, beautiful or good, can become Truth for some; so can entirely new beginnings within those spheres. Any kind of True (*verum*) can become Truth (*veritas*), the ugly and the evil included. Truth does not provide criteria for *verum*, *pulchrum* or *bonum*, for those criteria are set, upset and reset in different, connected, unconnected or disconnected language games.

To be edified by something means (for me) to be connected to this thing by the whole of one's existence. One's whole existence can be affected by contingent events; the whole existence can be involved in a bet, and also in living up to the object of that bet. In its most primitive understanding 'existence' stands for life; beyond it, 'existence' stands for the good or meaningful life. But regardless of whether we comprehend existence in a primitive or in a sublime fashion, Truth seizes, shakes, enlightens, changes, elevates this very existence. In this interpretation Truth is always the Whole.[32]

Let us assume that there is no dominating discourse. If this is so, there is no established hierarchy between truths ensuing from the hierarchy of spheres. Neither is there a prohibition against criticizing one kind of truth from the vantage point of another (which was the case in the philosophical theory of *duplex veritas*). Let us further assume that not only one thing, knowledge or anything else that is true, becomes Truth for you. You, as a person, can always establish a hierarchy among the Truths (for you) which do not stand in an 'objectively' hierarchical relation with one another. Truth as a Whole, then, is for the most part not a one-time event, a simple experience, but it includes a series of 'truth-events'. Truth-events build up, they are ordered hierarchically by the person whose Truths they are; certain Truths become relativized by higher – more encompassing – ones; Untruth will thus become the constituent of Truth itself. Something very similar happens here as in Hegel's *Logic*, except that there is no logic to it, and no absolute knowledge awaits us at the end of the journey. There is no logic here, for each Truth (for you) is intimately connected with your bet, as either the non-determining condition or as the undetermined result of this bet or of the series of your bets. Finally, not absolute knowledge but meaningful life appears as the highest *synthesis*, as the all-encompassing Truth.

The idea of Truth is, then, in the last instance, the regulative idea of a meaningful conduct of life.

The conclusion must arouse suspicion; this post-modern idea of Truth resembles too closely the well-known pre-modern concept that equates Truth with the recognition of the Goodness of the Good. There are, indeed, certain resemblances. After all, pre-moderns and post-moderns share something: they do not tremble in their boots while facing contingency; the ancients did not, because they knew nothing about it, hence they were not contingent at all, and the post-moderns do not, because they have just begun to learn to make peace with the consciousness of their contingency. And still an abyss divides post-moderns from pre-moderns. For the pre-moderns, the meaningful life and the good life were identical; but not so for the post-moderns. The synthesis, the all-encompassing Truth does not necessarily include the good in a moral sense, particularily not in a fully moral sense (as an end in itself).[33] The merger of the true and the good in the synthesis of life requires that one put one's stakes on the Good and stick to it.

The question of Truth is thus historical, but we learn nothing (or very little) about truth by just stating this. Throughout this chapter I have alluded to a stronger (or a slightly different) connection: the answer to the question of truth is the crystallization point of cultures. The dominating concept of truth of an epoch manifests the dominating culture of that epoch. Can we say that where there is no dominating concept of truth, there is no dominating culture at all? Or should we explore the possibility that the absence of a dominating concept of truth is actually the manifestation of the dominating culture of the contemporary (post-modern) world?

5

Culture, or Invitation to Luncheon by Immanuel Kant

1 On Accepting Kant's Guidance in the Philosophy of Culture

Philosophy of culture was invented by the men of the Enlightenment. They re-interpreted the old term 'culture' (or 'civilization') so that it encompassed several phenomena hitherto not seen to be strongly interrelated, for example crafts and the skills to practise them; arts and sciences and the skills (or the genius) to create them; sensitivity to beauty and taste in general; forms of social and private intercourse; urbanity, civility, the codes of honour and of decorum; the modes to carry out conflicts, be they personal, social or political. The idea of 'culture' was Kantian before Kant, for it was counterfactual and regulative from the beginning. The idea contained the normative presupposition that all phenomena encompassed by the term 'culture' should develop and flourish in harmony; yet the same presupposition transformed the concept of culture into a dialectical one. In fact, the different aspects of culture failed to match. One aspect may have flourished and grown while the other became impoverished.

Culture turned out to be a problematic, ambiguous phenomenon. It is misleading to blame universalism for this fiasco. Certainly, the idea and the concept of 'culture' is a universal. But neither the conception of this universal nor the perception of its contradictions is to be blamed for the fiasco – if there is any. Actually, the conception of the ideal of culture, and the renewed attempt to cope with the contradictions inherent in its counterfactual character, was an answer to the then emerging modern social and political arrangement. After two hundred years, none of the problems those early philosophers of culture once attacked has disappeared; the once detected contradictions have merely become more marked. The question is not whether

one keeps or abandons the ideal of 'culture' but whether one addresses sincerely those pathologies which were first discovered with
the help of this universal idea.

The idea can perhaps be blamed for being inflated beyond all proportions insofar as it included creative art. After all, one can imagine
a well-arranged society where no creative genius flourishes. However,
associating civility, urbanity, taste and sensitivity with the development of crafts and skills on the one hand, and with the multiplication
of independent and informal associations and societies on the other
hand, must not be regarded as an inflated expectation.

The philosophy of culture of the eighteenth and early nineteenth
centuries re-interpreted the old term 'culture' (or civilization) in order
to describe the promises and the problems of modernity in the making, and, incidentally, also in order to seek ways to remedy the
pathological aspects of an emerging world. Adam Smith, Hume, Dide-
rot, Rousseau, Lessing, Herder, Condorcet, Goethe and Schiller are
the best known of them.

The question of what is going to keep society together once time-
honoured customs lose their integrative power had already been
raised a century before. But the then usual answer, that the (modern)
state would take care of this task, seemed later hardly satisfactory
even for those who, like Kant, regarded the establishment of a modern
republican state as the necessary precondition of modern civilization.
The second, and then still recent answer, that the 'invisible hand',
the self-regulating market itself, will become the ultimate integrative
power, did not even satisfy Adam Smith who forged it. The fear
of civilized barbarism became widespread. A kind of mild social
hypocrisy was favoured by some (like Smith and Hume) in order
to moderate the cruelty of the laws of the jungle. Radicals rejected
mere role-playing with spite, and they either preached the absolutism
of virtues, both public and private (like Rousseau) or they juxtaposed
an aestheticized jungle to the one inhabited by the herd (de Sade
well before Nietzsche). Others again – early socialists, positivists
and some liberals – over-optimistically believed that the ambiguity
of modern culture is but a transitory phenomenon. To yet another
group of philosophers of culture, modernity appeared as the era
of general cultural decay, a self-destructive social arrangement,
where all attempts to inject worth or nobility into it are futile
(Ferguson).

As with all cases concerning the knowledge of the world, here too
a wise person is the best guide. This is why I invite Immanuel Kant
to be my Virgil. A modern wise man differs slightly from the ancient,

given that passing balanced and good judgements on matters concerning the modern world requires the mobilization of a few additional faculties when compared to the ancient. A sufficient degree of personal experience for the knowledge of the world, moral responsibility, seriousness, scepticism, humour, an understanding of human follies, *phronesis* – all these qualities were present in the character of the little man of Königsberg. Anyone who has doubts as to whether his personal experience was sufficient for the knowledge of the world, should read the Preface to Kant's lectures on Anthropology.[1] The great philosopher makes here exactly the same observation as does Miss Marple, the prudent elderly lady from Agatha Christie's detective fictions in our century, namely that one comes to know human character first at home, not by travelling around extensively. In addition, Kant refers to Königsberg as a proper place where a person can sufficiently expand both his *Weltkenntnis* and his *Menschenkenntnis*.

The very blood vessels of modern culture carried the viruses of the evil of the twentieth century. This means that modern culture can be the carrier (or the incarnation) of evil, but it certainly does not mean that modern culture (civilization) is the cause of evil or that it brings about evil directly; least of all that it is evil. There is no Auschwitz without gas chambers and without pathologically developed bureaucratic consciousness, but neither chemistry, leading to the production of poisonous gas, nor the invention of a soulless code of bureaucratic conduct are the causes of Auschwitz. Heidegger's equation of the Holocaust and technological imagination expresses nothing but the weak judgemental powers and the bad taste of a brilliant but morally unwise philosopher. Evil is a moral not a technological power.

To start with, in contrast to the English translator of *The Critique of Judgement* who did not catch the essential message and mistranslated the relevant passage in paragraph 83, Kant succinctly distinguishes between evil and evils (*Böse* and *Übel*). Had he known about the incarnation of Evil (*Böse*) in Auschwitz, he would never have dreamt of equating it with the evils (*Übels*) of modern technology. For Evil and evils were in his mind of a different quality or different kind.

According to Kant, we have reasons to assume that culture is the final purpose of nature, for it is culture that makes the rational creature fit to raise every possible goal or to serve every possible purpose. In this generality, culture has no affinity with morals, not even with ethics. The purposes can be good or bad as well as indifferent. But Kant also subdivides the realm of culture into two major branches: those of mere skills on the one hand and of discipline of the will on the other. The practice of mere skills can prepare the territory of Evil indirectly (although even then, it cannot cause evil) if it is not counterbalanced by the other kind of culture, that of the discipline of the will. Kant therefore obviously did not make a case for the ethical neutrality of the culture of skills. On their own, without being accompanied by the discipline of the will, technical skills, science (and sometimes even arts), serve as the means for satisfying the human hunger for wealth, fame and power. Since these major drives motivate humans towards the acceptance of bad (evil) maxims, skills can facilitate the actualization of that particular kind of Evil which follows from those maxims. Thus evil has indeed something to do with culture insofar as evil is perpetrated under the guidance of evil maxims. And evil maxims, like all maxims, belong to culture. But they do so, at least for Kant, only in a negative sense: insofar as culture fails to strengthen good maxims, evil maxims will be accepted. This is an important qualification in support of the initial argument. In Kant, there is no causal relationship between a concrete culture on the one hand, and Evil on the other hand, for man's inclination (*Hang*) to Evil is omnipresent and not culture-specific. In whatever culture humans dwell, they are inclined to evil maxims, unless a certain culture of the will (under the guidance of decent maxims) strengthens their original inclination to the good.[2] It may be added to this that although Evil does not follow from culture, specific kinds of evil maxims are formed under the unique imprint of particular cultures, and those unique formulations can be linked to the unique kinds of Evil perpetrated under the guidance of such evil maxims. Furthermore, even if the maxims themselves sound completely alike in two different cultural settings, they are not alike given that the worldview in which they are embedded, the arguments in their support, their underlying ideological or theoretical presuppositions, can be entirely different. And since evil as well as good maxims are intertwined in a network of cultural relations, the kind of evil perpetrated in the framework of one culture remains typical for this particular culture, even if it does not result from it. The Evil of Auschwitz (and of the Gulag) was perpetrated under the guidance of evil maxims which were forged in modernity, or were at least embedded in modern imaginary institutions.

Nothing but a reminder of its utmost topicality can be added, then, to Kant's philosophy of culture. For the answer to the question of 'what is to be done' remains unchanged. Political institutions are needed in the framework of which even the race of devil would behave decently. The discipline of will should be strengthened to make men and women well armed against the attraction of evil maxims.

Both issues are addressed by Kant several times. And both issues are addressed on different levels of his system.

Kant discusses matters concerning the application of the moral law within the system of philosophy; law (constitution) as well as virtue are to be treated in *The Metaphysics of Morals*. In Kant's mind, law and virtue participate in culture, but only insofar as they provide the formal precondition for both aspects of culture, particularily for its second aspect, the discpline of the will. *The Metaphysics of Morals* treats the relationship between Freedom and Nature under the absolute authority of transcendental freedom. Contrary to the philosophy of law and of morals, the philosophy of culture (philosophy of history and political philosophy included) cannot be discussed within the framework of the system of philosophy; it belongs exclusively to the system of critique, specifically to the critique of judgement, and to pragmatic anthropology. Although the philosophy of culture (including, again, the philosophy of history and political philosophy) also addresses the relation of freedom and culture, freedom does not occupy here the place of the supreme authority, but that of the supreme end. In Kant's global system, the supreme authority and the supreme end finally coincide. This is the story Kant tells us in the closing paragraphs of the critique of teleological judgement. But *The Critique of Judgement* as well as the *Anthropology* speak, after all, not about the transcendental subject but about *sensus communis*, not about law but about purposiveness and imagination, not about duty but about taste and *savoir vivre*; in short, about all those things which Kant encompasses in the word *Humanitaet*. Although *Humanitaet* cannot flourish where there are no good republican laws, and no *Humanitaet* can replace the goodness of the good person, a world of the best laws would still remain drab, joyless and deserted if it were lacking in *Humanitaet*. Kant writes: 'The cynic's purism and the anchorite's mortification of the flesh, without social well-being, are distorted figures of virtue, which do not attract us to it. Forsaken by graces, they can make no claim to humanity.'[3] In his philosophy of culture, Kant explores the different ways in which 'gesellschaftliches Wohlleben' can be lawfully enhanced. It was presupposed by Kant all the way along that private interest is constantly advanced in an unlawful manner, that is to say, by the instrumentalization of others and the breach of law, but he also assumed that 'social well-being' cannot be directly, only indirectly, enhanced by unlawful actions, via the ruse of nature.[4] A direct advancement of 'social well-being' can be asserted if the action or the judgement pleases in itself, and not only in terms of its otherwise unintended results.

2 Simulacrum; The Actor and the Spectator

The direct (positive) enhancement of well-being in the modern world presupposes the rule of good republican laws, the freedom of man, the equality of the citizen and the independence of the burgher.[5] It also presupposes that the process of men's (and women's) outcome from their self-incurred tutelage has begun. Social well-being can be enhanced directly in various forms and on different levels. All of those forms and levels are important, but not all them are unproblematic. The first level is that of the actors, the second is that of the spectators, and the third level is that of a group of people involved in speech acts in the form of a coversation of equals. The readiness of the human mind or soul (*Gemüth, Gesinnung*) to accept the moral laws is enhanced on all three levels, although in different ways. It is obvious that whatever enhances the readiness of human nature for the acceptance of the moral law in and for action is not the real thing, but only the simulacrum of the real thing, because it is heteronomous. The real thing is to subject ourselves to the moral law just because it is the moral law, an autonomous act. In the case of the spectator or in the case of people who participate in the cultural discussion of equals, one cannot speak of simulacrum, for this is the real thing. In Kant's terminology, both the spectator and the speech-actor mobilize, among other things, also their faculty of (reflective) judgement. This is why in *The Critique of Judgement* Kant only discusses the attitudes of the spectator and of the speech-actor. Apart from some sporadic remarks in the second *Critique*, and in particular in *The Metaphysics of Morals*, it is from Kant's pragmatic *Anthropology* that we learn most about his concept of the ethical as the simulacrum of the moral.

The world is, according to Kant, the human habitat, that is, the human theatre. We are both actors and spectators in it. Kant makes the fine distinction between knowing the world and having a world (*Die Welt erkennen*; *die Welt haben*). Insofar as we know the world, we understand the play; insofar as we have a world, we are co-players.[6] The specator knows the world (how well, is another question); the actor has a world. The speech-actor of a discourse is a combination of the two attitudes. He is a spectator, insofar as his pragmatic and interest-guided actions are suspended. Yet the attitude he assumes during a conversation is also practical; he participates in the play, he is a co-player. A symposium is a drama.

Ethics is a play, the simulacrum of the good. It is the social network of permitted moral semblance. In Kant's mind, humans become play-actors to an ever greater extent with the advancement of civilization. Paying lip service to Rousseau's spite, Kant rather subscribes to La

Rochefoucault's realism. Hypocrisy is certainly better than cynicism. While playing the role of good persons, Kant muses, men can get used to the role they play and the mask might grow to their faces. One must value even the semblance of the good in the other. Illusion in social intercourse is wholesome. Shedding illusions of this kind, for example, *politesse* or decorum, is a sign of barbarism.

> All the human virtue in circulation is small change: one would have to be a child to take it for real gold. But we are better off having small change in circulation than no money at all; and it can eventually converted into genuine gold, though at considerable loss. It is high treason against humanity to treat these coins as *mere counters* having no value at all. . .[7]

The metaphor of the theatre play is replaced here by the metaphor of the circulation of money. But the message remains. The simulacrum is far from being as worthy as the original; but it has still some worth. What is true about action in general, is true about artistry, particularly about political artistry. Political imagination can conjure up the image of the English Parliament when the freedom of people is being discussed, although in reality, the English Parliament is a mere formality of popular freedom; and the same can be asserted, in regard of equality, about the French Convention. Kant uses the expression 'in blossen Formalien besteht' (consists of mere formalities) to underline the commonness between ethical and political semblance; mere formalities are not merely formalities.[8]

Semblance can be pretension or betrayal. Mere accommodation to moral expectations is pretension, but it is not betrayal. Actions or gestures within the framework of that which is (morally) permitted cannot betray anyone. This is so, first, since everyone knows the rules of the game and no one takes token words at their face value, second, because even if they would take them at face value, no harm would befall him or her except a mild discomfort or a slight ridicule. As long as the game is played on the terrain of the (morally) permitted, a person can betray only him or herself. But the very moment s/he is confronted only with him or herself (with his/her own conscience), we leave the domain of ethics (legality) and we enter the realm of morality. Whatever happens between the person and his/her conscience is not a cultural matter. To mistake nature for freedom is a betrayal of morality, of pure practical reason and the moral law, and as such, it is self-betrayal. But in relation to the other person it is just the pretension of some ethical worth. Surely, in the case of unpermitted actions pretension becomes betrayal, because the actor does not play according to the rules, rather, dishonestly, he cheats in the game. Unpermitted acts are unworthy, bad, criminal and evil, regardless of the presence or absence of pretension.

The difference between man in his solitude and man in the network of the social intercourse is the less accentuated the more attention is shifted from the attitude of the actor to the attitude of the spectator. This shift is particularly noticeable in *The Critique of Judgement*. For example, in the deduction of pure aesthetic judgements the emphasis is put on sociability, in particular on the communicability of subjective experiences and impressions, and not solely in the paragraph on the empirical interest in the beautiful[9] where Hannah Arendt located Kant's 'true' political philosophy.[10] Immediately adjacent to it, in discussing the intellectual interest in the beautiful, Kant conjures up the image of the loner, of the man in his solitude who – without the intention to share his impression with anyone – adores and loves the beautiful shape of a wild flower, of a bird and so on. Here emphasis is on the non-social character of the aesthetic interest, for the man in solitude loves the *wild* flower and the bird, beings untouched by society. In this context, the imitation of the song of a bird or of the shape of a flower, in other words, the 'man-made', is called betrayal (*Betrug*), although this time not self-betrayal, given that the loner's enchantment with the mere form of un-social natural beauty is the twin feeling of his or her moral sense. The dual interest taken in the judgement of taste is even more accentuated in the chapter 'Of the Method of Taste'.[11] The 'culture of the mental powers (Gemüth-skraefte)' is enhanced, so Kant says, in the humaniora, because 'humanity on the one side indicates the universal feeling of sympathy, and on the other the faculty of being able to communicate universally our inmost [feelings]'.[12] But, Kant also adds, given that taste is fundamentally the capacity of judging sensitized ethical ideas, the true propaedeutic for the grounding of taste remains the furthering of ethical ideas and the cultivation of moral sense. The latter remains the task of men-in-solitude.

Both sociability and morality are furthered by the cultivation of the judgement of taste, the first directly, the second indirectly. It is enhanced directly as far as legality, indirectly as far as morality is concerned. There are certain differences in this context between the beautiful and the sublime, for the latter is not a pure judgement of taste. Both judgements of taste and the sense for the sublime result from the general cultivation of our mind and imagination. The first makes us love nature in the right way, the second makes us respect the ideas which are beyond the limits of representability. These ideas can, however, appear in a great variety of representations. In his

pre-critical work on the beautiful and the sublime, Kant remarked
that Evil, too, can be sublime.[13] Although in *The Critique of Judgement* evil itself can no longer be sublime, the sublime can still include
evil. After all, he enumerated war amongst the sublime events. Actually, Kant makes two moves in his discussion of the sublime which,
although different, are not unrelated. The sense of sublimity is culture, it indicates the outcome from the barbarism of our senses. But
the highest pitch of culture is achieved in this context whenever it is
the noumenal Freedom or the Good that elicits the sense of sublimity
and the respect for its object. The moral law in reflective judgement
is the sublime that stands beyond all other kinds of sublimity. But all
kinds of the sublime, including the lower ones, have something in
common: a certain greatness eliciting *Achtung*, the feeling of elevation
and respect, which invariably imprints the truth upon our mind that
freedom stands higher than nature. After all, in war we sacrifice our
lives for freedom. Kant would have agreed with Hamlet's reflection
on Fortinbras that there is greatness in fighting and dying for an
insignificant piece of land. However, it does not follow from this that
Kant would have agreed with Fortinbras nor that he would have
morally approved of Fortinbras' aims. For it should not be forgotten
that Kant discusses here the faculty of reflective judgement and not
the faculty of practical reason. Sublimity appears in the attitude of
the spectator. We are sitting in the real or metaphorical theatre, we
watch, we weep, we are elevated, we are even struck down by the
idea of freedom and the good, but we do not act. *Achtung* for the
Good in reflective judgement and *Achtung* for the Law in practical
reason are related, for both are *Achtung* for Freedom and the Good.
And yet, they are entirely different in kind. In the first case, *Achtung*
elicits enthusiasm and inspires our imagination, whereas in the second
case there is neither enthusiasm nor imagination. The moral good,
Kant asserts, should be imagined as sublime rather than as beautiful,
as far as it is judged *aesthetically*. But there is no direct access from
aesthetic *Achtung* to moral *Achtung*. 'The idea of the good conjoined
with [*strong*] affection is called *enthusiasm*. . . . Now every affection
is blind. . . . It can therefore in no way deserve the approval of reason.
Nevertheless, aesthetically, enthusiasm is sublime. . . .'[14]
    All kinds of aesthetic judgements (and not only the judgement of
taste) have thus a strong affinity with the good (and the moral), in
that they are not actions proper and insofar as they do not elicit
actions proper. This is why they are indirectly, and not directly, of
moral provenance. They also add an aesthetic dimension to an already
moral character (to the man of good will). The lonely aesthetic en-
thusiast of freedom and goodness thus joins the lonely lover of nature.

Ethics can be aestheticized in social intercourse, although it remains a simulacrum, a semblance. The actors there have a world, they are co-players, yet they are not identical with the role they play. There is a kind of a semblance in aesthetic judgement also, given that the sublime is also semblance of the good. But this is a free semblance; free play of imagination is at work in this semblance. Insofar as they form an aesthetic judgement, men and women are what they are. They do not imitate, they do not say 'this is beautiful' just because someone else said so; and they are not overwhelmed by the magnificence of the starry sky just in order to solicit a favourable opinion from a neighbour. But do they have a world? Or do they come to know the world better? Kant would say that through passing aesthetic judgements, men and women surely come to know the world better, if only in a negative way, by glimpsing a world which is unlike the sheer empirical one. But they can also carry this glimpse into a higher world above their activity through which they have a world. The actors and the spectators are, after all, the same persons. Aesthetic judgement as communication, as the vehicle of the culture (the cultivation) of social sociability, combines the attitudes of the spectator and the actor. Precisely this unity of the two attitudes, as a constant switching to and fro between the one and the other, appears in the culture of social sociability. Social sociability is also a simulacrum, a semblance, for it is the simile, the analogy, of the unity of freedom and happiness. Every small niche of social sociability that survives in the world of unsocial sociability here and now, is, for Kant, the *promesse du bonheur*.

Unsocial sociability is for Kant the paradox of human nature, this unique combination of nature and freedom. That men and women hurt their fellow creatures, rob them, murder them, compete with them, annihilate them, instrumentalize them, just in order that they should win their respect, love, esteem and recognition, is indeed paradoxical. There is nothing paradoxical about social sociability which is yet another combination of freedom and nature. In the world of unsocial sociability, freedom is in the service of nature, whereas in the world of social sociability neither freedom nor nature are instrumentalized – they are outbalanced. Social sociability, or, as Kant terms it, the world of *Humanitaet*, is the opposite of the state of nature. But so is the state of law, the contractual state, the modern republican state. The state of law does not cancel the world of unsocial sociability, for it is by the use of force that a lawful republic keeps unsocial sociability at bay. This has nothing to do with *Humanitaet*, although good republican laws offer the optimal framework for practising *Humanitaet*. Kant differentiates, implicitly at least, between political culture and the culture of social sociability. Political culture, insofar as it is the culture of action, remains a form of stage acting and a simulacrum in the same sense as is ethics. *Humanitaet* (social sociability) is, however, unlike stage acting. And yet, political culture and the culture of *Humanitaet* still have a common feature: both require a radical shift in the language game. They shift from an egoistic language towards a 'pluralistic' language. Pluralistic speech can be authentic as well as inauthentic, that is, it can be the manifestation of freedom or just the semblance thereof. In political culture, semblance suffices; in *Humanitaet*, it does not. More precisely, one enters the network of social sociability when the semblance of freedom in using a pluralistic language no longer suffices.

There are three kinds of egoism: logical, aesthetic and ethical (the egoisms of understanding, of taste and of the practical interest). The logical egoist does not give a hearing to other persons' opinions or judgements, the aesthetic egoist is indifferent to other persons' taste, and the moral egoist is exclusively interested in his own benefit or pleasure.[15] Kant juxtaposes pluralism to egoism. A person is a pluralist if he is a logical, an aesthetic and, surely, also an ethical pluralist. A logical pluralist is interested in other persons' opinions and judgements in a non-instrumental way. He is interested in them because they are the judgements and opinions of Others, for he is interested in certain (not all) Others as persons, and not in order to use this knowledge as an instrument to satisfy his hunger for fame, wealth and power. The same can be said about the aesthetic pluralist. Pluralists also benefit from their pluralism, but on the same plane on which they exercise it. For example, if someone is a logical pluralist, his judgements and opinions will improve as a result of his pluralism. Although it is difficult to fathom whether an ethical pluralist acts out of duty or out of moral sense, friendship or love – for all these motivations are, or can be exercised as pluralistic – the primacy of the ethical can be traced here also because the other person(s)' happiness or benefit is directly intended. But ethical pluralism, although it involves the refinement of the heart, is not yet the refinement of understanding and/or of taste. *Humanitaet* as the culture of social sociability is a matter of refinement, and it is an all-round pluralism, generating refinement, one which inheres in refined cultural practices.

In the chapter on taste as a kind of *sensus communis*,[16] Kant suddenly introduces, as a losely related issue, the problem of the three maxims of common human understanding. The first is the maxim which recommends that one think with one's own mind (autonomous thinking), while the third is the maxim of consistency. The second maxim recommends that one think as if one were in another person's place, to practise the kind of thinking that Kant has on other occasions termed pluralistic, but which he here termed '*erweiterte Denkungsart*'. Pluralism of taste and pluralism in common human understanding are, as we have seen, but two aspects of the same culture of social sociability.[17]

The maxim 'think with your own mind', that is, the maxim of autonomy in thinking, comes here first. Kant, who rarely resorts to historical references in his systematic works, makes it clear at this point that the maxims of thinking, and especially the first one, are the maxims of Enlightenment. In the *Anthropology*, where he presents the sketch of a speech-act theory, it becomes even more clear that the culture of social sociability belongs to the modern age.

Kant first associates egoism with speaking (and thinking) in first person singular, and pluralism with speaking (and thinking) in first person plural. But at some point, he makes a reference to the so-called *pluralis majestatis* (majestic plural), and from then on he ponders the assymetricality of speech acts in feudal society, where the use of the singular and of the plural in the second, third and first persons was strictly and hierarchically regulated. And he concludes as follows:

> All of this probably came from the feudal system, which was solicitous to observe the degree of respect befitting the nobility, from the royal dignity through all the ranks down to the point where human dignity left off and merely the man remained – that is the status of the serf, the only one his superiors addressed as *Du*, or of the child not yet entitled to have a will of his own.[18]

To cut a long story short: in the feudal world there is still pluralism, for men and women address one another according to the rank they happen to occupy in the hierarchy of the social whole. Pluralism and egoism are not entirely distinguished because the 'I' of the persons is inseparable from the 'we' of their rank. Respect is due according to rank; for non-persons (persons without rank), like serfs and children, no respect is due. It is the ideal of freedom that gives birth to the maxim of autonomous thinking, and it is the idea of political equality that requires the practice of the kind of pluralistic thinking that presupposes one's readiness to think with the minds of others who are as independent as oneself, and not mere specimens of their social rank. No networks of social sociability were needed for the pre-moderns, nor could such networks develop. Unrestricted egoism and the most subtle *Humanitaet* appeared together. Where the barbarism of uninhibited lusts feeds on the culture of skills and is constantly enhanced by the ever-increasing tempo of the expansion of needs, the culture of the discipline of the will can also acquire an unprecedented refinement – in and through the communication/conversation of free and equal persons.

3 Kant's Symposion. An Invitation to Luncheon

Kant enjoyed daily sharing an extended luncheon with his friends. After we became his friends, he extended to us, in his usual gesture of urbanity, a standing invitation to join him for luncheon.

'A good meal in good company is unsurpassed as a situation in which sensibility and understanding unite in one enjoyment that lasts a long time and can be repeated with pleasure so frequently', Kant remarked, in an insertion between the discussion of the beautiful and the sublime, in his *Anthropology*.[19] The goodness of both meal and company depends on the host's *taste*.

> The host shows his aesthetic taste by his skill in choosing with universal validity. This he cannot do by his own sense [of taste], because his guests might choose other foods or drinks, each according to his private sense. So he arranges for a *variety* that enables each guest to find something that suits his sense and in this way his choice has a comparative universal validity.[20]

The proper choice of guests for a reciprocal universal entertainment ('wechselseitige allgemeine Unterhaltung'), Kant adds, requires that reason should be applied to taste.

Regardless of whether Kant discusses the good meal (the condition of the good conversation) or the good conversation itself, he invariably uses the term 'universal', even 'universal validity'. What does 'universal' mean in this context? It means that in the judgement of each and every participant of the meal, they had a *good* meal as well as a *good* conversation, although each of them may have eaten something different, and each of them probably made a distinct contribution to the conversation. 'Comparative universality' concerning the table and regarding the guests is certainly not the same thing. In the latter case, Kant's term is reciprocal universal entertainment ('wechselseitige allgemeine Unterhaltung'). The diversity of food appeals to private tastes, which do not claim universal validity, only the taste of the host does. The diversity of opinions, however, consists both of private and non-private judgements (the latter claiming universal validity) and all of them enter into reciprocal relationship. Everyone needs to contribute something to the others' reason, understanding and taste, and vice versa, so that they all should agree in having been party to a good conversation. Only a bad host invites guests who are supposed to agree in all subject matters, for what kind of a discussion can emerge from such a get-together? But he who invites people having nothing in common, or some logical or aesthetic egoists, who are convinced that their views and their tastes are above discussion, is an equally bad host. What Kant terms comparative universal validity in matters of judgement is universality through diversity, or rather universality as manifested in diversity. Reaching 'consensus' in one or another concrete subject matter is not positively excluded, but it is not required. Reaching consensus in every matter under discussion would turn the discussion foul. After all, one exercises liberality in one's way of thinking ('liberale Denkungsart') by acknowledging and recognizing the difference.

In *Anthropology*, and also in *The Critique of Judgement*,[21] Kant frequently returns to the problem of the pluralistic character of judgements of taste. It is a problem for him, although it is not for many of his contemporary critics who never made an effort to understand him. No doubt, when someone asserts 'X. is beautiful', this judgement of taste is by definition a claim to universal validity. As Kant remarks, the very formulation that 'X. is beautiful' suggests that it is beautiful not just for me; it is beautiful for everyone. This is pluralism, for the 'I' speaks the language of 'we'. But if someone in a good company says 'X. is beautiful', and his fellow guest replies that X. is rather ugly, then in this situation of collision of judgements, pluralism requires that they mutually respect each others' judgement, although both claim universal validity. The person who insists that only his judgement matters because what he claims to be beautiful is beautiful and the others have no taste, acts in an egoistic way; put simply, he is a spoilsport. One cannot have a good conversation with people of such an illiberal disposition. On the other hand, one cannot have a good conversation on matters of taste with people whose taste is merely private. Taste can be merely private for many reasons, the two chief reasons being the lack of refinement and the absence of universal claim. Lack of refinement characterizes both untutored and heteronomous judgements of taste. Kant approves of an internal censorship which prevents men and women from subscribing to fashions in taste. One cannot have a good conversation with people who merely echo whatever is the *dernier cri*. Seemingly pluralistic, they are egoistic throughout for they are ignorant of the difference between 'I' and 'we'. It is a lesser problem for Kant, but not for those who are invited by him for a luncheon and who expect to have a good conversation, that there will be no good conversation in matters of taste if the guests, or at least some of them, do not claim universal validity for their judgements of taste. If one remarks 'I have enjoyed it', and the other that 'it was quite nice', and the whole exchange of opinions continues on this note, the good conversation will be buried before it could take off. If a single one of the three criteria of a good conversation is missing, i.e. autonomy, pluralism or the liberality of the mind, we might have a good time but not a good conversation.

We know well what to expect from a luncheon with Kant, for he gave us a detailed description of the modern symposion, under the title 'On the Highest Moral-Physical Good'.[22] He discusses there the possibility of combining (uniting) the supreme moral and the supreme physical good without mixing them (which would destory both). The right proportion of moral and physical good is the enjoyment (*Genuss*) of ethical happiness (*gesittete Glückseligkeit*). It is here that we return to social sociability (humanity) as to the simulacrum of the best social and political world. 'The way of thinking that unites well-being with virtue in our social intercourse is *humanity*.'[23] *Humanitaet* is thus a kind of thinking (and not a kind of action), but thinking as it appears in intercourse (in relation to others). The unity of well-being (good life) and virtue is possible only in intercourse (relation to others), for there are no private virtues. And yet, *Humanitaet* is not action nor can it be. In action proper, well-being and virtue are interlocked in a state of ongoing conflict where the latter must always gain the upper hand. Thus the kind of intercourse where well-being and virtue are united has to be interhuman, i.e. a social action or series of actions, and yet, *Humanitaet* must remain a way of thinking, and insofar as it is a way of thinking, also non-action. One gets out of this impasse if one accepts an invitation for an imaginary luncheon, and makes oneself comfortable in good company, around an imaginary table.

The imaginary Table is the counterpoint to Contract. It was mostly around symbolic tables that Socrates conducted his dialogues. Jesus of Nazareth had a predilection for the table. He provided fish galore; he liked to enjoy the pleasures of the table with his disciples and friends.[24] The contract, on the other hand, is the association of single persons. Once one enters a contract, it becomes binding; the contractor can be coerced into obedience. Quite different bonds are formed around the table: the spiritual ties of friendship, cameradery, those of freely chosen commitments. Parties to a contract are mutually dependent; they draw benefit, but no pleasure, from mutual dependency. One sits at the same table with others not in order to draw benefit but in order to draw pleasure from togetherness. There is no breach of contract here, no one can be forced to be seated, if unwilling.

For Kant there was no either-or; he wanted both contract and table: the legal state and the mystic union. The exterior of his mystic union is banal; but so is the exterior of all mystic unions. A luncheon is just a luncheon. The spirit is present, if at all, in the host and in the guests.

One can dance, listen to music or play games in company, but on such occasions one cannot have a good, not even a real, conversation, 'that requires the exchange of thoughs' ('welche wechselseitige Mitteilung der Gedanken fordert').[25] Playing games also opens the gates for the manifestation of uninhibited egoism. It is mainly around the table (where the good conversations take place) that the bonds of humanity, referred to by Kant as *Weltbürgertum*, can be forged. The model of freemasonry is unmistakable, although the external ceremonial elements of the masons' brotherhood are shunned by Kant; for him, these were just so much hocus-pocus.

A few rules are laid down for both host and guests of the noble *Tischgesellschaft*. The host should invite men of taste (at some point, Kant includes women too). Every participant (host and guests alike) has to share the *intention* to enjoy each other (and not only the meal). The number of the participants has to be proper: sufficiently large to ensure diversity, but small enough to allow for a common conversation. Private entertainment of neighbours around the table is in bad social taste; big parties are entirely tasteless.

For an imaginary presence at Kant's symposion, we need to be familiar with the ethical code of this noble *Tischgesellschaft*. There is such a code. 'Any symposium is somehow sacred and involves a duty of silence' even without special agreement.[26] Kant uses the loaded words of sacredness and of the duty of secrecy (without an oath), in spite of discussing a seemingly banal matter: parties to a *Tischgesellschaft* should not gossip about anything that was discussed there. Topics discussed, opinions aired, these are not bits of 'information' to be disclosed to an outsider. One does not participate in a *Tischgesellschaft* in one's public capacity as a citizen, but as such and such a person. *Tischgesellschaft* is a private community of communication. On an essential level, the seemingly banal example is not banal at all: Kant discusses here mutual confidence. If this is missing, if men and women keep their tongues tight and stop speaking their minds freely, if there are restrictions other than the participants' own taste in a company of men and women who get together with the intention to enjoy one another's company through the exchange of their judgements and opinions, one can rest assured that society is a mere jungle and nothing else. If the latter is the case, one should think twice about accepting the invitation for a luncheon extended by Immanuel Kant (or anyone else).

Assuming, however, that we have accepted his invitation gracefully, we are already in Kant's house, seated around the table. The various courses of food are served slowly, accompanied by the various courses of conversation. The latter unfolds (normally) through three stages: first, story-telling, second, *raisonnement* and third, joking.[27]

Story-telling is, for the most part, an exchange of political information. This whets the appetite and raises the conversation to the level of liveliness which encourages people to disclose their opinions and judgements. Opinions and judgements being different, conflicts emerge, and with the conflicts, the need for the bottle also increases. Finally, the over-heated discussion requires too much effort; a relaxation follows through the play of jokes. Erotics, too, enters the scene: men joke about women and vice versa – they joke for one another; women have the opportunity to show their wit. The meal ends with laughter.

As far as conversation is concerned, the second course is the crucial one. It is at this stage that judgements, tastes and opinions clash, that *contestation* (*Streit*) takes place. Neither disputation nor fight is appropriate around the dinner table. Kant uses the term disputation in regard of a proposition which is based on scientific or philosophical concepts. In disputation, there is only one true statement, only one possible true solution. In the course of a disputation, reasons convince the participants about the truth of one of the assertions (solutions), and consensus emerges of necessity. But disputations are conducted within, not across the disciplines, whereas the parties to the luncheon are not professionals of the same profession. For Kant, not even the most lively and most uplifting disputations among fellow-philosophers or fellow-scientists are closely connected with social sociability and *Humanitaet*. Disputation is not the simulacrum of the highest social and political good, it is not the 'highest moral and physical good', for its intention is to find out what truth is, and *not* to enjoy each other's company during the discussion. And while disputation is a-social, fight is anti-social. Fight is the kind of conflict that characterizes the state of nature, the well-known world of unsocial sociability. This is why it has to be avoided absolutely around the table which is meant to be a simulacrum of social sociability and a main practising ground of *Humanitaet*. ·

Contestation is a recurring theme in Kant's writings. It is the kind of conflict that can, in principle, be resolved but which, nevertheless, remains unresolved all the time. People contest each others' judgements and opinions. They do not reach consensus, at least not in everything; yet their conflict does not degenerate into fight, for it is carried out in the territory of the morally permitted. In the course of contestation people do not instrumentalize one another. Judgements of taste are exemplary kinds of those judgements which are open to contestation.[28] Judgements of taste cannot be disputed, but they can be contested. Kant stresses that whenever someone enters a contestation on judgements of (pure) taste, one implicitly raises a universal validity claim. All contesters do exactly this. Regardless of whether they make impure judgements of taste, other aesthetic judgements, political judgements or other sorts of judgements, all sincere participants in a contestation will equally claim objective validity for their judgement, although not necessarily universal validity as is the case with pure judgements of taste. But since all contesters alike dwell in the territory of the morally permitted, disagreement among them does not lead to a fight. No harm therefore, is done; people can even draw moral, aesthetic and intellectual benefits from the conflicts. They refine their taste, deepen their judgement, learn something new, get practice in paying attention to the other, that is, in pluralistic attitudes. But the main thing is that they enjoy the contestation itself; they love it for its own sake.

Before joining Kant for luncheon, we need to become familiar with the four basic rules of such a meal set by our host. First, the subject matter for the discussion needs to be chosen in such a way that every invited person could contribute to the discussion and add his or her voice to that of the rest. Second, the discussion can stop only for a very short time; no deadly silence is supposed to fall upon the company. Third, one should not jump too quickly from one subject to another; topics should be changed when, at least for the present, a discussion topic seems to be exhausted. Third, self-righteousness or showing-off are entirely out of place in a good conversation. Fourth, during the serious contestation, our mutual respect and goodwill for the people whose judgements we contest should always shine through our words. The tone is as improtant as the content. Kant attributes great importance to tone and intonation which is for him one of the most fundamental gestures in human communication. In particular, it is his concern that speech with a shrill voice or in an arrogant tone should be avoided around his table.

Kant compares the meal with a drama. After having seen or read a drama, we recall its most lively scenes in our memory. But this is what happens also at the end of the life of the 'rational human being' ('des vernünftigen Menschen'), Kant is in a hurry to add.[29] These two comparisons create a tension, but Kant's idea about a good luncheon requires both of them. The participation in a meal is action. Insofar as we are acting, the encounter is serious; we are on the stage and the drama we are playing is 'like' the drama of life; in fact, it *is* life. Kant mentions the 'serious debate' ('ernstlichen Streit').[30] Nonetheless, we are merely playing, it is not serious, nobody gets hurt. We are players indeed, but that which we play is not the real thing, it is a simulacrum. One must understand that 'since the conversation should not be a business but only a play, we should rather avert any such seriousness by putting in a suitable jest'.[31]

Joke and humour, together with tact, are thus constitutive elements of Kant's luncheon; they are constantly present long before they are put on the centre of the agenda which only happens at the end of the meal. The conversation taking place around the table is real-life action, but it is also unreal, simulacrum. Simulacrum of what? It has been presupposed that the good conversation around the table is the simulacrum of the best possible world. Certainly, this is what a good conversation around the table should be. But if the attitude of good will and of mutual respect does not shine through the collision of judgements, and if self-righteousness and showing-off is not going to be immediately eased by a light joke or a humorous remark, the conversation around the table can become the simulacrum of the world of unsocial sociability, and not of social sociability. The tension between utopian reality and non- (anti-)utopian reality makes itself felt during Kant's luncheons. Culture has, after all, two aspects – and the culture of skills is normally put into the service of the powers and drives of unsocial sociability. What is to be established during the luncheon is the primacy of the culture of will as against the culture of mere skills. During a conversation, the culture of skills is also mobilized; for adroitness in conversation is also a skill. Moreover, the culture of skills is not put into the service of the culture of the will, for if it were, the balance between morals and happiness (pleasure) could never be achieved. And it is this balance that the utopian reality of a good conversation around the table is all about.

One does not solve a momentary conflict between the culture of will and the culture of skills by preaching morals. Self-righteousness destroys the conversation altogether. At any rate, in Kant's mind, good persons compare themselves with the categorical imperative, and never with one another. Self-righteous people are not good, but they can still be ethical if they act as if they were good in the theatre of unsocial sociability. But they are not allowed to manifest their self-righteousness in the theatre of sociable sociability. Self-righteousness destroys the conversation by definition if members of the company are abused or put into an unsympathetic light. But it also endangers the goodness of the conversation by putting the comparison of people (instead of tastes and judgements) into the centrepoint of the conversation.

What happens if the culture of skills takes the lead over the culture of will, if moral preaching does more harm than good? Humour, wit and tact are the three compasses that help us in safe sailing in the small and narrow harbour of social sociability. A good heartful laughter afterwards seals the meal. But humour, wit and tact can help us out, because the meal is just a simulacrum, an oasis or a reservation where the wild animals of the social jungle are, for a few hours, tamed. But in these few hours the miracle happens, the utopia of social sociability is realized. And if the miracle happens, Kant makes us believe, then the final unity of freedom and nature, as the End and Purpose of 'Nature cum Freedom', might be more than just the regulative principle of the reflective teleological judgement. Our luncheon and the French Revolution stand for the same promise.

The end of the symposion is the end of a drama; so is the end of life. Close to the end of life, the rational and decent person ('der vernünftige Mensch') is preoccupied with remembering some of its major scenes; after a symposion one does the same. Kant has a special interest in the aftermath of the luncheon; to jump from one subject to another too quickly is unseemly, because if one changes topics all the time, the luncheon cannot be remembered, since our memory will lose the threads of the discussion too easily. The luncheon develops, it consists of stages, it contains drama, it is like life, in short, the luncheon is historical, it is history. Yet it is a specific kind of history: lived history. History lives in common experiencing which permits us to recall together that which we had experienced. In chapter 2, I have distinguished between primary and secondary lived history. Primary lived history develops in, and results from, close (or intimate) relationship based on mutual trust. The longer and deeper such a relationship is, the more the parties to the relationship share experiences, the thicker, the weightier lived history becomes. Secondary lived history does not pertain to relationships; it does not require basic trust. Empirical togetherness alone can bring about this kind of lived history (one particular generation of the same country, city, district, school, or one particular group of people who had been persecuted, and so on). Whatever the common experience consists of, it can be remembered together. If it is actually remembered together, that is, if it becomes constantly shared in remembrance as it had once been, one can confidently say that this generation or this group is historical, for their doings and sufferings are kept alive in their shared memory.

The luncheon with Immanuel Kant is neither primary history, nor secondary history, but a third kind. In contrast with primary lived history, it can be short-term. In addition, no intimacy is required for either participation or for remembrance. In contrast with secondary lived history, however, it demands commitment of a kind as well as a kind of confidence, confidentiality. It is also private. Put briefly, Kant discusses *culture as the third possibility of lived history*. If culture is a shared experience of communication in a network of symmetrical-reciprocal relationships, this experience can constantly be remembered, re-thought and re-enjoyed. But lived history remains thin if communication is nothing but a mere mental exercise; it will contain understanding without pleasure. The common meal, the bottle, the jokes, the mutual enjoyment in the presence of the other are as much the matter of culture as the contestation of judgements of taste (the Latin word *gustus*, Kant reminds us, refers to all of them). We remember together; we remember the judgements and the jokes, the last news of the papers we discussed, our passions, our follies, our opinions, and the taste of the food; all of these together we remember as we are remembering together. And we are happy that this meal took place, that we had the good luck to be there, that we drew enjoyment for ourselves together with others and not against others. We are happy to enjoy the utopia of the past. And as long as we enjoy the utopia of the past, the utopia endures: as long as we remember together that which we have lived together, we are still living, we are still living history.

4 The Difficulties of Returning the Invitation

Empirical Difficulties

Kant's cultural utopia is elitist. Elitism, so it is widely believed, is unfit for the democratic age. I would contest this judgement, yet without ignoring the empirical 'nature' of contemporary democracy that the judgement reflects upon. Kant's utopia is, indeed, elitist insofar as not every member of a society could be party to it. If they could, our luncheon would cease to be utopian. But Kant's utopia is the utopia of a modern society, of a society without rank and inborn status, that of a contingent society. Kant puts an emphasis on the initial contingency of the participants of the symposion. The two conditions of admittance, namely refinement of taste and a 'pluralistic' attitude, can, in principle, be met by every member of modern society. Neither wealth nor professional qualifications nor fame or might are required. And since to Kant's mind the three 'hungers' (those of wealth, power and fame) are the typical egoistic drives, one could reasonably assume that the least suited to being Kant's guest for luncheon are the socialites who chase fame, wealth or power.

It is generally questionable whether 'elitism' is so alien from the spirit of democracy. What can be termed 'social elite' rather emerges with the modern age, and in particular with open society. In the pre-modern social arrangements of asymmetric reciprocity men of the upper ranks were worshipped, respected, hated or served, but they could not be imitated. They could not become what modern sociology terms 'role models'. Aristocracy (or the gentry) became 'role-models' only for the early bourgeoisie; and the *bourgeois gentilhommes*, if they fared better than George Dandin, already heralded the nearing collapse of the *ancien regime*. In a typical mass democracy, elites still exist insofar as there are certain groups (almost) all others emulate without being able to become like them. The extremely wealthy, or the so-called 'cult figures', from pop singers to politicians, constitute this kind of elite. The gap between the few and the many is not smaller here than in the case of cultural elites; it is rather wider. Worse still, the small elite can only be imitated; in principle not everyone can become one of them, given that the pre-conditions for becoming like them are merely external and that the 'rules' guarantee a limited admittance. That is, the relation between 'the crowd' and the 'elite' remains that of a simulacrum. Imitation means to pretend, to 'look like', 'to behave like', to 'appear as if'. No authenticity, no choice of one's Self is required; not *to be*, but *to be similar* is what one chooses. Ethical life as a simulacrum works in exactly this fashion, Kant would say. But his elite is an elite precisely because for them (in that they constitute an elite) ethical life does not work this way. This is why the manner in which the luncheon is conducted becomes the simulacrum of the best world, instead of remaining the simulacrum of the summit of a world of unsocial sociability.

The rising democratic elite consists of the wealthy, the cult figures and the like. They are contingent persons, because their position on the top resulted from the combination of three elements. They started with the resolve to stand out by becoming similar; they used their skills well to serve their egoistic drives; and finally, good fortune smiled at them. The new elite is democratic, if being democratic means that there is no difference in attitudes between the top and the bottom, neither ethical nor cultural. While the new elite and the crowd that imitates them are quite alike, the guests of Kant's luncheon party constitute an elite, in virtue of their outstanding attitude alone, and not because they possess position, skill or wealth. Surely, Kant's cultural-ethical elite does not consist of people who have chosen themselves existentially, but their attitudes still include the readiness to *suspend* contingency. Moreover, they suspend the contingency of the others as well in the way that they converse and interact with them. They treat each other as autonomous (self-determined) beings, not just in their capacity as noumena, but also in their capacity as phenomena, for during the state of suspension of contingency (as long as the luncheon lasts), noumenon and phenomenon match each other and remain in balance. It depends on our interpretation of democracy whether we regard such a cultural-ethical elite as democratic or non-democratic.

Assume that democracy requires imitating people who are like ourselves and who merely happen to be on a higher position surrounded by glamour and success. If this is so, then what men and women imitate is merely that which is unlike them, namely glamour and success. But if our attitudes are entirely alike, the difference between us and them comes not from internal, but from external conditions or forces. This is why imitation as the mechanism of maintaining semblance plays a different role here than in ethical life. If one pretends to be good for a longer period of time, one may get closer to a kind of goodness, one may climb the ladder of decency step by step, even if inauthentically. But if one imitates the appearances of an elite that is totally undistinguished from the rest in taste, attitude, ethics and powers of judgement, no internal change can take place through imitation; there is no ladder to be climbed other than that of success. One does not grow through the imitation of the elite. One can only grow intellectually, culturally and ethically, and none of these faculties, abilities and practices are mobilized in the un-creative imagination of passive imitation. One can make the seemingly paradoxical observation that cultural-ethical elites are more democratic than any other elites can possibly be, as well as draw the conclusion that the greater the gap both ethically and culturally between an elite and the 'natural world of unsocial sociability', the more democratic this elite becomes. For if one assumes, in keeping with a long tradition, that democracy lives in those men and women who are involved in matters of justice to further the public good, and who pay due respect for each others' equality and freedom, one can also maintain the view that a vigorous democratic life requires the constant presence of a group of people, however small, to maintain these standards in their purest form. There must be a few persons in a group who suspend the rules of the jungle, if only for short periods, and who practise the norms of mutal respect for each other's freedom, rationality, good will and equality, without playing theatre, without aiming at collecting the chips at the end, and who do all this cheerfully, with pleasure. Such elites can be imitated in a manner entirely different from the imitation of socialites and cult figures. For those who imitate them can grow intellectually, culturally, and ethically; and that which is respected in an elite of this kind, is not just intellectual or cultural power, but the use of power without the instrumentalization of others.

Certainly, no ethico-cultural elite of the Kantian kind can put an end to the instrumentalization of knowledge, culture or intellect; all the less so, since membership in this elite does not bar anyone from instrumentalizing others. When Kant invited us to his luncheon, he did not ask the question of whether we ever instrumentalized another person in our daily lives. The existential choice of goodness is not the condition of membership in this elite, neither does membership result in such a choice. During the luncheon civil (everyday) life is suspended anyway.

Kant's luncheon party is a utopia; a utopian reality also for the participants who conduct a non-utopian life before and after. Or at least, it is not required of them to carry over the utopia into their daily lives. The elite of the luncheon party is a democratic utopia, because democracy cannot survive without this or similar kinds of intellectual-cultural elites. Without them, democratic reality is a dead body politic. Merely empirical democracy is itself an imitation, the mere shadow of the idea of a democracy. It was, after all, the elite gathering at the Symposion of Plato, and not the crowd cheering in Roman circuses while watching the fight of gladiators, that kept the idea of democracy alive for more than two thousand years.

The character of a common meal always encapsules the spirit of the times. Don Giovanni's lavish, comic and frightful *ultima cena* has remained the symbol of the collapsing *ancien regime*; Stalin's nightmarish and brutally menacing dinners remain the mementos of totalitarianism. Khrushchev describes them as 'interminable, agonizing'. Whoever was invited by Stalin had to go. Declining his invitation would have meant a 'punishment' from imprisonment to the death penalty. Night came, the diners (people aged both with Stalin's, and their own, crimes), were completely washed out, yet they had no other option but to stay and 'revel'. They were not hungry, but they had to eat, they could no longer hold their liquor, but they had to drink themselves to death. They had to listen for hours on end to Stalin's stories. Everyone knew that the stories were blatant lies, but everyone watched his tongue; no questions were ever asked. Stalin never touched food before others did. 'He didn't even trust the people serving him, people who have served him for years and who were undoubtedly loyal to him. He didn't trust anyone at all. . . . Every dish had its own appointed taster who would find out if it was poisoned or not.'[32] Modern ideology and power thus re-created the typical situation of the worst of pre-modern despotism, as a – not entertaining but threatening – satyr-play to Kant's luncheon.

There are at least one thousand and three empirical (sociological) difficulties in returning Kant's invitation. I will enumerate only a few of them.

We cannot assume that people of different occupations and professions would be interested in discussing the same topics or would express their opinions about the same works of art or forms of natural beauty. People of different professions can hardly talk to one another; they are interested in the internal matters of their own 'faculty' alone. And even if they showed authentic curiosity, they cannot ask the relevant questions, let alone discuss matters of a different kind of expertise on equal terms with the experts. Explanation takes the place of discussion. People read different books, they listen to different kinds of music. There is no longer a shared experience to be discussed. One can only give or receive various bits of information. A few political events alone stir a sufficient amount of interest to spur discussion. But then, sincerity is either discouraged, so that it will never come to real contestation, or the seriousness of the contestation destroys the utopian reality. Civility is non-committal and ritualistic, sincerity is uncivil. There is no social void between state (citizenship) on the one hand and private or intimate relations (business and family) on the other, that could be filled with societies of unique standards. Everyone is a member of some corporation, association, lobby group, party or else. The law of the jungle operates on a grand scale. In addition to the single beasts, whole packs of predators fight each other as the need for society can be satisfied in the horde; one does not talk but shouts. A luncheon that is not organized by the members of the pack for the members of the pack is unexciting, except if someone is present in the capacity of a spy or a spotter.[33] There is no confidentiality, neither is there trust. The common meal, in the form of dining out, became a matter of empty prestige; and this is true of culinary taste also. No real conversation takes place around the dinner table. The meal does not serve as an opportunity to enjoy the company of other persons but is strictly a pragmatic means for settling business, making sexual advances or simply showing off one's wealth. Nothing is done for its own sake.[34] As Kant observed, loud music and dancing obstruct conversation. So do big parties, and this is why they are preferred. Silences are created artificially – not the kinds of silence that result from the difficulty of finding words for the expression of obscure ideas, pregnant with emotions, but the kind of silence that result from indifference, from the absence of ideas, feelings or the interest in communication.

Kant himself could have listed one thousand and three empirical (sociological) difficulties of the above kind. All of them, plus the ones I did not mention, are no excuse for not returning Kant's invitation. But there are empirical (sociological) difficulties of another sort. We may be able to find people of different occupations and professions who can discuss the same works of art, who are interested in similar problems, who can offer their opinion and judgement (which would neither be entirely professional nor irrelevant); who can conduct a conversation gracefully; who are liberal-minded enough to contest opinions without self-righteousness, without the air of superiority or the demureness of false humility; and who enjoy each other's company, being together for its own sake. However, the question of how many of them will *believe* in the Kantian spirit of the luncheon, in this luncheon being a utopian reality, the simulacrum of the best world where freedom and happiness (pleasure) can be harmoniously fused, still remains. One should not forget that we were not simply invited to a meal but also to participate in what Kant has termed 'the highest moral-physical good'. To return the invitation for luncheon to Kant without understanding what we are supposed to share, when we share this meal with him, would amount to foul play.

The ways in which one imagines and perceives the world, the matters one believes or no longer believes in, are empirical factors of life to the same extent as are the division of labour and station. If the kind of people we would hypothetically invite with Kant for a luncheon did not believe in the message of the luncheon, this would cause a far stronger empirical difficulty than any of those which have been noted so far.

Most people would perhaps agree even today with Kant that the need for the unity of freedom and happiness is present in thinking beings (of nature) insofar as they think. And for Kant and his luncheon party, that was all that had to be presupposed in order to entertain the rational hope (not the knowledge) that the best possible world will come to earth, although only in the remote future. In all probability, people we can now invite will not share this hope. Neither will they believe that a conversation around the table is an end-in-itself for the participants, or that they should not instrumentalize one another. In all probability, they will tell Kant that the End he envisaged, though only in hope, is an End-that-can-not-be, and that the simulacrum of something that cannot be is nonsense, or rather, an illusion of distorted rationalist minds, these leftovers from the age of the Enlightenment.

Sceptics who maintain that the best possible world cannot be, do not necessarily disrupt the luncheon. It depends on the substance of their beliefs, on their reasons for rejecting even the regulative principles of the best world (based on hope) whether they play fair in the game of table-discussion. No harm is done to the utopia of the luncheon if it is not regarded as the simulacrum of the best possible world. After all, a utopian reality stands for itself and it does not need to be related to a future world, possible or impossible.

The real difficulties arise when the authenticity of the desire for the unity of freedom and happiness itself will be questioned and thus the utopian message of the model itself undermined. For even if it were true that the unity of freedom of happiness is desired by everyone insofar as he or she thinks, the question would still arise whether thinking is the manifestation of the innermost regions of the person or rather the distortion thereof. In Kant's model, transcendental freedom is autonomous, and the unruly desires – together with all their sources – are heteronomous. One can also reverse this model, that is, the relation between the upper and the lower faculties of desire, and perceive men and women (among them also ourselves) as mere containers or manifestations of an autonomous anonymous desire that keeps breaking through heteronomous rationality, good will included, as Schopenhauer suggested. Although the Schopenhauerian challenge underwent many modifications, what was done by him cannot be entirely undone, at least not in the framework of our contemporary historical consciousness. Most people with 'refined taste' perceive one another, as well as themselves, as desire-machines. They imagine their autonomy as a kind of a state of unhindered manifestation of their anonymous desire-machine, but with a twist. The unconscious, or rather the concept of the unconscious, is responsible for this twist. The relationship between the desire-machine and our actual desires and thought is twisted, because the former is unconscious, a thing in-itself. The unconscious desire-machine is the parody of transcendental freedom. In this scenario, it is the transcendental freedom of un-reason and un-lawfulness that directly determines our will through the contingent objects of concrete desires. People who never read Schopenhauer, Nietzsche, Freud, Jung or others, will also raise serious doubts about the authenticity of the participant members of Kant's luncheon.

The reversal of the division of functions between the lower and upper faculties of desire, and the re-interpretation of the relationship between phenomenon and noumenon, especially in practical employment, makes the Kantian utopia look phony for many of our contemporaries. It will be doubted whether a luncheon, where all participants are free and happy, is possible at all, whether even in a small group of people all would desire to be happy or to be free, whether all can leave the luncheon with good memories, whether the relation between the participants can be symmetrically reciprocal, and so on. If we think in terms of the contemporary imaginary institutions, something that only few of us will avoid, all previously enumerated doubts hit home. He who desires (in his unconscious) either unhappiness or unfreedom, will not have the experience of the unity of both. He who desires both unfreedom and unhappiness, at least unconsciously, will not enjoy completely freely and happily even their temporary unity.

The company gathered around the luncheon table will look different if we cast a glance at it from below the table or above; yet it does not follow from this that what we see is distorted in either case. It would be distorted only if we pretend that by looking at them from above the table we also know what they look like from below and vice versa. The utopian unity of freedom and happiness is not psychological but cultural in nature. Kant insisted that in his model encounter, no one will be hurt, and everyone will be entirely pleased, if only we proceeded tactfully in our conversation, playing due respect to each and every person's vulnerability. This is as far as culture can reach. But we do not and cannot know for certain where other people are vulnerable, to what extent and why. Moreover, the persons concerned do not, in all probability, know anything or much about the sources of their own vulnerability either. As they remain hidden, below the table, our sense of tact will move in the dark and some of the participants are going to get hurt. But looking at the table-companions only from below the table and pretending to see what is indeed going on above is also unwarranted. A person who felt hurt and uneasy during one or another point of the conversation without knowing why can still share the happy remembrance of the utopian events in retrospect. The discussion can still remain an integral part of his/her lived history. Depressive characters have few happy moments, and sometimes none at all. Psychologically, they will never enjoy the unity of freedom and happiness. But if they feel only as comfortable as they are able to feel with their unfortunate psychological make-up, then they have enjoyed the utopian reality as much as the rest. Nothing else or more can be expected from a cultural utopia. And the cultural utopia of the luncheon can do better here than any other utopia, for the very reason that everyday and institutional constraints and actions are suspended, that the discussion takes place in a social no-man's-land, and that secrecy protects the participants.

Yet one or another person's feeling of discomfort or of being hurt without knowing why and by what or by whom, is the least significant kind of trouble that has been inflicted upon the promise of the Kantian utopia by the unconscious desire-machine. In addition, the text (the texture) of the discussion is also the outlet of such desires, as is the process of contestation.

Whether the text is distorted and to what degree is a decisive matter in many situations, but certainly not in the situation of the Kantian luncheon. Here people are not expected to talk about themselves, and thus the distortion of their self-image plays no role in the discussion. They are expected to give their opinions, pass judgements and tell jokes. In neither case does the term 'distortion' make any sense. Distortion of what? There is no truth or truth claim here that can be possibly distorted. All judgements are accepted as authentic *at their face value*, in a literary sense. One is authentic in passing judgements if only one says what one thinks or means. To think something else, for example something that is difficult for someone to think because of psychic constraints, is by no means required. Nothing is more rational than jokes; one normally does not even notice that one laughs about oneself when bursting into laughter; when jokes distort unconscious or semi-conscious language or meaning, this just belongs to their character as jokes.

Contestation is another matter, and Kant's belief in a total symmetricality during contestation may well be naive. Stalin's dinners, the most extreme exercises of macro-power, will certainly not be mistaken for situations of symmetric reciprocity. But macro-powers of this magnitude sensitized us for micro-powers also. After Foucault, one is inclined to describe a conversation like the Kantian one as just another (hidden) power-game.[35] Rendered in the language of micro-power relationships, every contestation is a power-game, and it certainly is. There are only a few situations of 'pluralism' where 'egoism' has been completetely left behind, and none of these seem to be entirely discursive. The partially suspended 'egoism' still asserts itself, that is, the ego asserts itself vis-à-vis the other(s), to certain degree(s) also against the other(s). In a chess game, even if nothing but winning or losing in that single game is at stake, one tries to win and is pleased if one does. Moreover, if one rather lets the other win (for example, to cheer him up) one is a cheat, for not trying to win runs against the spirit of the game. And there is still something wrong with the player's personality if playing for him becomes a mere means for winning and ceases to be and end-in-itself, a pleasure for its own sake. The conversation during the Kantian luncheon is supposed to be a game, a drama of the kind where there are neither winners nor losers. There is no check-mate in interpretation; there are no rules to measure the 'scores' with, and the contestation is open-ended.

One can describe every conversation as a game played in the field of micro-powers. This would not be a false description. Social sociability, the use of a pluralistic language, does not amount to practices via acts performed under the guidance of the categorical imperative. We still want to achieve the other's love, respect, acknowledgement; yet we do not trample the others underfoot in order to gain the conditions of our happiness but rather play ball with them. Not exactly the power of knowledge, but the power to exercise one's own judgement is exhibited throughout the Kantian conversationalist ball-game. There is indeed a field of power there. But symmetric reciprocity can be actual, even if the participants to a discussion perform their speech acts in a power-field. A power-field is a field of tension, and good conversation needs tension. It needs excitement. If the main pleasure comes from being together and from the free exercise of our judgement in the absence of external censorship and conscious internal censorship, no harm is done if one draws additional pleasure from having caught the ball well, and having thrown it skilfully too, so that the other could properly catch it. The exercise of conversational generosity contributes to creating good cheer, and if someone pays jealous attention to a kind of quantitative equality and makes mental notes about a particular X or a Y who spoke too much and 'dominated' the conversation, he just spoils his own finest day.

We cannot return Kant's invitation if it turns out that the utopia of the table-conversation (*Tafelgespraech*) is no longer perceived as a promise of the unity of freedom and happiness, not because the tension is too great, but for the opposite reason. Since all tensions and excitements of such a common enterprise are gone, freedom becomes meaningless and happiness shrinks to the level of a low-scale entertainment to give way, finally, to boredom.

The ethical, aesthetic and emotional weight of the free exercise of judgement increases in proportion to the weight that a person and his or her interlocutors attribute to that judgement. Although Kant was right that whenever one says 'X is beautiful', s/he actually claims universal validity for his/her judgement, one can also add a discursive disclaimer to this claim. In the present, one does not even need to add a disclaimer, for the public perceives a claim for universal validity of a judgement of taste as an inadmissible overstatement. On the other hand, all cultural matters can be directly politicized. If they are, the judgements passed on them will cease to be reflective and become determinative. Consequently, contestation is translated into the language of disputation, and the drama of the free exercise of judgemental powers degenerates into a fight. The social grace is gone, there is neither trust nor secrecy, nor, for that matter authenticity; hostility and compromise replace pluralism and tact.

Thus as long as the discussion remains on the level of a friendly conversation, the opinions and judgement are viewed as relative, subjective, and so without having much weight. There is freedom here, but not much excitement and pleasure. Sometimes, judgements are perceived as extremely weighty, but then they are determinative judgements (of others), and thus the freedom of the encounter is lost; so is its pleasure. The laws of the jungle take over the dining room.

Modernity saw major waves of politicization and depoliticization of cultural judgement in general and of aesthetic judgements in particular. Contrary to what one might expect, no relevant interconnection can be discovered between the changes intrinsic to the aesthetic sphere on the one hand, and the waves of politicization and depoliticization of cultural, and particularly of aesthetic, judgements on the other. For example, extreme cultural relativism can be coupled both with the politicization and with the depoliticization of aesthetic judgements, and not only subsequently, but also simultaneously.[36]

Can one invite to the Kantian luncheon people who politicize aesthetic judgements? If one answers in the affirmative, one destroys the luncheon. If one answers in the negative, one destroys the 'universal' (or rather the general) appeal of the utopia of the luncheon. The third option is to require the guests to behave. To behave is not tantamount to withholding their judgements, for if they did, they would not be free. But they should not claim universal validity for those judgements. This may sound odd, for non-politicized aesthetic judgements do claim universal validity to themselves. But the political aspect of judgements, that which makes them determinative judgements, is derived from standards, either from the standard of morality or from the standard of true knowledge. No universal claim for the application of a standard is permitted, unless an inquiry into the rightness and/or into the truth of the standards themselves is simultaneously undertaken. The truth of the rightness of the standards cannot be taken for granted if there is only one person in the luncheon-company who denies their validity. (If no one does, we have no problems, provided that the group of guests is heterogeneous enough.) No disputation can take place in a Kantian luncheon, and a meta-discourse about the standards is a disputation.

Disputation is either a professional or a public matter; disputation concerning political standards is eminently a public matter. The encounter at the luncheon table is private. It is conducted not among citizens but among private persons who practise themselves in social sociability, in *Humanitaet*. Those who politicize cultural (aesthetic) judgements need to adjust themselves (within this framework) to the requirements of *Humanitaet*; so need all who make political judgements. In the case of determinative judgements this requires the suspension of the claim for the universal validity of the judgement, without curtailing the *judgement's claim (and right) to recognition*. The claim for recognition is to be accepted by all interlocutors, given that the situation of symmetrical reciprocity includes the right for the recognition of such a claim. But if the yardsticks (the principles, ideas, laws or rules) of a determinative judgement remain unchecked or unaccepted, the insistence on the universal validity of this judgement is not pluralistic but egoistic in character, even if the judgement is passed in the name of, or by, a group or a collective agency.

These difficulties do not arise whenever reflective judgements are contested. But others will.

The feeling of having been party to a utopian reality will never be enhanced, and the utopian reality itself will miscarry, if reflective judgements are taken too lightly and their contestations remain insignificant. The absence of yardsticks, of the quest for the absolute, and, as has been already mentioned, the reluctance to claim general validity, all contribute to the loss of significance of aesthetic judgements of any kind. Certainly, one does not apply here yardsticks or standards; just the opposite is the case: one connects the single phenomenon, the thing of beauty, or rather one's own perception of that beauty, with an imaginary rule, or one just expresses or manifests one's enchantment by, and enthusiasm for, the greatness of natural phenomena, of human actions and of ideas. And still, although one does not apply standards, one is confident that there are such standards. After all, one cannot speak about the refinement of taste, if there are no obscure and vague standards one needs to hit, once one has attained a certain quality of refinement. At the same time, those standards need to remain obscure and tentative, for otherwise good taste could be learned which is not the case. Concerning aesthetic judgement, Kant would have endorsed Hegel's remark that one needs first to jump into the water in order to learn to swim.

Provided that we return Kant's invitation, we cannot avoid inviting men and women who will maintain that all standards are props of domination and that to tell refined taste from unrefined taste is but an act of violence. Others will add that each culture has its own standards and none of them is superior to the other. Some others will remark that we still have a standard of our own, namely that we do not have any, because we recognize all.[37]

Cultural relativism recognizes the other, and in so doing, it also satisfies the Kantian norm of pluralism. But this is a phony kind of pluralism, one of asymmetrical reciprocity. In the situation of authentic pluralism, everyone utters his or her judgement of taste with full conviction. These judgements are different. They can also be incommensurable. But they matter. The contestation remains open after each participant has clarified his or her point up to a degree. And thus, everyone becomes richer. But if one of the participants apologizes for her judgement or for having formed a judgement at all, and if she adds that the others' judgement is as good as hers, then she plays unfairly. And if everyone plays unfairly, there will be no relation, neither symmetrical or asymmetrical. Normally, however, only one party plays unfairly, whereas others make strong claims to their judgements. If this occurs, reciprocity becomes asymmetrical, and pluralism will become just a cover-up for a masochistic kind of egoism.

Cultural relativism is but one of the reasons for shying away from too strong commitments in judgements of taste, especially when it comes to passing judgement on artworks. There are many other reasons for this. The ugly thing of yesterday is the thing of beauty today. Everything that happens to have been brought on to the surface from the 'well of the past' acquires the dignity of beauty and becomes an exhibit. All creatures of personal imagination are legitimized, limits and constraints are lifted. One no longer dances in chains. There are no dividing lines between artistic genres. Every day brings some surprise; unheard-of monsters are created, and lines thought banal re-appear in quotation marks. These are not, however, reasons for judgemental bashfulness, but rather for increasing judgemental pluralism. Moreover, none of these developments annuls the distinction between refined and unrefined taste. The question is not whether one *can* still pass judgements of taste, aesthetic judgements, or reflective judgements in general, but whether it *matters* at all that one passes such judgements, and for whom and for what.

Theoretical Difficulties

Culture, as a philosophical Character, has entered the stage of philosophical speculation quite recently; so has Meaning.[38] Their co-existence with the old, venerable Characters such as Being, Substance, Reason (*Logos*, *Nous*), Nature (*Physis*), Universe or World (*Cosmos*),

Will, has been troubled right from the beginning, or became troubled soon afterwards. Culture and Meaning turned out to be twin sisters who pushed out the old Characters step by step (particularly metaphysical ones) from their leading role, and discredited them. They became leading Characters of modern philosophies in the last two centuries. Philosophy first benefited from their presence, but soon they began to spoil the game that they have recently joined. The Characters called Culture and Meaning, which were begotten by modern historical consciousness, stabbed philosophy in the back.

In Kant, culture becomes a dominant 'character' in social philosophy and anthropology, but it is not allowed to occupy the position of a main 'character' in his system of philosophy. Kant shields the venerable ancient heroes – Knowledge and Reason (the latter as a kind of Jack of all trades) – from the impending danger carried into philosophy by the new intruder. There is a beautiful state of balance here. Old metaphysics is discredited and the main gate opened before modern philosophy, but the absoluteness of a few old 'characters' is still protected against all forms of historicism. This balance required that Culture should be introduced, together with her twin sister, Meaning. The latter makes her first appearance in the guise of the need for metaphysics, and her decisive debut in a leading role takes place in the sub-section on the sublime, and in the critique of teleological judgement.

But the new philosophical 'characters' – Culture and Meaning – already play key roles in Hegel's philosophical staging; that they are twin sisters is now beyond doubt. In Hegel, the sphere of Absolute Spirit is distinguished from the other sphere, that of the Objective Spirit, as the 'highest',[39] the locus of meaning providing Religion (in general, that is, including art and philosophy) is understood as the primary source of the ethical, political and cognitive *'powers' of life*. It is the main principle of this highest sphere[40] which inheres in everything (in the family, the state, and so on) and which provides the *unity* of life, its kind, character and form of freedom. The principle is not an *arche* in an ontological sense, but it is an *arche* in a cultural/historical sense. The whole life of the 'congregation' depends on the spirit of the congregation, it is its spirit. If the principle that dwells in the sphere of Absolute Spirit changes, everything changes with it and through it. A world will be emptied of meaning, and after a state of sheer 'positivity', it will crumble and disappear. Among those aspects of Kantian philosophy criticized by Hegel, Kant's treatment of the Absolute, the emptiness, the 'abstractness' of his conception of the Absolute is reproached most harshly. In Hegel's mind,

Kant constitutes his Absolute in such a way that it should not and could not provide meaning. But Hegel has still some praises in store for *The Critique of Judgement*, especially for Kant's discussion of the sublime, precisely because it is here that the question of meaning appears, of course in conjunction with the question of culture.

After meaning has occupied a central role on the stage, a philosophy of culture, in which the question of meaning remains marginal, is somehow deficient. To avoid misunderstanding, this is so certainly not because of its deficiency in meaning. We can perhaps render meaning to our life experiences through Kant better than through Hegel. When we chose Kant rather than one of our closer contemporaries (e.g. Heidegger) as our guide to understanding evil, we have already expressed our confidence in an approach where the quest for understanding excludes rather than includes (in our interpretation) the quest for meaning (sense). But in our own (contemporary) perception, we also render meaning to something by refusing to do so. The issue cannot be avoided. The life of philosophy is similar to the life of persons. What has been told cannot be untold by simply pretending that it has never been told; it remains in the back of one's mind. One has to face it, spell it out, reckon with it, and afterwards, perhaps it can be left behind or, alternatively, it will be re-asserted.

Since both Culture and Meaning are latecomers to the cast of philosophical Characters, one almost naturally assumes a historical position in questioning them. No sophistication of a Heidegger is needed to discover the non-ontological difference between Being and meanings; but an immense speculative effort is required for thinking through this difference, by putting it into a broader philosophical perspective.

One speaks about cultures (in the plural); *whenever culture is thought, difference is thought also*. The same holds true about meaning; it is understood that 'the meaning' is one meaning among many possible meanings. Whether forms of life are thought to be holistic or fragmentary, they are perceived as being inhabited by different meanings. The old philosophical 'characters' are assimilated to the newborn ones; Reason, Being, the Good, Truth, the Subject historicized, temporalized, and, as a consequence, relativized. Nothing has remained eternal and a-temporal, except temporality (historicity) itself.

In Kant's usage, the term 'culture' still carries the traditional meaning of 'cultivation'. The more thoroughly one cultivates a garden, the finer, tastier, more beautiful will be the yield; the better one cultivates one's mind and soul (*Gemüt*), the more beautiful and refined one's tastes, judgements and habits will be. But as cultivation does not render meaning to the garden, so cultivation of the mind and soul does not render meaning to the mind or the soul. What is, then, that which renders meaning to the soul or the mind? Kant does not raise the issue as a problem. Tasteful things exist, beautiful flowers exist, decent persons exist, knowledge exists, there are *a priori* synthetic judgements, and we can also hope that the world progresses towards something better.. Hope, that which gets closest in Kant to the Hegelian 'need of reconciliation', is not a cultural issue in the strict sense of the word. But the term 'high culture' and its distinction from 'low culture' acquired an entirely new meaning with the emergence of the question of meaning. 'High' culture is now seen as the meaning-provider (the Hegelian absolute spirit), whereas 'low culture' is seen as the meaning-receptacle or the meaning-absorber, although the material (*Stoff*) for meaning-providing can also emerge, so it was believed, from 'below', i.e. from the ranks of the so-called 'people' (*Volk*) which has just been discovered (or invented).[41]

The question of Meaning and Culture is modern, not because meaning is modern, but because the modern social arrangement opens up the possibility of meaning-problematization, and modern men and women experience a strong meaning-deficiency and hence develop a deep need for meaning interpretation. One can even suggest that historically (though not necessarily also chronologically) meaning-problematization and meaning-interpretation are closely linked. Meanings were often questioned in traditional cultures as well; and whenever they were, interpretation became crucial, because the problematization of meaning brings about a level of uncertainty that humans rarely endure with a sane mind.[42] But it is only the moderns who pillage everything (texts, graves, the life of the primitives) in the ongoing exercise of meaning-providing. Meaning-providing (for ourselves) is also meaning-attribution (to the other). Modern historiography and anthropology are, among other things, ongoing enterprises in meaning-attribution. No matter whether the meaning-providers are structuralists or hermeneuticians, functionalists or Marxists, everyone has been busy for almost two centuries attributing meaning to all past and present practices. And everyone did attribute different meaning to (almost) all of them in the 'bad infinity' of interpretation. As a result, there is very little left to pillage in this territory, not only because the material has been exhausted (there are very few 'primitive' people left and they have already been over-interpreted) but also as a result of a certain kind of hermeneutical saturation. A new cycle (or new circle?) is to be opened up: a cycle of attributing meanings to the meaning-attributors (anthropologists and historians) and their 'cultures'.[43]

It would be difficult to describe the modern practice of 'meaning-providing' as an 'ideology', or a kind of 'false consciousness'. In the early nineteenth century this was still possible. After all, when Marx proposed to 'turn' Hegel from his head to his feet, he expressed a general impatience of a then existing 'scientific' trend with deficient explanations, or rather non-explanations. Hegel certainly did not explain why the Absolute Spirit took leave from one place and moved towards the second and third. There was no answer to this question, nor was any prediction possible. As every cultural-interpretative exercise, Hegel's philosophy is also retrospective. The story of the Absolute Spirit lives on the 'matter' (*Stoff*) of the ancient cultures it creates (as cultures), and so it must end in the past-of-the-present. For Marx, reality was only that which could be explained, that which operated according to laws, and science became science by its power of making predictions.

One cannot deny that there is something fishy about 'the fusion of horizons'.[44] We do *not* know whether the horizons have actually been fused, we only believe that they have.[45] Since the others are long dead or they do not think in our terms of meaning and meaning-interpretations at all, knowledge and belief do merge, not in the stage of the beginning, as Hegel knew they were, but in the end-result. Drawn from the deep well of the past, the bucketful of water shows our own faces.[46] One should add that if someone maintains (as it sometimes happens) that those horizons can never be fused, he or she practices a kind of meaning-attribution also ('*we* shall never know what *they* meant').

The interpretation of meaning as meaning-attribution or meaning-rendering developed as the most forceful imaginary institution of modernity. To use Hegel's 'characters', it is the main principle (*arche*), or at least one of the main principles of our 'absolute spirit'. This imaginary institution, this *arche*, sends us along this single track and we proceed from there. Philosophy of culture is perhaps the only kind of philosophy that has remained 'active', that is, alive, in our century.

One can issue a report on the present age in its own terms by speaking about the imaginary institution(s), historical consciousness or absolute spirit of the present age. The three terms are partially overlapping, but they are by no means synonymous descriptions of our possibilities and of our predicaments.[47] But there is something common to all of them; they manifest our consciousness of contingency, either directly or indirectly (in their hopeless effort to overcome it). Pre-modern ages appear as successful meaning-providers, whereas our ability to provide meaning still seems to hang in the balance.

Assume that it does not make much difference what kind of judgements men and women pass on cultural and related matters and that the form of judgement is of little significance. Assume, further, that we convene a Kantian luncheon party just to reciprocate the great old man's invitation. The discussion that might take place here would remind us of the dialogues of an Ionesco play. The party could still proceed properly, at least *formally properly*. Men and women could still smoothly pass judgements of taste and other judgements, although it would not matter whether they pass them or not, nor would it matter what they have to say. They could raise universal claims for their judgements of taste as before, they could also proceed with the stage of contestation so that no one gets hurt. They would perform just like marionettes, playing a language game that they do not understand, because there is nothing to understand. They could cultivate certain skills in playing this particular language game rather than another, but they could not cultivate their so-called 'will' for either they have none, or they are entirely detached and uninvolved. Instead of happiness, there remains entertainment, instead of decency, there remains indifference. But the luncheon might not lose its utopian character after all. As a utopia within the present, it would stand for the possibility of a world where indifference replaces hostility, and entertainment (passivity) is substituted for the active effort of passing independent judgement. The combination of entertainment and indifference is utopian in the above sense, but by no means in a Kantian sense.

Kant is a pre-romantic author.[48] Rousseau's problems were problems for him; Rousseau himself was not. Kant's subject was not yet subjective; he has not yet discovered 'subjective spirit'. 'Subjective spirit' is born together with Absolute Spirit; they are chained to one another – and to the same boat.

Modern tradition holds that Reason is universal, whereas feelings, emotions, interests are particular and individual. We differ in our opinions and judgements insofar as we are bodies and not minds or insofar as our bodily character affects our minds. Were we not bodies, were we not pulled by the strings of egoistic feelings, desires and prejudices which keep us in ignorance, we would all think the same; we would share knowledge, and, among others (or first of all) our knowledge of the Good. Transcendental philosophy is not part of this tradition, but it streamlines this tradition. Kant's Transcendental Subject is objective.

The intersubjective constitution of the world, no matter whether it is conceived of as the paradigm of consciousness (where 'consciousness' stands for absolute spirit, sometimes writ large, sometimes writ small), or whether it is conceived of as the paradigm of language, opens the theoretical space for a subject which is *neither transcendental nor empirical*. There are different philosophical ways to achieve this. The paradigm of communication preserves the Kantian duality between reason and feelings.[49] One such way is to conceive of modern destiny as a result of the existential choice of oneself. Assume that X as a contingent being is aware of her contingency; she chooses herself as such and such (e.g. as a good person); she chooses all her determinations; she leaps; and thus she becomes what she is (a good person). She also becomes autonomous and free. To go one step further, the modern tradition holds that autonomy equals internal determination and that internal determination equals determination by reason. In case of an existential choice, one aspect of the modern tradition prevails, the other does not. The person who has chosen herself is free in that she has determined herself 'internally' (by herself alone). But she is certainly not determined by reason. The leap is a holistic act; the whole person leaps, existence leaps. The person re-chooses her determinations (the 'intersubjectively constituted world' as one's contingency, and her own, unique being as just another contingency) together, without creating a hierarchy among them. All contingencies are moulded together anyway in the gesture of choice, into one single destiny. That this 'destiny' cannot be equated with the transcendental subject is a matter of course.

But the same 'destiny' cannot be termed an 'empirical subject' either, if only for the reason that it is (self-)constituted. There is much common ground between the world of a self-chosen person and the world of her contemporaries, namely the intersubjectively constituted world itself. However, this world is not 'alien' to the self-chosen person, precisely because she re-chose all her determinations existentially. But the self-same person's world will not be entirely identical with the world of her fellows either, for she chose herself and not others, and thus she also chose (re-chose) her personal, unique determinations, her idiosyncracies. She dwells in a common world and she dwells also in her own. She 'has a world' which is shared and not shared by her at once. There is a world 'according' to her, and according to the other and to the third and so on. These worlds are identical, but also different; difference and identity together make our condition modern.

A person who 'has a world' is a subject. Those who 'have a world' also 'know the world' – they know it differently. They do not claim universal validity for their aesthetic judgement. If Kant will point out to them that 'this is beautiful', a statement which implies by its form a universalistic claim, they will answer, that according to them, the sentence 'this is true' does not of necessity imply such a universal validity claim either. And this is not said because truth or beauty does not matter for them; it does matter, it matters most of all. But it is rather because truth (or beauty or goodness) matters so much to them that they question the criteria of a universal rationality that allegedly obtains a timeless power to make such claims good.

In all probability, few modern men and women have chosen themselves existentially; there are few autonomous persons. Although, one may add, there are far more men and women who are capable of making relatively autonomous decisions or passing relatively autonomous judgements. However, within the horizon of a hermeneutical universe, every person becomes a subject, that is, every person dwells in a shared world and a world of her own; there is a world according to *everyone*. The Heideggerian *das Man* is not a metaphor that stands for the end of the subject – it rather stands for the generalization and the trivialization of the subject. Nothing is nowadays more trivial than the subject. The title *The World According to Garp* tells the story better than philosophy could. There is a world according to everyone. 'Everyone' is the subject, because everyone is a subject.[50]

Let me briefly return to the historical dimension. The subjective spirit and the absolute spirit were born together (in Hegel and in the world he stood for). For Hegel, subjectivity (Christian, modern, romantic) is the mirror image and the realization of the infinite form (of freedom) which is adequate to the absoluteness of the Spirit and thus contains it. In its relation to the Absolute Spirit, the subjective spirit is 'deepening' itself. The higher its fellow-(intersubjective) subjectivity stands, the deeper the subjective subjectivity becomes. If one imagines for a minute that there is no Absolute Spirit there, 'high up', because the spirituality of the age is gone, one must also assume that there is no 'depth' left in the subjective spirit either. Then there is a world 'according to everyone' but all these worlds are equally shallow.

I am somewhat reluctant to return Kant's invitation for luncheon, because I am afraid of disappointing him. But a wise man, especially if he is also a sceptic, cannot be really disappointed; he learns. And, as experience teaches, hope, as much as good cheerful spirit, comes from the character rather than from the world in which the character dwells. For as we know, the world of a cheerful character is always different from the world of a man of sad disposition.[51] This is why this whole chapter, full of 'ifs' and 'buts', was, nevertheless, written as a reluctant, but heartfelt, invitation to Herr Professor Immanuel Kant for luncheon.

6

The Absolute Spirit

1 The Absolute Spirit in Hegel and Beyond

Paragraph 554 of Hegel's *Encyclopedia* presents the Absolute Spirit in the following words:

> The absolute spirit is eternally in itself and also to itself returning and ever returned identity: it is the one and universal *substance* as spiritual (substance), the judgement (diremption) in itself and in a knowledge, for which it is just such (a spiritual substance). *Religion*, as this highest sphere may be generally designated, is to be studied as issuing from the subject and having its home here, as also objectively, as it is issued from the absolute spirit, which as spirit dwells in its congregation.[1]

(English translation modified, the words in brackets were added by me for the purpose of clarifying this very dense text; emphasis by Hegel.) In the commentary Hegel adds that 'God must be apprehended as spirit in his congregation'.[2]

In what follows, I take the liberty of disregarding, at least for the time being and in the main, the Platonic-theological interpretation of Hegel's philosophical system. Not because I find such an interpretation irrelevant, but because its acceptance would by no means modify the tasks of this sub section, but only remove some of the theoretical difficulties. The sphere of the absolute spirit of a (preliminarily) decapitated Hegel is roughly, but not entirely, identical with the sphere I was calling earlier 'the sphere of objectivation for itself'.

In an un-Hegelian fashion, I attributed empirical universality to this sphere,[3] and I did this in the spirit of my (our) congregation. Hegel certainly ascribed religion to all cultures of the human race, and for that reason alone absolute spirit could have been described as omnipresent. But it is decisive for the whole of the Hegelian philosophy that the absolute is universal, and that the total presence of the absolute on the one hand, and its recognition (qua spirit) on the other hand, cannot be fully separated: the absolute spirit is after all constant revealing (*sich offenbaren*). Before the Greeks there was no universality (in Hegel's view), before Christianity there was no revelation (also in Hegel's view). Hegel's absolute spirit (as absolute) appears in Western (European) cultures. This vision is almost intolerable for the spirit of our community, and not only, not even first of all, because of its 'Eurocentrism', but because of its blunt identification of the absolute with that which has been, and is going to be, recollected and made transparent by the modern age.[4]

The conscious limitation of the actual story of the absolute spirit to the European culture is a productive limitation for Hegel. First, it was not perceived as a limitation within the spirit of his own congregation. Second, it provided the conception with a productive centre. Gathering all the essential elements for the Hegelian Absolute Spirit was made possible by this productive limitation.

It is from Greek art (and religion) onwards that the Spirit appears as the Absolute One, the historical actualization of the logical Absolute Idea. Actualization is self-determination in process. As is well known, the spirit marches through three major epochs in this process: those of Greek art, of revealed (Christian) religion and of (modern) philosophy. The three major forms of the spirit (intuition, representation and concept) concretize the absoluteness of the spirit. But only when the 'determination of free intelligence is the content of the idea that the absolute spirit is for the spirit',[5] and so is the process fulfilled. The Absolute Idea is the Whole, that is, the Truth, which encompasses the idea of the True (knowing) and the Good (willing) on the one hand, and the idea of Life on the other. It is the unity of universal, particular and individual. It is freedom; it is healing; it is reconciliation, for the diremption between spirit and nature is sublated. All these determinations appear, and appear wholly (become transparent) in the Absolute Spirit of the presence.

To apprehend the 'limitation' of the 'spirit' of Hegel's 'congregation' is a very Hegelian thought, although with a twist. For in Hegel's mind it happened in his time that all limitations had finally been removed in and by absolute knowing. Certainly, absolute knowing does not mean that one knows everything, which is anyhow impossible, and for Hegel, entirely uninteresting. There is only one kind of infinite knowledge that makes sense, for it satisfies, and this is self-knowledge, self-consciousness, knowledge of the spirit by the spirit, put briefly, meaning. But it is the kind of meaning that is also knowing insofar as it knows itself as final. Absolute knowing is the knowledge of the absolute principle, which, on its part, dwells in our (his) congregation as its 'living spirit'. For it is this principle that makes the human universe transparent as the work of the world-spirit (reason) in its march towards freedom.

Could it perhaps be asserted, with a slight modification of the Hegelian formula, that every epoch's knowledge is absolute? After all, no epoch knows that which it does not know; and the meaning it knows is absolute insofar as it is not, or only marginally, queried. Hegel would respond to this unwarranted extension of his theory that the knowledge of those epochs is not yet absolute, but not because they are unfamiliar with electricity or neutrons, but because they are ignorant of absolute knowing. Their consciousness is mere natural consciousness, they take things for granted, they have not even proceeded towards sheer reflection, negation, let alone speculative thinking. The spirit of absolute knowledge enters the congregation as freedom; the free spirit rejects taken-for-grantedness. It is not mere substance, but also subject. For Hegel, absolute knowing always includes not knowing, and the overcoming of negation. After all, paragraph 553, quoted above, mentions not only a returned, but also an ever-returning, identity.

Absolute spirit (or absolute knowing) is an ever-returning *identity* that makes us wonder *which* communities can be imbued with the absolute spirit at all. Not every community is a 'Congregation'.[6] Congregations are communities that can carry out conflicts, can endure collisions, can even sublate contradictions without the loss of their (cultural) identity, the very identity where the (absolute) spirit can return and where it has been returned.[7] But the Greek community was finally dissolved, giving way to Christianity and its new principle, and Christianity, though never failing to reproduce its identity through schisms which kept it alive, now finds a more adequate form in philosophy. Absolute Spirit is absolute knowing now, because it is in modernity that the identity of the spirit as substance/subject is reconfirmed through opposition, contradiction, schism. Nothing can bring about this identity (of the absolute spirit, absolute knowing) without ceasing to be (an identity). Put bluntly, it is precisely because modern historical consciousness is omnivorous, because it includes everything (it does not exclude anything) that modern spirit (knowledge) is absolute. Everything means something for us, we make sense of everything, we interpret everything, we understand everything. For us, nothing is entirely false, we only have to put it into context, that's all. Absolute knowing is at loggerheads with relativism, not because it excludes relativism (it does not exclude anything), but because it 'sublates' its one-sidedness, and ridicules its narrow-mindedness.

This reminds us very much of the spirit of our congregation. After all, we share our 'world spirit' with Hegel, the first 'philosopher of culture'. But a strong resistance to Hegel's 'absolute spirit' is also in the air, and not only owing to the many misunderstandings concerning its message. There are a few questions to be asked. Can cultural identity be maintained without exclusion? Or, put from the other end: is the Hegelian Absolute Spirit not the most radical gesture of exclusion with the illusion of all-inclusiveness? The first issue is directly tackled by A. MacIntyre[8], and we shall come back to it. The second runs like a red thread through the whole of Heidegger's middle and late philosophy. Whatever else 'forgetfulness of Being' is all about, it certainly means at least this much: to presuppose the absoluteness of (our) absolute is not warranted. It is actually in these terms that Heidegger discusses Hegel's concept of experience.[9] He does not take the traditional approach to Hegel, pointing out that he presupposed his absolute (and thus his philosophy was, after all, not without presupposition), an approach already taken by Feuerbach.[10] Heidegger rather asserts that Hegel presupposed the absoluteness of the absolute – and this has nothing to do with the traditional reproach. There is absolute knowing of meaning if there is no forgetting of meaning. The problematic of Hegel's universal recollection is the erasure of all that which had been forgotten. (Needless to say, the absolute cannot be presupposed but absolutely, so, finally, the non-Feuerbachian argument falls back to the Feuerbachian.)

There is one common element in these two queries (can cultural identity be maintained without exclusion? is the Hegelian absolute spirit not the most radical kind of exclusion?). Both questions are asked because the questioners regard the constant 'returning' (and 'having returned') of the absolute spirit of 'our' congregation as a menace rather than as a blessing. Both want to negate the 'spirit of our congregation' in a non-dialectical sense, so that its identity should not be restored but disrupted or annihilated. One opens these queries if one contends that this 'absolute spirit' turned out too poor in spirit. But such and similar philosophical queries can easily be accommodated by our omnivorous Absolute Spirit. For all the attempts at radical negation, given their impotence to break through towards a new (or old) positivity, are but reconfirmations and manifestation (revelations) of the still vigorous spirit of (our) congregation – they just add more determinations to it.

Hegel speaks about one principle (one *arche*) that lends unity to the spirit of a culture, a people, an epoch. This is not to say that everything is somehow 'determined' by this arche – 'determination' is, in Hegel's mind, a very primitive concept of necessity. The principle of the spirit comprises the core of cultural-political imagination. To pull an old Platonian metaphor: it is like a sun, the rays of which reach everything, the closest as well as the most remote, but not with the same intensity and not to the same extent. Necessity includes contingency.

As long as the sun shines (that is, as long as the principle of the spirit remains alive), the whole culture is being reproduced (the spirit is always returning and having-returned). But the life of the spirit is not mainained by the institutions of the objective spirit as such, only through the 'subjective spirit's' engagement in the Absolute as well as through the institutionalized (or quasi-institutionalized) collective practices, similarly related to the Absolute. The first is termed *Andacht* (piety of thinking), the second *Kultus* (worship) by Hegel.

Let us accept the Hegelian vision as a starting point. If the spirit of the congregation is only kept alive by piety of thinking and worship, it is a minor miracle that modernity has survived so far.

The adequate form of the Absolute Spirit in modernity is, in Hegel's mind, philosophy. Whereas in ancient Greece the sculptures and the temples of the Olympians, as much as the tragedies of ancient heroes, were the genuine centres of worship and texts for the piety of thinking, and whereas in the 'romantic' (early modern) epoch the crucified God was worshipped and the trinity remained the subject/object of all pious speculations, no practice of similar magnitude and kind surrounds philosophy now. Certainly a kind of piety of thinking has remained, for some men and women ponder meaningful issues speculatively and, ultimately, every serious discussion on a philosophical topic is a kind of worship. But it is more than doubtful that these practices keep modernity, the spirit of our congregation, alive.

And yet, Hegel may prove right all the same. The Absolute Spirit (of philosophy) is also the 'infinite form' as freedom, and the fundamental principle of modernity is, for its part, the universal idea of freedom. Hence, the principle of modernity is philosophical in a strictly Hegelian sense. The dynamic concept of justice was born with philosophy. After all, philosophers invented meta-reasoning with terms like: 'not this is good, but that is good, not this is just, but that is absolutely just'.[11] And it is exactly this kind of meta-reasoning, particularly in the form of contestation of justice, that has been universalized in the modern age and that keeps modernity alive so that it can constantly 'return' into itself. So if one 'worships' freedom (for example in the form of general elections or by protecting the rights of citizens, etc.), or if one practises piety of thinking (by recalling the wisdom of the founding fathers or reflecting upon Parliamentary debates), one thereby worships philosophy and practises the piety of thinking towards the spirit of philosophy.

Philosophy is conceptual thinking. Freedom is a concept and a universal one. A universal concept is certainly not abstract; freedom is being constantly concretized. And it could be asserted that, whatever concretization of freedom our congregation will worship, it does, in the same act, worship philosophy.

However, the constant determination (or self-determination) of freedom, taken in itself, generates institutions, but it does not provide meaning. If philosophy, as the main imaginary institution of our congregation, is reduced to the bare minimum of re-confirming and re-defining a few universal concepts and to the practice of meta-discourse, then the absolute spirit will become a mere *function* of the objective spirit.

If this is what philosophy as the principle of the absolute spirit 'yields', there is absolute spirit no more, and Hegel's challenge adds nothing to Kant's cautious and rational scepticism. A free (liberal) constitution has to be based on the philosophical principles of an enlightened age in Kant's view as well. But, as is obvious from his philosophy of culture, Kant could affirm the idea of freedom and of a political constitution based on that idea, without mistaking it for a so-called 'totality', or hailing it as the ground of reconciliation.

Hegel, too, came to see gradually that in the just emerging modernity the absolute spirit as religion is about to leave the congregation. He closes his lectures on philosophy of religion in 1831 with a gloomy diagnosis of the Spirit of the Christian congregation: it is in the stage of dissolution (*Vergehen*), or rather, of decline or disappearance (*Untergang*). But, Hegel adds, the Kingdom of God is everlasting; how can it then be dissolved? 'Thus, to speak about dissolution meant to finish on a false note. Yet what good does it do to us? This false note is there in reality.'[12] It is here that philosophy comes to the rescue of Spirit. Only conceptual speculation can keep Spirit alive in a world which, all of a sudden, reminds Hegel of Imperial Rome. Modern thinking is private and negative, it serves 'particular well-being' as its end and purpose. Speculative philosophy set the task of reconciling philosophy with revealed religion. In other words, it must keep alive both the absoluteness and the spirituality of the absolute spirit. It must remain a meaning-providing speculation, a kind of *worship*. However, this worship should not be grounded on faith but on knowing. But whatever task speculative philosophy can accomplish, its life as absolute spirit will remain restricted.

Yet this reconciliation is in itself only a partial one without external universality; philosophy is in this respect but a secluded sanctuary, and its servants compose an isolated priesthood that cannot go out into the world and has to protect the estate of Truth. It is left to the temporal, empirical present to find its way out from this split [ambiguity], how it is going to do it, how it will develop itself, is a matter that does not belong to the *direct* practical concerns and tasks of philosophy.[13] (emphasis added by the original editors)

The congregation of philosophers respects the torch-holding Lady on Liberty Island; it was, after all, the spirit of this congregation that has begotten the Idea of Freedom. But what the congregation actually worships (as the highest) is *itself*. And it worships itself by telling its own story, by recollecting its first two stages in the language of the last, in that of conceptual speculation. The absolute spirit has only past, but no foreseeable future. The small congregation of philosophers hold the torch, they shed light on the past, and enliven the spirit of past congregations, so that meaning should not be entirely lost. They keep the torch bravely, so that the world can change and perhaps become more sympathetic to spirituality again. We have learned, that philosophy has no competence to counsel the objective spirit amid its further vicissitudes in empirical reality, nor does it belong to its immediate practical tasks to do so. But, for Hegel, immediacy is the lowest level of consciousness and of the concept. The practice of self-understanding in the form of conceptual recollection (the speculative recollection of the present included) must be comprehended as a kind of intervention, albeit a mediated one. Otherwise the Absolute Spirit of our epoch could not be the spirit of our epoch at all, at least not in the Hegelian sense. For the absolute spirit of an epoch must render meaning to its own epoch, having the 'practical task' of contributing to the life of its own time, and not to previous, not even to forthcoming 'times', at least not to the same extent.

In Hegel's story, the absolute spirit has impregnated both the objective and the subjective spirit since its entrance into world-history, and entirely so. If philosophy (the absolute spirit of our epoch) does not impregnate both the objective and the subjective spirit of our congregation to the same extent and in the same sense, as art and religion (presumably) did their own, does the absolute spirit remain absolute after all? Or, to reformulate the same question: if the Absolute Spirit of our time lives, at least in its totality, only in the minute 'congregation' of (speculative) philosophers, can this congregation be regarded as the heir to the ancient *polis* or to the Christian community?

There is an undercurrent of tension here between the Hegelian philosophy on the one hand, and the situation of the Hegelian philosophy in the modern world, on the other hand.

The Hegelian system (Heidegger was right on this point) presupposes the absoluteness of the absolute. But the absolute spirit of the speculative philosophy, or rather the absolute spirit as it is embodied in speculative philosophy (the absoluteness of the absolute), is not returning to itself, nor has it returned to itself (in its absoluteness) in the modern world. Hegel's remarks quoted above indicate that he never expected this to happen. The world goes on (empirically), and philosophy thinks itself, it returns constantly to itself, in the minute community of speculative philosophers alone. On the one hand, speculative philosophy is the highest culmination of the absolute spirit by definition, and not only 'so far' or 'hitherto'; this is also why it is absolute knowing. On the other hand, *absolute knowing touches the world which it had made appear, and which it simultaneously contains, only tangentially.* There was no free life for a Greek man without the *polis*, neither was there freedom for a Christian without Christianity, but there is free life for moderns without the Hegelian philosophy, or without any philosophy. Hegel's system was supposed to encompass the 'Truth' of everything that had ever been entirely or partially true, the truth of everything that had ever been. On the other hand, the Truth of all truths as totality is accessible only for the self-elected few, not for the whole. Given that in Hegel's terms there is no such thing as 'unrecognized' Truth, Truth as a Whole is, and remains, Truth *for the speculative philosopher alone.* It is not Truth for *us*, if 'us' stands for the representative individuals (subjects) of modernity.[14]

There can be no greater contrast than the one between Kant's *Tischgesellschaft* and Hegel's *Gemeinde.* Play or drama rather than worship, difference between subject and object rather than their unity, contestation rather than peace, balance between the ethical and the physical rather than mere spirituality, happiness rather than blessedness are on the Kantian agenda. The pluralistic setting for the question of culture was accessible to Kant because culture does not belong to the spheres of world-constitution.[15] Members of the *Tischgesellschaft* have a world, they also know the world up to a degree, yet they do *not* constitute the world.[16] Yet Hegel's starting-point was precisely the total rejection of all these distinctions, and this becomes now the source of his dilemma. Absolute spirit, i.e. the core of culture, i.e. the core of meaning-providing, i.e. Truth (True+Good+Life) have, all of them, to coincide in the last instance. Yet the world does not accommodate the grand design.

Instead of out-Hegeling Hegel, let me rather un-Hegel him to a degree. First, we can try to separate content and form of the Absolute Spirit contrary to the Hegelian philosophical presentation. I do not have in mind here the nowadays frequently recommended remedy that philosophy should return to intuitional or representational forms (*Anschauung, Vorstellung*). There is philosophical poetry, there has always been, and the limits between *genres* are not rigid. In addition, philosophical concepts are conceptual characters, and they do not need a poetic touch to become resources for the 'piety of thinking'.[17] To separate content and form in Hegel's philosophy is not to separate spirit and concept, but to separate the sphere of the Hegelian absolute spirit from its claim to absoluteness. '*The self-knowing reason*' of the last syllogism of the *Encyclopaedia*, the coronation of the Hegelian system,[18] will then cease to be the over-arching 'moment'. It will simply carry the message that modern philosophy thinks, or rather recapitulates in thoughts, whatever it remembers from the history of the human race; it will mean, furthermore, that everything that had once lived, sometimes without having been thought at all, becomes now, through us, by virtue of our effort, a thought, because we are thinking it through and through. The past, and the present too, becomes a thought-thing, for it lives as thought. What we assimilate are not thought-things 'in themselves', they become thought-things 'in-and-for-themselves', for us, and what they are for us is but the most concrete 'idea' a thing as concept can assume for us. We meet our past, the past we recollect, including the past of the present, and it is thus we encounter the 'spirit' and it is in-and-by the spirit that we confront the spirit, and that we become, in this restricted sense, identical with it, though we remain different. We do not claim that we recollect everything, nor do we claim that our thoughts are richer in meaning than all the previous thoughts we cannot re-think, much as we try.

Piety of thinking (*Andacht*) – this is what conceptual thinking (speculation) is. Philosophy is absolute spirit not insofar as it is absolute recollection (a claim one cannot redeem) nor insofar as it is the rational thought through and through. For whether or not we redeem this second claim depends exclusively on our understanding of rationality *within* our philosophy – thus it is either irrelevant or tautological or untrue.

Philosophy is Absolute Spirit insofar as it is *Andacht*. *Andacht* is the thread that binds together philosophy, religion and art; it is the spiritual disposition that can be actualized as 'living spirit' every time the 'spirit of the congregation' is sympathetic to the close association between art, religion and philosophy rather than to their disunity. It is not the form of their respective objectivations that establishes their unity through difference, but the mode of their reception, the way in which we, moderns, approach them, let ourselves be elevated by them. Elevated is the right expression, for the absolute spirit is supposed to be the highest of all spheres. The reception of works of art, religion and philosophy is not passive, but active. The initial stage of reception is 'immediate', to use Hegel's expression; one surrenders to the 'higher' with the gesture of a pleasurable admiration (of beauty) or in faith (in the truth of the religion). In Hegel's mind, philosophy does not require this kind of self-surrender, but he is wrong. However, the initial immediate gesture is just the beginning – whatever has been received will be 'mediated' by the subjective spirit (the person), transformed into thought, into thinking-that-which-is-the-highest in manifold ways (such as recalling, phantasizing, reflecting and the like). What we receive and keep alive in the piety of thinking is neither spatial nor temporal. In *Andacht*, the most remote becomes the closest, there is no distance nor is there time. In *piety (of thinking)* we are 'presencing'; there is 'eternal presence' (*parousia*). Presencing is immortality. Whatever we receive while we are receiving becomes immortal through the piety of thinking and in it; and those who practise *the piety of thinking* (the finite spirits), also become immortal (infinite) insofar as they practise it. Immortality, Hegel contends, is also a disposition; it is the disposition of the subjective spirit. The spirit is not immortal in some undertermined future or place, but it can be immortal here and now, through presencing. *Piety of thinking*, though a-temporal, changes the subject through and through; the subject's subjectivity deepens through the piety of thinking.[19]

When, in his lectures on the philosophy of religion, Hegel discusses the three regions (*Momente*) of the Absolute Spirit in Christianity, he allocates a 'representational' temporality and location to each of them. The Kingdom of the Father is eternal and it is 'up there', the Kingdom of the Son is temporal and it is 'down here', whereas the Kingdom of the Spirit is 'presencing' and it is *within us*. This is a very important point. Although the spirit lives in the congregation (in modern terminology: it is intersubjective), the Spirit of the Spirit itself lives in the internal space of the personal subject. The more the Spirit appears (reveals itself) in a conceptual form, the deeper and broader the metaphorical 'internal rooms' of the personal subjects need to become in order to keep the spirit of the congregation alive. And here I would agree with Hegel. The spirituality of the modern congregations (if such a spirituality is possible at all) cannot be based on one or another time-honoured tradition as a consistent whole. It cannot be grounded in faith beyond questioning, given that the very principle of its spirit is one of questioning (freedom, dynamic justice). It cannot express the undistinguished identity of an 'I' and the 'we'.[20] It seems paradoxical, but it is also plausible, that the more pluralistic an age, the more the spirit of the congregation needs to be rooted in, and needs to be reconfirmed by, the piety of thinking (*Andacht*) of the members of the congregation.

It has been presupposed that it is the 'absolute spirit' as the spirit of the congregation that keeps an epoch, a world, going, that makes it return to itself. But there are doubts whether this is still the case in the modern age. Perhaps it is not. Perhaps modernity is verily a Marxian, rather than a Hegelian, universe. Perhaps it reproduces itself, as long as it does, precisely as a system, or as a system of heterogeneous sub-systems. Marx was perhaps right in attributing a strong determining power to the 'base', and in pointing out that the spheres of the objective spirit (particularly the economic one) reproduce the *whole*, insofar as it can be reproduced at all, without an essential contribution from the absolute spirit (the sphere of the 'forms of consciousness'). Certainly, one can argue, Marx was wrong in prophesying the doomsday of capitalism, and he was also wrong in attributing a world-historical role to the proletariat, as well as being proved wrong in many of his economic theories and much more, yet was right in one important point: modern society can maintain its identity without the contribution of any kind of absolute spirit, and also without the subjective spirit. Modernity can perhaps kept going with a kind of psyche, but without spirit.

This seems to be one of the major points of disagreement between Luhmann and Habermas. In Luhmann's view, persons who dwell in a complex (modern) social system are unable to bring to consciousness the system's identity (that is, to work out the system's self-consciousness). If this is so, no consciousness (self-consciousness), and hence no 'spirit', subjective or absolute, is needed for the reproduction of the modern system's identity.[21] If this were so, modernity could be described as a world that can 'return to itself' without the contribution of the 'spirit'. But whether or not we believe that this can be so, for the time being this is not what has happened. As pointed out, until now, the idea of freedom (a philosophical idea) has been accepted by a gesture (of faith), and this is what kept modernity going.

Yet another question can be asked too: need one equate spirituality as the condition of a world's identity with the self-consciousness of that particular world? Only Hegelian true-believers are compelled to do so.

On his part, Habermas, in the highly interesting essay, 'Can complex societies develop a rational identity?', takes issue with Hegel on two fronts. On the one hand, so he believes, Hegel's 'spirit of modernity' is too restrictive: 'Not the idea of freedom characterizes modern consciousness alone, but also an unrestricted objectifying thinking and a radical future- orientation.'[22] I think that Habermas puts his finger on an important point here. Both objectifying thinking and future-orientation are philosophy-begotten ideas as much as freedom, and they also enhance modern phantasy so that they contribute to our identity-maintainance as *spiritual attitudes* and not as psychological 'motivation'. But freedom on the one hand and objectifying thinking or future-orientation on the other can still not be equated. The latter spiritual attitudes do not inhere in all spheres of the modern world as freedom certainly does; they are general but particular ideas, whereas freedom, as an idea, is both general and universal.[23] But Habermas makes also the opposite reproach to Hegel: his Absolute Spirit is too concrete, too dense, unfit for modernity; Hegel conceives of philosophy as an ersatz religion.[24] Modern societies do not constitute their identity in total world-pictures (*Weltbilder*). This is true. But Hegel's philosophy was not meant as a 'world-picture' at all. Just a few cosmetic operations on this philosophy are needed to present it as a normative diagnosis rather than an ersatz religion.

Let me return to the attempt at separating the content of the absolute spirit from its form which is the concrete Hegelian philosophy sealed by the third syllogism. We are then left with the following constituents of the contemporary absolute spirit:

(1) It appears as *thinking*, more closely, as speculative thinking. Not every kind of thinking is speculative. Speculative thinking is not problem solving and it is not put to any direct use. It is thinking for thinking's sake, telos-in-itself. It is meaning-providing thinking. That is, it is the kind of thinking that satisfies our need for metaphysics, without being metaphysical itself. It is suited for rendering meaning to the contingent person's life. Given that modern men and women are contingent and that they are also aware of their contingency, they suffer from a 'sickness unto death' in the form of constant 'meaning deficit'.[25] In the absence of a taken-for-granted traditional faith in divine providence (a condition shared also by many who were actually calling heads in the cosmic wager), the need for rendering meaning by thinking also increases. Many a thing can be meaning-rendering by being thought and re-thought, so much so that nothing is by necessity the thing that must be thought, and an infinite number of things (or at least an unaccountable number of them) can become thought-things. One can go as far as to assert that the original *what* of thinking becomes almost indifferent, given that it is via thinking

that the thing receives, by being re-thought speculatively, its philosophical significance. This is why modern (speculative) thinking is, by definition, non-metaphysical, even if the *what* of thinking is a metaphysical character or object. If one can practise speculative thinking *a propos* of a cloud, of the psyche of a single man, of a poem of Auden or of the emanations of God, this is not metaphysical thinking. But speculative thinking of this kind suits the contingent person well. The things that are transfigured (*verklaert*) by one person's thinking do not have to be transfigured by the other person's thinking. Our meaning-provision has also a personal dimension, although the practice of speculative thinking is in-and-for-itself universal and thus 'the spirit of our congregation'.

(2)   The constant practice of speculative thinking as an end-in-itself and as meaning-providing exercise is *Andacht*. It is the piety of thinking that transfigures the thing that one thinks. Piety of thinking, as we know, deepens and broadens our 'internal rooms' or spaces; we are presencing. We can 'presence' infinite things through the piety of thinking.

(3)   But the absolute spirit *is* the spirit of our congregation. A congregation requires common practices, the exercise of worship (*Kultus*). What has to be worshipped is the piety of thinking itself. But the modern (post-metaphysical) piety of thinking is rather personal and, as personal, unfit for common worship. The spirit of the congregation itself has to suggest certain representative objects for worship.
    Philosophy is the owl of Minerva; it casts a retrospective glance. Speculative thinking is this retrospective glance. The things of worship are the representative things of the past. But everything of the past becomes representative once it becomes 'presenced' by the piety of thinking. *And this 'piety' need not be pious; it can be irreverent, ironical, destructive or deconstructive, for not the mode of 'presencing', but 'presencing' in thinking as such makes the act one of piety.* Thinking means to think the past thing and to 'presence' it.
    Modern men and women are diggers. They dig out the past to recollect items bygone.[26] What we dig out is the past, but it is dead past. Dead past is not history. There is only living history. History is alive as long as, and to the extent that, men and women can remember together, by virtue of their shared experiences. Philosophy, religion and art perform a minor miracle in the life of modern men and women: they create the perfect illusion of a lived history. By taking a philosophical work, an art work, a religious vision of the past as

the object of thinking worship, and in transfiguring it by thought, one lives historically; though not here, and not in this time, nor there and in that other time, but in the spaceless and timeless kingdom of meaning.

Both Hegel's 'minimalism' and 'maximalism' are rooted in the spirit of our congregation. There is one spiritual thing that originates in our congregation, and this is the universal idea of Freedom. Yet nothing else *originates* in it. Freedom offers the possibility of re-thinking everything that once was, that was originated far before our times. Freedom gives us liberty to re-think those past things in practically infinite ways and modes and to 'presence' them. This is *repetition*, a kind of meaningful, moreover meaning-providing, repetition. It is the repetitive transfiguration of the repeated by subjective thought – yet repetition it remains.

Our world does not originate new meaning; our spirit is spiritless, for it lives on borrowed meaning. Moderns discover culture and meaning precisely because they live on borrowed meaning. Ours is an omnivorous age. We have no special taste, our thought digests all tastes. After an extraordinary outpouring of the modern philosophical and artistic creative genius in the 'romantic' age, we became un-creative. Philosophy paints grey in grey; it became philosophy of culture. The spirit of modernity has begotten democracy on the one hand, and hermeneutics on the other hand.

This is, in short, Hegel's story (rendered in an un-Hegelian way). An illuminating story it is, and many aspects of it ring the bell of truth. But Luhmann's point could also be reconsidered. One need not be a systems theorist to ask the question of whether the self-consciousness of our overly complex society could at all be developed from the inside. For if it cannot, our 'omnivorous' memory is then not necessarily the sign of a general deficit in the capacity of originating meaning. It can equally result from the incapacity to give a comprehensive account of the meanings that are still originated and generated.

2 On the Spirit of our Congregation

Absolute Spirit, Historical Consciousness and Imaginary Institution(s) (in Castoriadis' rendering) are not just three names for the same philosophical character that happens to make its appearance in different philosophies. They play similar but distinct roles. So do other main characters of the contemporary philosophical dramatology, such as Language, Text or Writing.

Paradigm-pluralism, or rather the commitment to, and the consciousness of, paradigm-pluralism *is the negative theology of the spirit of our congregation*. Not in the sense that the spirit 'has' many names, but insofar as it 'gives' many names. Paradigm-pluralism is essential for the spirit of modernity, yet the self-same pluralism bears witness to the elusiveness of the spirit of our congregation: no single and comprehensive self-consciousness of our age can emerge. We know about the spirit of our congregation absolutely through its absence. Absolute spirit appears also as absolute knowing in the night of this negative theology. He who says that there is only one paradigm in modernity will be regarded as a fool; he who says that there should be only one paradigm in modernity will be regarded as a madman coming from the moon or from a pre-modern congregation.

To provide a comprehensive self-consciousness of modernity is beyond possibility. Subject and object, substance and subject are not about to meet; they are not a match; their marriage will not be consummated. The spirit of modernity is a treacherous imp that makes us choose among a great variety of paradigms and thus eludes us. The world as a whole is not recognizable in that which it originates.[27]

On the other hand, whatever paradigm is put to theoretical use, the theorist, the philosopher, the art critic or the interpretative historian behind it will do nothing else but provide self-consciousness for modernity. There are self-consciousness-providing factories producing wholesale. The finished products remain unfinished, odd fragments, and none of the fragments will match the others. They remain fragments precisely because the spirit of our congregation is such a treacherous imp. The theorists cannot help but take dictation from the imp. Since all paradigms are 'given' to us by the spirit of our congregation, none of those paradigms has the privilege to aspire to the position of the 'only', the 'real', or the true one, let alone to receive such a privilege. Every theory is just a version of self-interpretation and self-description without the slightest hope of becoming the sole 'real' or 'true' one. Certainly, the philosopher, the theorist can insist that his, and only his, paradigm is true; but insistence does not move the impish spirit of our congregation. Claims to absoluteness do not transform a fragment into a whole, the monadic universe into the divine universe, neither do they diminish its value, provided that the spirit of our congregation inhabits the fragment or the monad.

The treacherous imp eludes us – it cannot be caught. But it is omnipresent, and everyone is aware of its presence. It lures us into the deep forest, the virgin land, the wide seas, and just when we get to work and start to enjoy our intellectual comfort, it appears as a stern censor from within, and starts to whisper: do not go further, this is pathetic, things like that cannot be done anymore; do not lie! Indeed, we are not supposed to know what the truth is, nevertheless, we should not lie. What is a lie? Everything is a lie that becomes intolerable for the spirit of our congregation. To 'lie' means to think *against* the spirit of our congregation. There is no external pressure; the spirit of our congregation has no institutions at its disposal which would suppress ideas that contradict the spirit. Actually, no idea is 'evil', if by evil transgression/total negation is meant. The spirit of our congregation is not familiar with formal transgression; it is, after all, this spirit that lures us into the unknown. As we know, neither poets nor philosophers dance their pirouettes in chains. But there is such a thing as spiritual transgression or transgression against a spirit that is unfamiliar with censorship administered according to formal barriers. One transgresses if one gets out of touch with the spirit – and this can happen with the best of intentions. Yet it is from the inside, from the 'subjective spirit' that the voice comes: 'This is a lie! Do not lie!' One can decide to listen, one can also decide to disregard the voice.

Talents have an intimate relation to the spirit of the congregation; the talent of the moderns is no exception to this. But the modern condition requires an exceptionally refined and over-sensitive *phronesis*. One has to develop a 'feel' for when and how far the voice of the spirit of our congregation should be listened to, and when and to what extent it should be neglected, in order to go one step further in the direction of the unknown. The warning of the spirit needs to be taken seriously, for one should not lie. Cutting the umbilical cord that ties the subjective spirit to the absolute spirit, in other words, lying, causes the spiritual child to be stillborn. But the warning of the spirit need not to be taken at its face value: our absolute spirit is, after all, a treacherous imp. One can dismiss the internal voice and venture a few steps further. How many, in which direction, when (and when not) – this is exactly what *phronesis* decides.

Who has never heard the voice of the spirit of our congregation does not dwell in the sphere of the absolute spirit. The closer one gets to the centre of that sphere, the more one exposes oneself to the censorship of our *daimonion*.

Hegel was in a way right. Only the recognition of the message of the spirit of our congregation makes authorship free. And he was also right that freedom is not there initially, only as a result, if at all. As usual, the worshippers put enormous pressure on their fellow worshippers. This time they cannot brand anything as heretic, immoral, so, as a rule, they brand it 'untimely'. But the spirit of our congregation can play a few tricks on this account, too. Our spirit is also a good listener. What the fellow-worshippers consider untimely (as Nietzsche's *Untimely Meditations*), often proves to be extremely timely, and vice versa.

There is no other way to catch the spirit of our congregation but to listen to its voice, directly or indirectly. One can catch it directly in the autobiographical mood. The spirit of the congregation speaks also through the subjective spirit. In modernity, there is a world according to everyone, since everyone became – in this sense – a subject.[28] This theory (if it deserves the name) is certainly one of the cornerstones of my own vision of modernity, it belongs to modernity as it is 'according to me', but it is the kind of idiosyncratic theory which, so my *phronesis* suggests, got the green light from the spirit of our congregation. I can support this theory not only with introspection but also with general observation. Everyone can notice that works of art became more and more autobiographical as modernity developed. I owe to MacIntyre the discovery that in the twentieth century not only continental, but also Anglo/American, philosophy took a sharp turn in this direction.[29] Introspection was not alien to modern philosophy in general, from Descartes to Rousseau. But this introspection was meant to be methodological rather than world-constitutive. Or to put it another way, the individual/idiosyncratic person could not be recognized as the source of world constitution. The bodiless, insentient, universal Subject prior to experience, this monster of a Subject had first to be invented, and it in turn proved very helpful in construing a 'true', that is a common, world from scratch.

Idiosyncratic world-constitution is secondary world-constitution. It must be so in principle, otherwise we could not communicate. To acknowledge, as much as to practise, idiosyncratic (secondary) world-constitution is not only allowed for, but also encouraged by, the spirit of our congregation. It follows from its very core, its very centre. Idiosyncratic world-constitution is no longer regarded as a blemish to be removed, a source of error to be overcome, but rather as the only way to participate in the Sisyphean labour of developing the self-consciousness of modernity. By terming it a Sisyphean labour I only reconfirmed a previous point: it is a task which is impossible to accomplish. And yet, one must try the impossible if one dwells in the sphere of the absolute spirit, the absolute spirit being the self-consciousness of an epoch. And the impossible is tried, since tried it must be, but it is tried through that what is perhaps within the author's reach, namely through the practice of secondary world-constitutions, that is, idiosyncratically.

It would be a mistake to believe that if personal experience pours freely into the work of art or philosophy, these works will stand out more in their individuality or their greatness. For the time being, rather the opposite is to be observed. Perhaps Nietzsche was right: one can dance more gracefully in chains. Artists and philosophers of our century cannot hide a subtle envy they bear towards their colleagues of the past. Those old ones did not run into any difficulty in shaping their works as the self-consciousness of their age; even the early moderns could still do it, for the consciousness of their age was split between the pre-modern and the modern. This subtle envy is as much misconceived as the nostalgia it normally accompanies. Those who develop nostalgic feelings, for example, towards the Greek world, imagine themselves to be free Athenian citizens, never slaves or women, nor even citizens of a lesser, insignificant city. Furthermore, idiosyncratic modern authors do not really want to dance in chains. They imagine themselves rather in the place of the very few who rid themselves of those chains. But the stark and essential contrast between the genius on the one hand, and all others who just follow the rules set by a genius on the other hand, had already begun to shrink. There is now rather a continuum than a contrast. Apart from the question of whether this stark contrast carried the same weight for the contemporaries of all those 'geniuses' or whether this immense weight has only been poetically added by certain authors of the age of the Enlightenment and Romanticism, is of little relevance. More importantly, in the last half-century we run short of new geniuses – we discover rather new ones among the oldest.[30] Since no one is dancing in chains, no one needs to make a tremendous effort to get rid of those chains. Everyone is idiosyncratic, a subject. To be a subject is not a privilege. Our contemporaries are no longer the lucky or the blessed children of nature. They are the children of the inter-subjective constitution of the world, the children of historical consciousness as such (in-and-for-itself). Whether they are lucky or unlucky is another matter. Yet even if that which has been a contrast becomes a continuum, there is still no accomplishment without blessing. The intimate relationship between the subjective and the absolute spirit did not change essentially. Blessing cannot be wrought out, it can only be granted. It still comes 'from above'.

I want to summarize a few points in retrospect. The denizens of modernity are unable to present the self-consciousness of modernity. The absolute spirit of modernity appears fragmented, or monadic, and the fragments do not make a whole. Works become idiosyncratic, the presentations of the subject's (or the theorists' and artists') experience. Philosophy fixes its gaze onto the past (or the past of the present). It thinks thinking; it transforms every object into a thought-object while piously presencing it. One can draw from these observations the preliminary conclusion that *instead of making their (our) epoch self-conscious, modern theory, philosophy, and to an ever greater degree also art, rather make the past self-conscious.* It seems as if the self-consciousness of all of past history would amount to the self-consciousness of modernity. What we know of our own self-consciousness is the consciousness of the *Other*, not the consciousness of one's self.

The core of our historical consciousness is its being qua *the* historical consciousness of historical consciousness, or, in Hegel's lingo, as the idea (the concept) of historical consciousness. It is our historical consciousness that construes historical consciousness. The consciousness of historical consciousness itself is not historical. Everything is being 'presenced' through it by being thought. As long as historical consciousness remained unconscious, people could generate the self-consciousness of their time. They had their incontestable Truth – all their stories confirmed it. Since historical consciousness became conscious (around the time of the French Revolution), whereby the Truth of History became unveiled, the capacity of establishing Truth-for-us was gone: as if our age would have coined the Truth for all those dead ages from the previous metals of contemporary mines that got exhausted before having been put to use for the sake of the living. Being became through and through historical. Moderns have shut themselves up in the prisonhouse of historicity and they have lost the key to this prisonhouse. They cannot gaze upon it from the outside; they cannot suspend its existence, not even in their dreams. We are no longer in Plato's cave, because we now know (or rather, *this is what we know*) that every epoch is a prison, and everyone a prisoner. No one has ever left his or her own prison. The cave and the sun and the shadow and the things whose shadows the shadows are – all of them are just different items coming from the same prisonhouse. It does not make much difference whether or not the self-consciousness of historical consciousness assumes the form of a grand narrative. We need not believe that our prisonhouse is the broadest and that it encompasses all the previous prisonhouses, and still, we continue to live in our prisonhouse as it is. Many escape-routes had been tried; the social sciences are one of them.[31] Experimenting with escape routes in the social sciences did not prove futile. A few new and also representative idiosyncratic worlds were presented through these language-games. Many of them contributed to our self-knowledge, as all fragments do, even if they overlap, cross each other or contradict one another. *The absolute spirit cannot be overwritten.*

The consciousness of historical consciousness, the historical consciousness in-and-for-itself, is not a paradigm. It does not qualify as a paradigm, but it is the condition of all paradigms. Moveover, the discovery that we put together our worlds in paradigms is already one of the manifestations of the spirit of our congregation. It is certainly not an *a priori* form of experiencing, at least not in the Kantian sense. First, it cannot be said to be a form, for it provides contents and takes contents away, and we do not have the means anyhow to distinguish between 'form' and 'content' in something that eludes us. But one can say that historical consciousness in-and-for-itself is the condition of *our* experience, because it is through it that we have experience at all. The single person does not need to be conscious of this all-emcompassing historical consciousness; but it is omnipresent and all-pervasive whether one conducts the business of everyday life, or one is busy with a profession, or one is doing one's act in the political arena.

Paradigms themselves have a positive explanatory power, while self-limiting paradigms have a negative explanatory power. But both have this power, or claim to have it. Take only less obvious cases. For example, Castoriadis proposes the imaginary institution of society which is a paradigm with positive explanatory power, insofar as it offers us an explanation for the radical changes in social imagination. These changes allegedly originate in the psyche. Castoriadis' ontological difference, if I may use this idiosyncratic expression out of its own context, is the difference between the historically programmed and manufactured men and the timeless psyche which, like an eternal volcano erupts in emitting originary imagination, taking or not taking root in the world, forming or failing to form institutions of imagination. If an ensemble of such new institutions is formed, then, in a Hegelian language, a new epoch in the life of the spirit is established. Here Psyche is functionally equivalent to Heidegger's Being.[32] Paradigms of language, on the other hand, are employed sometimes, but not always, as self-limiting or negative paradigms. In asserting that everything is language (consciousness, of course included), one can achieve a complete closure. Nothing is within or without, since the distinction becomes irrelevant. But even the most extreme versions of the paradigm of language have a negative explanatory power, because they claim the power to explain why all other paradigms are wrong. The inclusion of everything amounts to exclusion, because if everything is included, there is no alternative left. Extreme paradigms of language manifest the omnivorous character of the spirit of our congregation as much as the Hegelian philosophy or radical hermeneutics.[33]

The historical consciousness in-and-for-itself (the self-consciousness of historical consciousness) has no explanatory power. This is only another way of saying that it cannot serve as a paradigm. The problem with all our paradigms is not that they try hard, but that they entertain the illusion that nothing has eluded them, for they have been entirely successful in their venture. It is far easier to collect the concrete manifestations of the spirit of our congregation than to assert something about its core.[34] In order to discuss the core, one needs to have recourse to metaphors, similes and a traditional, sometimes metaphysical, philosophical terminology.

For starters, the term 'consciousness' can be misleading, because historical consciousness in-and-for-itself is not an epistemological category. One could assert, if one's Hegel has a Spinozist colouring, that it is the ultimate subject/substance of our age and that everything modern is, in a fashion, the modification of that substance/subject. Modification is not meant in term of causation. Let me use the simile of the tree of life. The core of the spirit of our community is like the trunk of the tree. This tree has several (practically an infinite number of) branches and they are divided into sub-branches which carry leaves and flowers. The leaves are the souls of men and women. These souls are entirely different, yet they are all souls born out of the same bough or of another bough of a branch of the selfsame tree. This is certainly a simplistic account even of the little which is in sight. Branches are connected with one another also directly, not simply through the trunk. To speak with Spinoza, one has to distinguish between a vertical and horizontal chain of 'determination'.[35] I put the word 'determination' into inverted commas, although we cannot think the chain of horizontal connection nor can we form sentences about it, without using the language of determination; but we do it in another way which is better suited to the spirit of our (own) congregation.

The longevity of the trunk temporalizes its own branches, while it remains the same trunk all the time. I termed these branches 'historical consciousness'. There are many kinds of historical consciousness on the same tree of historical consciousness. Or, put the other way around, the consciousness of historical consciousness itself establishes (or brings about) its own stages. The past, while 'sucked in' and made 'history', has to be identified. Its layers are identified as the stages of historical consciousness. One need not use this terminology; in fact, one rarely does. One normally speaks about cultures, civilizations, social formations, modes of production, epochs, ages and the like. One lines up stages of historical consciousness in a spatio-temporal field. The labels are important, so are the ways of temporal/spacial ordering. Each label belongs to a different theory, mostly also to a separate paradigm. The past becomes spatio-temporalized in the process of having been sucked in by the presence. The past becomes history or anti-history when it is 'presenced', and people living in the remote places of our planet were discovered (and temporalized) when their world was sucked in by the presence. The great interest and devotion for the otherness of the other (culture) is the surest sign that this (other) culture has already been sucked in, and that what happens is just 'presencing' it.

It seems as if I just said the same thing about the consciousness of historical consciousness that I disapproved of in the extreme version of the paradigm of language. The extremist version of the language-paradigm holds that since everything is language, everything is included (in language), and since everything is included, there is no otherness left (there is nothing outside language). Despite similarities, the assertions are still not identical, because I do not use consciousness of historical consciousness as a paradigm. I have remained deliberately on the level of an approximative description. The consciousness of historical consciousness is the permanently self-repeating process in which the past and the future are sucked into the present, and otherness becomes otherness within the consciousness of historical consciousness. As a result, sequences or stages of historical consciousness appear, a few of them pertaining to a past that had been sucked up, others, however, being the manifestations of the consciousness of historical consciousness itself. They are those branches of the tree which have grown in different times.

Yet I would not state that there is nothing external to the consciousness of the historical consciousness at all. If I knew whether or not there was anything external, I would not have introduced the idea (and the practice) of the cosmic wager. The cosmic wager remains the manifestation of the spirit of our congregation, but our bet is unmistakably ours. By staking our life and happiness on calling heads or tails (or on betting for not betting), we manifest and, at the same time, challenge the spirit of our congregation.

I described the consciousness of historical consciousness as the core of the spirit of our congregation.

I employed the terms 'conciousness' and 'spirit' not merely in order to pay Hegel his due. One of my reasons was to find a concept which, in my interpretation, does not qualify for paradigmatic use. My second reason was to de-psychologize the core institution of contemporary imagination. In my mind, there are no instinctual, emotional or volitional forms or attitudes built into the core of the spirit of our congregation. One can assume, even if one can make the opposite assumption as well, that those forms of attitudes are somehow 'external' to that spirit, for example, that they encompass empirically universal elements also. One can also assume, although here too one can make the opposite assumption, that certain other emotional, volitional or motivational factors are bound to certain institutions of the 'objective spirit' directly and not through the mediation of the absolute spirit. Whatever is strictly non-historical cannot be consumed by the consciousness of historical consciousness either – this is what I meant by 'external'. However, unlike Castoriadis, I do not regard an 'external' psychic force as the sole resource of our imagination. Furthermore, the term 'consciousness' carries an anti-psychological connotation in another respect also. I called the spirit of our congregation 'consciousness' in order to emphasize that it is not something unconscious. It is not a kind of an unconscious essence which somehow fails to appear, which bars us from developing an adequate self-consciousness of our era. Rather, it is over-reflexivity, the multiplicity of overlapping and only partly fitting fragments of consciousness that characterize the incomplete mosaic which is the self-consciousness of the age. It is that which is conscious, rather than that which is not, that is chiefly responsible for lack of transparency. We *know* that we are contingent, and it is because of this that our access to the Absolute is barred. We *know* that we are historical 'products' and whatever we produce is of short-term relevance. We *know* that we are 'complex', and that all the simple self-descriptions are lies, and so on and so forth. If we did not know what we know we would not be what we are.

As has been pointed out, it is the consciousness of historical consciousness that constitutes historical consciousness itself, together with its stages. Hegel told the real story. It is from the consciousness of the present that the story of historical consciousness can be told, because it is now that it has become 'recognized'. One can, unlike Hegel, know that historical consciousness is not 'the truth' of all those stages, and yet one is no less entrapped. For one cannot help knowing that this knowledge too is only 'granted' by the same Spirit that has granted what Hegel knew.

The consciousness of historical consciousness is the core of the spirit of our congregation; it is not its whole spirit. There is no 'knowledge' of the whole spirit, but we do perceive many aspects of it. We perceive first and foremost that the spirit of our congregation is in a constant flux, that it is changing, that it is a dynamic spirit. What is termed 'dialectics' is also a modern life-experience. The core of the spirit remains the same, and yet the spirit does not remain the same; for the most part, it is composed of opposites or of countervailing elements. The core/spirit relationship is unlike the centre/periphery or the essence/appearance relationship; there is no binary opposition here. The core is, rather, a kind of disposition. All the imaginary elements that share the disposition of the core can emerge, transform themselves, live and also die in the world where the spirit of our congregation holds sway, and where nothing else can.

3 The Imperialism of the Objective Spirit: Culture Versus Absolute Spirit

So far I have been borrowing Hegel's language to tell a part of my story I have already told many times, and each time in a slightly different version; all of them were conceived in the spirit of our congregation.[36] I now have to return briefly to my original language and narrative.

There are two spheres indispensable for the very existence of social-human life.

One of them is the sphere of everyday life which encompasses all those heterogeneous activities that are necessary for the simple reproduction of the particular social unit as well as all kinds of knowledge and aptitudes that are needed for the exercise of these activities. Contents of activities are changing, so are the kinds of knowledge and aptitudes. But all activities require three aptitudes: the use of ordinary language and of man-made objects and the observance of customs by distinguishing between good and bad, right and wrong.

Another sphere is the meaning-providing sphere, or the sphere which yields authorization, legitimation for a particular form of life as it is. I termed this meaning-providing sphere, which also establishes the identity of a society and thus becomes the repository of its self-consciousness, the sphere of objectivation for itself. It happened only at the dawn of our civilizations that the meaning-providing sphere was divided into two spheres. One remained chiefly meaning-providing, whereas the other differentiated itself as the sphere of institutions. It is from this stage onwards that the distinction between the objective and the absolute spirit becomes relevant.

The split between the sphere of the absolute and the objective spirit goes with a spatial and temporal differentiation. The more explicit the split, the more hierarchical will be the relationship between these two spheres. Gods do not dwell anymore between humans, they become more remote and majestic. They are separated, placed 'up there'. At first, they become immortal, then eternal. The absolute spirit is the sphere where God dwells; it is the higher sphere, or rather, the highest. When Harold Bloom contrasts the Book of J with the later biblical texts, this is exactly what he points to. In the earliest texts of the Torah, Jahweh was a character figure who lived among his peoples, whereas in the later textual versions of the story he became a remote, majestic, just and powerful King of the Universe. A similar development can be observed among the Greeks. While the Olympians, though immortal, appeared among the crowd and mixed with mortals, Plato invented deities (sometimes only one) who were removed from worldly life and who were also a-temporal, eternal. A-temporality (eternity) became the hallmark of things that are 'higher up'. Neo-Platonism divided the highest into lower highest and higher highest and so on. Mystical philosophies of emanation broadened the gap between the absolute and the objective (earthly, institutional) spirit to the extreme. What Hegel termed the piety of thinking (*Andacht*) became a preoccupation with things 'high up'. Absolute spirit created its own institutions. The worship of the absolute spirit became removed from the worship of political institutions, as in the case of Buddhism, monastic life, or Aristotle's *bios theoretikos*.

At the dawn of modernity, the relation between the objective and the absolute spirit became ambiguous and full of tensions. The moderns preferred the pragmatic spirit, earthly matters, things which are primarily useful. Yet, as Hegel acutely observed, they have transformed the Christian God into a remote Spirit, a thinking thing. It was their taste that made the trifle, the banal, the prosaic nonsense suitable for artistic representation. Yet they were the ones who began to worship genius and originality, and they were also the ones who transformed artworks into autonomous objects of divine worship. They were the mouthpiece of the deification of man. They claimed the highest place for the man who vanquished all gods. But they also felt alienated and abandoned, thrown back into helpless anxiety under an empty sky, and they yearned for salvation.

For five centuries, the absolute spirit has remained suspended in the same ambiguity; it still is. It is just that in the last half a century, as our consciousness changed to post-modern,[37] the manifestation of this ambiguity became less and less direct. In the manner of an omnivorous spirit one can make a case for everything and for the opposite of everything. One person prefers Plotinus, the other William James; it does not really matter.

Absolute spirit can take three forms: art, religion and philosophy. They are the meaning-providing objectivations proper. All of them consists of three aspects: first, the creation of the object of worship, second, the object of worship itself, and third, the piety of thinking or worshipping, that is, the personal and the common, the theoretical and the practical reception of the objects of worship. If one wants to determine whether the gulf between the absolute and the objective spirit is deep or superficial, one has to consider all three aspects at once.

The birthplace of modernity, the European sub-continent, was poor in original religious imagination, but it was rich in philosophical phantasy and in the ability to invent (to create) a great variety of art-forms. Art-forms and philosophies have constantly enriched religious reception, particularly since the emergence of Christianity. Religious artworks and philosophies helped to bridge the gulf between absolute spirit on the one hand and objective spirit on the other hand. Philosophy, the so-called handmaiden of theology, raised her lady very high up on the level of speculation. Not only the object of worship (God) was placed into a remote highest sphere – for this to happen no philosophy or art was needed – but the handmaidens themselves get highly placed. When the quality of a painting becomes of primary concern, one can no longer tell who or what is actually worshipped here, the Saviour or the beauty of the painting. It was through service that art and philosophy prepared the ground for their autonomy. Between the Renaissance and the Enlightenment, they succeeded in occupying the highest position in the Kingdom of the Absolute Spirit. Religion is not self-worshipping, but needs god(s) as the object of worship, and so do art(s) and philosophy. The independent deities Truth and Beauty were thus enthroned. They were not brand-new deities. But after having been degraded to the position of predicates or attributes of the Highest for more than a thousand years they returned to their throne with a vengeance; they declared that they alone were going to occupy it.

Nietzsche said that God is dead; it was a philosopher who said that God had died. He meant that god is for us no more. The God of the philosopher, the philosopher remarked, is no more. But the god of the (modern) philosopher is not the God of the religious worshipper. If the religious worshipper says that God has died, this is a religious statement. God has, indeed, died, but he was also resurrected. The God of religion is (always) resurrected. But the god of the philosopher is Truth. When Nietzsche, the philosopher, said that god was dead, this meant that god was no more (the philosopher's) truth, or that truth was no more (the philosopher's) God. He said 'God' but 'God' meant the philosopher' truth.[38] The heavenly governance of the philosopher's Truth and of the artist's Beauty proved short- lived; or so it seems. For what happened is not a return to the status quo ante, but *the ascendancy to the throne of the practice of worshipping*. It is not Truth or Beauty that is now worshipped. The old god of philosophy – Truth – is not the object of devotion, nor is Beauty which shines through the work of art sought in that work; rather, works of art and works of philosophy themselves have become the objects of worship.

In a way, philosophy has returned to its previous –pre-modern – practices. It renders a service, yet not to its own deity, at least not directly. Rather, it renders services to services rendered. Primary services are (were) rendered in religious devotion (to God), philosophical devotion (to truth), and, at least so it was believed for a few centuries, in artistic devotion (to beauty). Now, philosophical services are rendered for those other services – for philosophies, artworks, and forms of religious devotion, as well as for sciences. After all, sciences, too, worshipped Truth for its own sake so that they could become relevant objects for the practice of secondary service. The yield of the primary service is now termed culture. The God of philosophy is dead; long live the philosophy of culture! Philosophy of culture is the philosophy of the omnivorous absolute spirit without identity. Contemporary philosophy *services* itself (the spirit of our congregation) indirectly, because it is impotent to service it directly. 'Impotence' may be a too harsh expression. The spirit of our congregation does not tolerate direct service, it is dismissed as a lie; and a lie it is. This impotence is not the absence of potency, but self-imposed abstinence, the abstinence of sincerity and honour, yet also of convenience.

This is how philosophy became philosophy of culture in the service of the spirit of our congregation.

Philosophy of science is philosophy of culture, so is every meta-discourse, so is deconstruction, so are all ordinary language theories. Rehashing or re-formulating traditional 'arguments' (e.g. the three-world argument) is certainly philosophy of culture. These are the happy philosophies of culture, because they do not care; existentialists are the unhappy philosophers of culture, because they do. But hermeneutics is the most adequate self-expression of the spirit of our congregation.

Hermeneutics is all-pervasive: the anti-hermeneuticians are also hermeneuticians. Hermeneuticians mediate the past to the present, they re-think (or believe that they have re-thought) what had once been thought, they re-interpret what had once been (or they believe to have been) interpreted, or they subvert it. They render meaning with borrowed meaning, they infuse life into the present with alien blood.

Hermeneutical practice is authentic 'piety of thinking' (*Andacht*), whatever forms it takes. That which is re-interpreted and mediated to the present is resurrected or preserved from oblivion by having been re-thought. Re-thinking can be ironic and playful, one can also read a text against the text; and the text is preserved even if one reads it 'against itself', or irreverently, ironically. Perhaps this kind of reading is more redeeming than the rest. True enough, hermeneutical practice is frequently manifestly devotional. Every text becomes sacred if it is tendered in a devotional manner. Each word will thus have its significance, each variation of a sentence religiously accounted for.[39] Viewed from this perspective, there is no difference between commentaries on the Talmud and on the *Critique of Pure Reason* just that when one writes commentaries to commentaries on the Talmud, one interprets interpretations whose primeval source is supposed to be the Divine Law, whereas when one writes commentaries on Kant-commentaries, one can cherish the hope of getting closer to Kant's mind, but certainly not to the Divine Mind.

Parousia is presencing. While recalling a tradition into the timelessness of the present, hermeneuticians are redeeming this tradition. They certainly do not redeem tradition for tradition's sake, but for their (our) own sake. Alien blood is infused into modern blood vessels; alien blood keeps the moderns alive; aliens are not allowed to rest in peace because *we* want to survive. That some of those aliens never wanted to rest in peace is another matter. For example, Greeks were yearning for immortality, and they achieved immortality through all of their successors as well as through us a thousandfold, with the added satisfaction that their (allegedly) immortal gods owe their immortality to mortal men.

Owing to the omnivorous appetite of our epoch, redemptive reading (thinking) does not discriminate. And it is this non-discriminative redemptive practice that occupies the pride of place in the spirit of our congregation.

Whether the absolute spirit can now keep the elevated position that it had occupied since the dawn of our civilization is a serious question. That many a civilization survived, even flourished, without worshipping 'absolutes' is true, but those ancient civilizations did not face dangers that ensue from the quest for the deification of man on the one hand, and of private narcosis on the other hand.

Everyday routine from time to time has to be suspended. The sheltered independence of the self becomes psychologically unbearable without the regular occurrence of its opposite, that is, the surrender to the other with the momentary suspension of ego barriers.[40] In modern life, where business as usual offers very little respite from routine, and practically none from an externally regulated formal self-discipline of body and mind,[41] where the natural practices of other-experiencing are lost with the break-up of communities, even the satisfaction of elementary psychological needs must be met by practices provided by other spheres. We could even mention higher spheres without inverted commas, because this is how our dwelling in those spheres is normally experienced. Overcoming self-limitations and routine actions is perceived as something beyond and above our normal self, for it requires the concentration of physical and mental powers, phantasy, as an exceptional moment that stands out and is always remembered. Men and women strive for actions or things which can be remembered, which leave a stronger impact on their memory, because this is what life is. It is heightened living.

A sphere is removed from everyday life if it becomes more remote, 'higher up', if one can really dwell in it, that is, if it offers a 'world'. One does not live constantly in this world, but one can and one does live there by adopting a set of attitudes different from those one normally has. It is not itself but normal everyday life that this 'world' provides with meaning. The three aspects (meaningful, shared, out of everyday pattern) pertain to the 'highest' sphere of 'the absolute spirit'.

The psychological needs, mentioned above, can be satisfied without a 'high' sphere. One can get 'high' on drugs, but no lasting meaning will be rendered thereby to everyday experience. In addition, the aspect of 'sharing' will be a sham, and no experience of shared memory will ensue. One can share the remembrance of having drunk pink champagne together,[42] but pink champagne is not a world where one dwells and it certainly will not render meaning to one's life.

Ethically demanding acts, especially if shared by a collective of similarly-minded people, satisfy all the needs men and women normally carry to the sphere of the absolute spirit. They are utopian realities, just like artworks, philosophical works and religious visions.[43] But the difference between those two kinds of utopian realities remains enormous. One cannot return at will to the period of the war, the revolution, or to the foundational moment of one's *urbs* save in recollection, but one can always return to the sphere of absolute spirit whenever one feels the need to dwell in it. The ethical utopia is one of action, whereas the utopian world of the absolute spirit is utopian *in* contemplation, although not, or only infrequently, also the utopia of contemplation.

None of these utopias are moral utopias. This is obvious in the case of the absolute spirit, but less so in that of ethical utopias. Yet men and women can be ethically elevated by a morally ambiguous cause (for example, a war) so that they experience the uplifting moments of friendship, unity, and cameradery. The moral utopia is the absolute utopia, but the absolute utopia is not the utopia of the absolute spirit. The good person is the absolute utopian reality.[44]

Piety of thinking (*Andacht*) is the tribute paid to something 'higher'; not necessarily to something morally higher, yet always to something that is spiritually higher. The term 'spiritually higher' stands here for the *intensity of meaning*. The meaning of a world is intensive if it is ambiguous and manifold, so much so, that one can return to it in a practically infinite number of cases, one can understand it always in a new way, as well as experience it in an (emotionally) new way. In the sphere of the absolute spirit, Heraclitus' truth holds sway: one cannot enter twice into the same river. The same is said to be true about every kind of practice – but one is hardly aware of it and it does not matter. But when one enters into a sphere which is meaning-intensive, one is fully aware of the uniqueness of each distant occurrence of experiencing. One enters the river for the second or the third time because one has a presentiment that one will experience the same once over again, but also that something new will occur. Without such a presentiment that seduces us into stepping into the river for the second, third, and infinite time, we can be sure that the object, the story, the vision we first encountered does not belong to the sphere of the absolute spirit, or merely to its lowest periphery. Absolute spirit is the sphere of repeatability, of repetition and of having been repeated (of returning and of having been returned, as Hegel said) where each repetition stands out in its unrepeatable uniqueness.

Before the Absolute Spirit one bows one's knees – so Hegel said.

Bowing our knees is a sign of humility. Men and women indeed enter the sphere of the absolute spirit with humility. The attitude carries the message that there is something that stands above us, that *Man is not the Highest that Is*.[45]

Early moderns had pushed the sphere of the absolute spirit higher and higher to drive home this message. At times when European man's pride in his power began to assume unheard-of dimensions, the gap between the objective and the absolute spirit had to be widened. Omnipotent on one level, capable of ruling his own destiny, man must still remain aware of his limitedness and make peace with it. Goethe's *Faust* contains all the ambiguities of this story.

A meaning-intensive sphere as a merely human, man-made product no longer makes men and women bow their knees simply on entering there. Men and women need to approach this sphere with humility. One no longer approaches a creature born to an earthly woman with humility. That was done in pre-modern times when the serf approached the nobleman with humility, the nobleman the king (and all of them God). But then the defiant Spinoza ensured us that humility of the old sort is no virtue at all, and that the intellectual love of God, the kind of contemplative devotion that suits free men of high dignity, should replace it. Hero-worship is the mockery of the absolute spirit, given that it is not the human author of the work, but the work itself that embodies higher meaning. But if one approaches the higher sphere without 'contemplative devotion', the enounter with the absolute will be a flop. The absolute is, after all, not simply 'there', it is not something factually contained in an image, an idea or something that one sees or hears or tastes or feels, whatever original posture one takes. Without the readiness to receive the absolute, one will not receive it. It is this readiness, this gesture of coming forward, humility, intellectual love, contemplative devotion – you name it – that disposes men and women for the encounter with the absolute.

The core of our historical consciousness, the very spirit of our congregation bars direct access to Truth and the Beautiful. Our *daimonion* warns us that we should not cry out in wonder: this is the Truth, this is the Beautiful! For that would be just a lie, and one should not lie. Our absolute spirit turns us around; we are facing the past – true things and beautiful things we must wrest from tradition. But why should anyone bow one's knees before tradition? Tradition consists of human works, artifacts. They are meaning-intensive things; this is why they belong to our Absolute Spirit. We are presencing them, we offer them *parousia*, salvation, with the gesture of reciprocity, for it is salvation too that we seek. But what kind of salvation is this? Can Aristotle save us, or Plotinus or Descartes? Their Truth, perhaps, could, but it is not their Truth that we seek – for *their Truth is certainly not Truth for us*. Or rather, we seek their Truth, but not as Truth-for-us. What we rather seek is the continuation of the *discourse about truth*, just as we seek the continuation of the discourse about the beautiful and about the good. In this topsy-turvy way, we are 'presencing' ourselves, too – just by not letting the discourse about Truth disappear into oblivion. The meaning we may render thereby to ourselves is to keep up the spiritual exercise of meaning-rendering, of not closing the shop down. *Servicing the absolute spirit is maintenance work.* But in rendering service through maintenance, we do not bow our knees.

The denizens of our congregation redeem tradition in expectation of reciprocity. But the congregation will not be redeemed, because the Truth of the ancients is not Truth for us. But Truth became subjective; our Truth is subjective. What is true in religion, in art and in philosophy are topics for ongoing discussions; opinions differ. Truth is, however, not dependent on opinions, it cuts across them. That which is True can be the Truth, provided that it is the truth for me or for you.⁴⁶ It is such that certain exploiters of tradition do receive what they seek, namely their own, *personal* Truth, and sometimes also their own, *idiosyncratic, private salvation* (Hölderlin for Heidegger). The Truth is not only personal, but also immanent, and so is eventual salvation. Man is the saviour of man all the way. Yet it is not one's neighbour, friend or lover who is one's saviour, but man's creation in the fragile body in which the spirit of ancient times or of yesteryear has become encapsulated. The spirit seems still to be 'higher than men', even if one does not bow one's knees.

The 'saving power' of artworks and works of philosophy is personalized, or rather custom-made. A single Homer was enough for all the Greeks, a single Torah for all the Jews, a single Gospel for all the Christians – now each of us needs his or her own. The omnivorous character of the spirit of our congregation is extremely forthcoming. In the heaven of the cultural heritage everyone can find that which uplifts him, in the supermarket of the tradition every taste can be satisfied. The Heaven and the Supermarket are the same. It depends on the approach of our contemporaries whether it will be a Heaven or a Supermarket for them. The one who approaches the heritage with humility, who seeks Truth, meaning or even personal salvation there, glimpses into Heaven. He who looks for entertainment or for a rare topic to promote his academic career, walks through the Supermarket. No use or abuse of the Supermarket will prevent men and women from seeking Truth in the Heaven of tradition, and no Truth-seekers, headed for Heaven, will prevent anyone else from using and abusing the Supermarket and expanding the supply. Both attitudes reinforce one another; in addition, both attitudes can also be combined in the self-same persons, if not simultaneously.

The privatization of salvation liberates; men and women are now free in their relation to the absolute spirit. There is a world according to everyone – this is what I called 'the subject'.⁴⁷ If there is a world according to everyone, there is also a slightly different, idiosyncratic way for salvation for everyone. Yet one pays a heavy due for this liberation. One cannot discuss personal/private salvation, for the experience is entirely incommunicable. We can communicate that which we experienced together. When the same tradition is the source of meaning of a congregation, the congregation 'worships' this tradition. Personal/private salvation and worship, however, do not match. Where there is personal/private salvation, there can be no worship, just the lousy substitute for worship, a secondary worship. The more spacious the supermarket, the more primary worship is shrinking. In nineteenth-century Germany every literate boy and girl read Goethe, they shared a primary experience here. If a Gundolf analysed his life-shattering Goethe experience, others could join in. That was still worship in the grand old syle. These days, Heidegger's Hölderlin-studies are widely discussed, even religiously worshipped by many an American student. They seek edification from Heidegger who on his part was edified by Hölderlin. Very few of them ever read Hölderlin, and I am not very far off the mark in assuming that no more than a handful of them experienced 'the Truth' by reading those poems. This is what secondary worship is about. And there is tertiary worship as well, for example when the person who has worshipped Heidegger's worship of Hölderlin is in turn worshipped. This exercise has to be seen as worship, for it is not private. Groups are practising it; members of the group speak the same lingo, they understand the small and fine points of distinction; they are like Scholastic philosophers or Talmudists, they feel 'connected'. But since secondary worship has little impact on the form of life in a world where truth is subjective, (contrary to all the worlds where it was not), one loses the redeeming force that one wants to catch in worship.

There is a contradiction here which has to be solved practically and separately in each and of every occasion. Salvation (search for Truth) became idiosyncratic; there are no more schools, or tendencies, or 'isms'. Each and every philosopher or speculative thinker is on his or her own. Foucault's irritated reaction at being labelled a 'structuralist' or a 'post-structuralist,' his emphatic protest against pigeon-holing, became a paradigmatic gesture. Every philosopher will say nowadays that he or she does not want to be pigeon-holed, that he or she does not belong to any 'isms', not even to a 'non-ism' such as post-modernism. Without divine pretensions, philosophers and thinkers repeat the (mistranslated) divine claim: I am what I am, I am myself and nothing else. But the moment one's uniqueness has been established by initiating an idiosyncratic way of *Andacht* (piety of thinking) and one begins to exploit the tradition in his or her own way by interpreting a segment of it within the aegis of a subjective world (the world according to him and her), the philosopher runs the risk of a group of worshippers congregating around him or her in no time and transforming the original 'anti-ism' into an 'ism' of a novel kind through the practice of secondary and tertiary worship. It is in this process that absolute spirit becomes encapsulated in objective spirit. The problem is not that the sphere of absolute spirit develops its own institutions and institutional constraints – insofar as this is the problem, it is an old one. On the contrary, it seems as if the sphere of absolute spirit ceased to be the direct source of institutions or the main content of their ongoing practices. It is, rather, the system of the objective spirit (the system of systems) that circulates, distributes and assimilates whatever has been generated by the absolute spirit, together with much else, and in a democratic fashion. This is small wonder given that the access to the absolute spirit has become personal/private (with the exception of traditional religions, but not with the exception of theology). The Kantian *Tischgesellschaft* is gone, or rather, it has never been fully developed. The sphere of the absolute spirit is becoming thinner, but its withering is hardly visible in the bacchanalia of universal interpretation.

Absolute spirit is not part of 'culture'; it can become culture in and through the worship of a tradition for tradition's sake. The creation of artwork does not belong to culture; artworks become items of culture in relation to their own traditions such as continuation or disruption. For this to happen, the autonomy of certain arts has to be acknowledged to a certain degree. Arendt remarks that the Romans were the first people of culture – she is in all probability right.[48]

In modernity creative art became culture, moreover 'high' culture.[49] Today, it has become a part of tradition too. Since culture has always been linked to tradition, everything cultural in nature aspired to become a part of tradition and to acquiring immortality through it.[50] Modern creative art understood itself as culture so that it could aspire, in its own right and not as an interpreter, to immortality. It saw itself as the tradition of the morrow, but not as the tradition of the present. These days, works of art become tradition at the time of their conception; not traditions of the morrow, but the traditions of the present.

What is frequently called 'post-modernism' is, in the main, not a new trend nor a new style in art; least of all is it adverse to modernism. If one takes many a single work separately, one gets the impression that modernist tendencies go on unabated. But on the whole, there is a change here and a remarkable one. Something is happening to art similar to what has happened to philosophy. Single artists no longer join schools or groups – there are no more 'ists'. They are not obliged to heed aesthetic strictures or external yardsticks as if they still were in times of high modernism. They can do whatever fits their talents best; all of them conjure up a world according to their idiosyncratic personalities. They are also interpreters, they plunder the tradition. There is only one voice they have to lend an ear to: the voice of the spirit of our congregation. And the spirit of our congregation encourages interpretation, quotation, re-thinking, re-dreaming, re-petition.

Freedom from the pressure of external standards allows artists to seek the way of their personal Truth (or salvation). What was termed worship is, however, even more institutionalized in art than in philosophical thought. The institutionalized worship of art criticism and aesthetic discourse is joined by the institutionalized speculation of the institutions of the art-market. There is a greater variety than ever, there is difference, there is something most pleasurable for the eye, for the ear, some tasteful fodder for imagination; and still, the objective spirit swallows the absolute. The sphere of the absolute spirit becomes thinner, the concentration of meaning less intensive, the scope of interpretability narrower, timelessness more questionable. As if the two interpretations of freedom, the Hegelian on the one hand and the existential (ours) on the other, would join hands at this point and ridicule everyone who believed in their incompatibility. Who is after all the thinker or the artist who seeks her private, idiosyncratic, salvation? Is she not the same person who has chosen herself as a philosopher or an artist, and who became through this choice what she already was? Is the way and mode of conjuring up a world according to you and me, of becoming witness of my Truth or yours, not the greatest freedom after all? Is it not autonomy, determination from within, is it not the royal road to shedding all external constraints and obligations? Yet the core of the spirit of our congregation is the consciousness of historical consciousness, the spirit that makes us face the past, which we embrace through 'presencing' the tradition. And if someone becomes disloyal in her heart and flirts with the possibility of a new metaphysics or ontology, the spirit of the congregation will immediately whisper in her ear that she should not do this, because it is a lie, and one should not lie. And she will not lie. What else is this if not the 'recognition of necessity'?

4 Is There Truth for Us? The Challenge

The discourse on Truth (chapter 4) concluded with the question of whether the absence of a dominating concept of Truth is actually the manifestation of the dominating culture of our (post-modern) times. To maintain that historical self-consciousness is the core of the spirit of our congregation is to give an affirmative answer to this question. Historical consciousness opens the way to personal/private salvation. In the sphere of the objective spirit, no salvation, not even reconciliation, is accomplished.[51] But there is a plurality of discourses, and all those discourses constitute their own criteria of truth. In the sphere of objective spirit there can also be consensus concerning what truth is (e.g. in a court procedure or in reporting the results of scientific experiments), but this consensus will differ both in its mode and in its strictness. The 'saving power' of Truth, if there is any left, rests on the absolute spirit. But since private persons interpret the tradition on their own while ransacking it, and since there is a world according to each of us, there is also a truth according to each of us. Or rather, there are many truths according to each of us, one Truth on Monday and another on Thursday. This is not to say that our congregation lacks (common, shared, absolute) spirit; it is, rather, tantamount to putting our finger on the very message of this spirit. One cannot stress too often that the spirit of our congregation liberates us; but it also ensnares us. After having taken account of this apparent contradiction, there remains nothing shocking in the discovery. The first modern intellectuals became so intoxicated with the very novelty of the modern social arrangement that they could not imagine how one can be ensnared by a world where everyone is born free. They sought a culprit. But why should the modern arrangement differ in this respect from the pre-modern ones? Is it possible at all for a world to survive without a (shared) spirit of the congregation? But a (shared) spirit must also ensnare individuals. There is always a circle out of which there is no escape. To speak with Heidegger: Being always withdraws; the question is, how narrow or how large is our own chalk circle. Hegel may have been wise to insist that we should turn towards the circle to recognize ourselves in its content (the whole), for this is what his injunction to look at our world rationally means. Yet, modern men and women do not heed Hegel's advice. If one is ensnared by the spirit of one's own congregation, one hardly notices that one is so ensnared, and Hegel speaks to those who do. Yet if one notices it, one will try to escape, or one will realize that there is no escape route. Either way, Hegel's wisdom will appear as cheap comfort.

The spirit of our congregation presents us with a very big circle, the circle of the past (the past of the present included). The content of the circle is the interpretandum, and all the interpretanda and all their possible interpretations constitute Truth as Whole. Truth is whatever there is *within* the Whole – within the circle – for there is nothing outside the Whole, at least so it is presupposed. Truth is entirely immanent. Within the circle everything is permitted; Truth is subjective, after all. But the circle cannot be transcended. If one tries to transcend the circle, the spirit of the congregation will whisper into his ears: this cannot be done anymore – You should not lie!

The two assertions 'Truth is the Whole' and 'Truth is Subjective', imply one another; they together manifest the spirit of our congregation. Infinite possible truths offer themselves, and the saving power of their merchandises, to the subjects, who on their part recognize themselves as being thrown behind the bars of the prisonhouse of historicity.

This is not what Hegel intended to arrive at, but this is what he saw arrive. Thinking can become an exercise of mere *formal* freedom, and if this is so, everything and its opposite can be thought of as 'truth', depending on the momentary mood or whim of the thinker. This is what Hegel called 'irony'. There can be but one Truth, and yet, alas, the retrospective glance that closes the circle of the past can be indifferent to the content of this past. If this is so, anything goes. To disentangle himself (and his philosophy) from the ironical praxis of interpretation and thinking, Hegel seeks refuge in Christianity. Religion is withering because its (presentational) form has been discredited; but its content has not. This content is the true content. The difference between a modern philosopher and a devout Christian is that the devout Christian turns towards the truth in piety of feeling (*Gemütsandacht*), whereas the philosopher who acknowledges the truth of the same truth, thinks this truth. Not only the form of modern philosophy, but also its content, has to be Freedom.[52] But on what grounds, apart from his own pre-philosophical faith, does Hegel identify the content of Christian religion with the true content? On the grounds that Christian truth is 'necessary', that it had developed necessarily. But which 'truth' did not develop 'necessarily'? If one thinks in a Hegelian way, all truths did. So the content of the Christian religion is the true content (truth as freedom) because it is the end result of the development of all previous truths (in plural). This is a circular argument, and as such, it is in its proper place; the argument is an argument for circularity. The magic chalk circle that surrounds and defines us moderns is a result. The absolute, which is the result, is necessary, all-encompassing and true.

The spirit of our congregation is Hegelian up a degree, but not quite as Hegelian as Hegel himself. Much of Heidegger has transpired, even prior to Heidegger's time, to philosophize through it. We understand ourselves as members of a congregation that has been thrown into the prisonhouse of historicity, and not into another prisonhouse. It is a prison because its denizens came to know that all peoples of all epochs were chained to their respective epochs, that their minds were held captive by their times, only they did not know what we know. Just as people of past epochs were held captive, so, too, will all people of future times. The inmates of the present prisonhouse can know something about the prisonhouses of past cultures, at least that the inmates of the latter were unaware of their historicity. But they know nothing about the future ones, not even whether or not their citizens will be aware of their historicity, not even whether there will be future epochs at all. Moderns turned out to be deficient Hegelians. For it seems to run against the grain of the spirit of our congregation to detect necessity in all that which has happened and to claim knowledge of it. Truth as the Whole is an absolute, but it is not an absolutist claim. To paraphrase Heidegger: The absoluteness of this absolute is *not* presupposed. It is not meant as the One and Only Truth; it is meant as the Truth – for us.

What Hegel termed 'mere formal freedom' seems to carry victory as the source of all truths.

Everyone can seek his or her private salvation. Yet the old veneer and dignity of truth could still be maintained in the congregation of happy and unhappy hermeneuticians if the ransacking of the tradition were limited to the works, images, concepts, ideas, etc. that were recognized in their own times as major representations of Truth. But there is no such self-restriction and there cannot be. The whole of the past became Wonderland, and the more out of pattern something seems to be, the 'curiouser and curiouser' men and women like Alice will become to figure something out.[53] After all, the treasure can be found in the most remote corner of the house called history; and only a treasure that has not been found by anyone else prior to us can become our private treasure which might attract, at least for a while, a considerable entourage of worshippers.

Happy and unhappy hermeneuticians decipher the hieroglyphs of history, seeking many a different thing, such as good fun, mental exercise, satisfying jobs – or salvation – salvation not from sin, but from contingency. But whatever they seek for, they contribute, wittingly-unwittingly, to the 'thinning out' of the sphere of absolute spirit. This is not the hermeneuticians' 'fault' – the spirit of our congregation is a fraudulent imp.

Not such a very long time ago, hermeneutics brought the good news that it can build a bridge between our world (consciousness, language, text) and the Other. Although the conversations with a practically infinite number of significant and insignificant 'others' go on unabated, yet the more such bridges are built, the more we became (or remain) captive in the prisonhouse of historicity. Building those bridges is exactly what the spirit of our congregation (and not of the congregations of all those others we play bridge with) dictates. The old correspondence theory of Truth, the pride of early modernism, became marginalized in art, and it is about to lose ground in most theoretical endeavours, not only in philosophy. *Irony* begins to underscore all speculative and theoretical forms and modes.[54]

Awareness of our contingency, formal freedom and the consciousness of historical consciousness are the main constituents of the spirit
of our congregation. This spirit is absolute insofar as it is omnipresent: in the subject and his/her world, in institutions and in cultural
practices. There is no escape. The small sub-spheres can still defend
their – relative – independence. For example, one cannot survive in
everyday life without remaining true to the correspondence theory,
not of 'truth', but of true knowledge. If the cat is not on the mat, it
does matter whether someone says that it is, or that it is not. The
awareness of the limits of interpretation are as vital as interpretation
itself.[55]

The Unhappy Hermeneuticians are those who are unhappy in their
dearly won freedom, although they do not want to forego this freedom. What they want is to use this freedom not formally, but sub-
stantively. They want to challenge, they do challenge the spirit of our
congregation itself. Instead of indulging in the fine exercise of philosophy of culture, they yearn for philosophy of the old kind – the
Presocratic, the Socratic, the Platonic, the Aristotelian kind. They
yearn to ask the question 'what is this?' directly, bravely, without
footnotes. They want the 'real' thing, instead of the simulacrum. They
want to read the hieroglyphs of the divine text, not of the text of a
text of a text written by a minor commentarist of Kant. They yearn
for metaphysics. The more modest ones want to communicate their
own life experiences in conceptual speculation, without donning the
costume of a dead man to serve as a 'bridge' to the present. They do
not want to remain the interpreters of the past. Certainly, they know
that they should not lie; they hear the whispers of the spirit of our
congregation. This spirit cannot be betrayed; more precisely, to betray
this spirit is self-defeating. In an absolute sense it is also impossible.
But this absolute sense cannot be absolutely explored. Our absolute
spirit is not transparent. One can try the impossible, because one does
not know whether it is impossible in an absolute sense.

In one of the scenes in Kafka's novel, *The Trial*, a mysterious priest
tells the story of a man who yearned for admittance before the Law.
So he went upwards, till he arrived at the walls of the Heavenly region
and noticed a gate in the fortification. So he went there and sat down
to wait. Before the door, there stood the doorman watching him.
After a long wait, he turned to the doorman and asked him for
admittance. He was told to wait. So he waited and waited till he
returned to the doorman again and asked about the conditions of
admittance. The doorman asked him again to wait. To cut a long
(and beautiful) story short, after waiting on and on and on the man

despaired, for he realized that he would die without ever being admitted before the Law. Sorry, the doorman said, closing down the gate and leaving himself, for this gate was destined only for you.

What can a philosopher do in the age of universal hermeneutics? To keep banging at the door of the prisonhouse of historicity.

7

On the Railway Station

1 On the Railway Station

Many people made their home on railway stations and still do. Hippies liked to live there in the sixties and seventies, and, regardless of whether or not they like it, the poor and the homeless live there today – from New York to Bombay – they have no other option. For these people, railway stations are still temporary lodgings. However, the metaphorical railway station, where the denizens of our world just begin to settle in, is no longer a temporary lodging. One settles in there for a lifetime.

For Hegel, the present was the terminus of history. This terminus was like a port. After several thousand years of sailing, the boat of history has finally returned home. Arriving at Descartes in his history of philosophy, Hegel ruminates that we are like sailors who shout 'land!' when we recognize the well-known shores – we have finally returned. Hegel's vision of the voyage culminates in the moment of 'returning', like the vision of Odysseus or that of Beethoven's sonata *Les Adieux*.[1]

It was in the year of Hegel's death that the railway was born. The nineteenth and most of the twentieth centuries stood under its spell. It is the train and the railway station that, consciously or unconsciously, begin to dominate historical imagination. The physical railway and the metaphysical railway are fused in the images of social phantasy. Impregnated by this vision, even the traditional seafarer phantasy is less and less linked with the desire to return. In Baudelaire's *Invitation au Voyage* one sails towards the alien, the unknown but paradisiacal destination. The novelty of the train/locomotive phantasy is exemplified by the reception of Turner's painting, *The Great Western Railway*. In 1844, most of the critics complained that it was very difficult to identify the thing on the painting as a train. A decade later this would have been obvious for every ten-year-old kid living in any big city of Europe.[2]

The train moves ahead; history, too, is supposed to move ahead. The train moves ahead on tracks, from station to station. History, so it is widely believed, has its inherent laws, and it cannot move ahead but by following these laws, from one future station to another. Certain passengers climb the train, others get off. Passengers change, but the train keeps going or rather running. Whoever is on the train will be carried to the pre-set, known or unknown, destination. We know the future stations and destinations of our journey if we are familiar with the train schedule; the same holds true of history. The schedule of the train of history needs to be scientifically established. The train is pulled by a locomotive; so is history. The more powerful the locomotive, the faster the train; the same is true of history. Sometimes, history is identified with the locomotive itself. The locomotive is handled by machinists; history also needs machinists, who know how to feed progress, so that its speed continues to accelerate.

All the major railway stations of London were constructed or substantially rebuilt at the very time Karl Marx was working on his *magnum opus*, withdrawn in his modest lodgings: King's Cross in 1851–2, Paddington in 1854, Victoria Station in 1861, Charing Cross in 1866, St Pancras in 1868.[3] Not necessarily the physical train, but rather the phantasy-field that emerged therefrom, that is, the image of the metaphysical train and the metaphysical railway station, must have exerted a deep influence on the historical imagination of this eminent German emigrant. What happened to Napoleon also happened to the train. From the mid-nineteenth century onwards, and increasingly so, images of the train, the railway, the locomotive, the railway station, the tracks, the viaduct, the tunnel, and the train trip itself became objects of dreams as carriers and manifestations of unconscious wishes and desires.

It is still the train phantasy that dominates the nightmares of the heroine of *The White Hotel*.[4] But here the meaning of the train metaphor has already become confused, because the grand voyage, as Semprun called it, the grand train voyage that the heroine of the novel could not yet place, turned out to be the trip toward the destination 'Man-Made Hell'. It is a railway station that serves as the metaphor of the Holocaust: the railway station of Auschwitz. The very real people, though unreal passengers of real trains, are carried by the locomotive of historical progression to their final destination, code-named the final solution. Auschwitz destroys the dominating images of the train as the vehicle of history by realizing one of these images. Here is a journey towards the unknown, the itinerary of which is known by the planners, not by the passengers, here is the place from which there is no return, here is the end as the absolute future.

After having reflected, though never seriously enough, on this journey, and also on that other trip which carried men and women to the remote arctic regions of Siberia, the islands of the Gulag, our generation became reluctant to jump again on those historical fast trains. This is how the denizens of the modern world came to realize that it is better for them to settle in, in one way or another, on the well-known railway station of the present.

The railway stations, and particularly the head-and-terminus stations of the nineteenth and the first half of the twentieth centuries, were characterized by the stark contrast between the functionalist arrangement of the building complex and the magnificent facade. Before the nineteenth century, the facade was just the over-emphasized aspect of the exterior of a building, be it a church, a town hall or a palace. Palaces sometimes harboured hideous dungeons, but the palace's exterior was not the facade of those dungeons. Representation matched the represented lifestyle. There may be some doubt about this in our mind in case of certain representative bank buildings (e.g. The Bank of England), but there was none in the contemporary bankers' mind. They saw themselves as princes of their age, and they indeed became new princes. At the other end, in a lawless port city, the port appeared what it indeed was: colourful, dangerous, busy and dirty. What 'was there' became visible; the belly of the institution was turned inside out. The (dialectical) unity of the internal and the external was, in the main, taken for granted. Hegel, indeed, lived before the construction of the first railway stations.

The discrepancy, moreover, the contrast between the internal and external can be latent or explicit. Nowhere is it so explicit as in the case of railway stations, not even in the food-market buildings. The facades of railway stations suggest magnificence. The first Euston station is classicist; it promises the inside of a Greek temple. However, most of the facades are romantic or romantic-eclectic in style – they look like palaces. The clock on the Railway Tower associates it with the church-tower. But he who enters a railway station finds himself in an entirely different world. What the facade covers is otherness: the otherness of the world of function and of the machine. It is the factory belly that no one can escape, for everyone has to enter.

The facade of the nineteenth-century railway station is an architectural phantasy constructed from some beautiful elements taken from the world of the dead. What this facade covers is disorder, disharmony and ugliness, but something that is very much alive. (By contrast, on the terminal station of Auschwitz, where the train of our century's history was heading, the facade was the semblance of life that concealed death by murder.)

The architectural phantasy of the facade does not call for poetic embellishment; only the inside, the hidden belly of the station does. The complexity of the visual suggestiveness of the interior of a railway building can best be exemplified by Monet's series of paintings of the ancient Gare Saint-Lazare.[5] The locomotive and its smoke dominate these paintings. The liveliness originates from the locomotives, be they stationary or just entering from afar. People are also there, but they are painted in masses. Single individuals are not made to stand out in their singularity, not even as miniature figures, as they usually are in Monet's other city-paintings, for example the paintings of Saint-Germain-L'Auxerrois and the Boulevard des Capucines. It is the darkness of the station and the smoke that fuse single persons into undetermined masses. But something else, something much deeper, appears through this seemingly technical consideration. People on the station are contingent. They do not belong to the station either as individuals or as members of a social class. They just happen to be there because the trains are there. Tomorrow others will be there. People on the railway station are undetermined, undefined, they are non-persons. It is this indeterminacy, this contingency of their presence that moulds men and women into dark and undistinguishable masses in this railway station. The trains, the rails, the locomotives are the real heroes; they, particularly the locomotives, are the individuals. They are the ones who stand out. The locomotives are not contingent, they belong to the railway station by necessity. The railway station is their home and their life-breath, the smoke, fills it. A one-eyed locomotive, an iron Cyclops, dominates Monet's most powerful railway painting from 1877. Though a man happens to be in the foreground, he remains just an enlarged blot, whereas the massive machine-hero stands out clearly and distinctly, resembling a sad, tired, but unconquerable Working Man. The nineteenth-century myth of the proletariat is also tied to the imaginary institution of the railway station.

The railway station is located in the city. It mediates between the city and the railway, between the traditional and the novel, between *topos* and *eutopos*, between the past and the future. The facade turns towards the tradition, the past and the habitat. Eclectic borrowing from ancient architectural motives and quotations from old styles belong to its typical features. Many railway facades face a main square like a church would. Others tower over all other buildings at the end of a wide avenue; they inhale the city air and they exhale it. But the interior structures of the railway stations turn towards the novel, the unknown, the future. Vis-à-vis the facade there are the flaneurs, men and women take their time. Men use their walking sticks, they are at leisure. The closer one gets to the entrance, the less the facade can be seen, the greater becomes the speed. The forms vanish and people become encapsulated by Time. One can miss something forever if one is just one minute late, so one cannot afford to be late; one needs to elbow oneself through the crowd. One looks for the porter, one shouts; here are the suitcases, one cannot leave one's habitat naked so one carries into the future a suitcaseful of tradition and manages to also squeeze in one's personal history. The conductor blows the whistle, the engines start, you catch the rail and jump. You believe that you have finally caught the train, but it was the train that has caught you, carrying you away towards unknown destinations.

The railway station mediate between the past and the future; it encapsulates the absolute present. Men and women on the platform are already standing outside the tradition. But they are still dwelling on the soil of the city, they have not yet left, they could still stay and return. But returning, the great dream of the seafarer, is not the dream of the train-passenger; his absolute present is the moment of departure. The moderns, Faust, Rubempré, Peer Gynt, all dream of departure. If they return, which they still might, they return as failures; alternatively, they can bid farewell to the dream of the great railway of progress.

There have been only a few big port-cities; good waterways are rare. But all cities, be they located on the top of a hill, in the desert or in a fertile valley, can have their representative railway stations. The artifice sets itself free from nature; the track, the viaduct, the tunnel criss-crossing the map of the continents. Every state, nation, city can become historical. The facades of the great railway stations might also mirror the ambitions of states and nations. Not only individuals try to catch the metaphorical rapid trains of modern history – nations and states do likewise.

The dominating metaphors of the seaport, the railway station and the airport stand for the stages of the development of modern consciousness. As metaphors, they poeticize or demonize the actual seaports, railway stations and airports as the sources of imagination. The metaphoric seaport is associated with the sailboat. The early steamer still fits into the picture, yet none of the contemporary floating vehicles does. The sea-voyage is now 'privatized': it became associated with sport or luxury, but not with history. The railway-phantasy surrounds the steam-driven locomotive; the motor car does not evoke fear and attraction as did the iron monster that once carried the weight of historical imagination. The airport started at the point where the seaport ended. The grassy spot where small planes took off and landed fed the private rather than the historical imagination, whereas war-planes were a part of history in such a direct sense that they were prevented from becoming metaphors for history. The international jet-airports and the big passenger carrier planes became, finally, the late heirs to the legendary harbours and sailboats; as if modern historical consciousness had returned to the once forceful image of returning home.   ·

The one-eyed monster of the Monet painting is gigantic; he looks strong, powerful, dirty and tired. I said 'he', for the locomotive is of the male sex. As I pointed out, he reminds us of a working man; he is the machine version of the machinist who feeds him. He carries no person in his underbelly, his load is his own food: coal. Nothing reminds us of a sailboat here. The sailboat is a woman, a mother, a wife or whore. She carries all the sailors in her body. She is white even when dirty; she is protective even when miserable. They curse her, but they love her. Finally, the plane is a hermaphrodite, or rather a sexless bird, a steel albatross, elegant from afar in its rapid flight, but clumsy on the earth, like a minor ship in the docks. The early moderns dwell in their histories, the moderns are running after History, whereas the post-moderns are the voyeurs both of History (with a capital H), and of the histories of a colourful past.

The boat is not a vehicle but a habitat. It is the home of the captain and the crew; it is also the shelter of all passengers, an island of relative security. He who embarks on the boat subscribes to the law of the sea. The ship is a city where there is contract, yet also command and obedience. People sharing a boat trip get to know each others' character through everyday encounters and also in borderline situations. Their private stories are woven into the fibres of a common experience. Shared history, collective history, is at once the history of each.   ·

The typical model of a metaphorical boat-voyage can be described in the following sequence: (1) departure: one leaves the firm land under one's feet to discover unknown worlds, to get rich and to return; (2) establishing a new community on the boat; conflicts, maybe also disaster, but finally deliverance; (3) discovery of new lands and people, thereby the satisfaction of the needs of curiosity and hunger for wealth and power; (4) return – the end of the cycle. For it is a cyclical concept of history that dominates in the metaphysical seaport. Each trip is an adventure, a history on its own.

There are many trips, with their own conflicts and adventures, thus there are also many histories. But no Universal History makes its appearance. On the level of generality it is still Space, and not Time, that holds sway. The Other is divided from us by the Ocean in space, not by the Ocean of Time. This is why the seafarer can return to his absolute present, to the harbour, to the seaport which has remained almost the same, though he – and his travelling fellows – had changed. The latter aspect underlines the novelty of the early modern cyclical vision of history. Every trip is a new experience, a new history that changes everyone who lives it. If a boat encounters Sirens, their song will be heard also by the passengers and the crew, and not only by a mythological captain, who, unlike Odysseus, will not keep the experience – and the temptation – just for himself.

The metaphysics of the railway is the metaphysics of linear history. The locomotive pulls the train ahead, always ahead, on the rails of history. The train knows no obstacles. The sea is irrelevant, given that in the nineteenth century, 'universal' history means 'European' history. The passengers do not matter much in this vision. They are the dark shades crowded on stations, the cacophony of indistinguishable sounds of human and non-human origin. Only the sinister and impersonal voice of the loudspeaker and the noise of the locomotive, spitting its steam, remain distinct. The passengers are isolated in carriages and compartments. They can sit there throughout the voyage without ever exchanging a single word. The passengers' co-operation is not needed. As far as the success of the trip is concerned, they are irrelevant entities. It is only speed, the business of the machinist, and the destination towards which the train is heading that matter, yet the passengers do not matter at all. There is the total absence of any connecting line between the passengers' action, ethos or communication on the one hand, and the speed of the train, the success of the trip on the other. There is the total isolation, atomization of the passengers, who have abandoned themselves to an Iron Monster and its merely mechanical powers, and let themselves be carried wherever the tracks are heading.

The airport is separated from the city, even from its outskirts. It is extra-territorial, rather than extra-temporal. Though airport buildings, even more than railway stations, are divided into exterior and interior complexes, there is no contrast between the two. Airport buildings are eminently functional, they have no facade. They do not need one, for they do not link the image of a rapidly progressing linear history to an urban tradition. Modern railway stations or bus stations look like airports, too. Architecture follows the change of a historical imagination where railway stations are no longer protagonists.

The vision of the plane is fixed upon ascending and descending. The plane ascends from where we are, but it descends somewhere else. This is a dual spatial vision: up and down, here and there. The second spatial move (here and there) may remind us of old sail-boat cruises. But 'coming home', returning, that is, the cyclical vision of history does not play an eminent role in the imaginary institution of airports. Given the short duration of a flight, no community is forged among passengers, captain and crew. (A disaster of considerable duration where the stamina, courage and honesty of crew and passengers are tested is a 'boat-story', even if it happens on a plane. The language used, for example, the expression 'air-pirates', is apposite.) Although passengers do not play a greater role in the air-journey imagination than in the rail-journey imagination, they are not subjected to the imaginary historical necessity, but to the necessity of the laws of nature. Rail-phantasy is history-centric, air phantasy is *geocentric*. The passenger is no longer related to his city, land, country, to his historical habitat, but to the earth in general, to his or her geological habitat. Not even the re-temporalization of the air-journey image through the rocket-spaceship-space-journey phantasy has anything to do with the metaphor of universal history. The past and the future of science fiction are eminently a-historical. The cyclical model can here play some role; the return of the spaceship (again, a ship!) is the culmination of the drama. But the spaceship returns to the Earth, to the geological habitat of homo sapiens in general, and not to a particular home. Tradition, this hallmark of historical phantasy, is totally absent; behind the operations of all the desensitized mechanical artifacts, the natural reality and solidity of Mother Earth stands out in her full majesty.

The railway station, a link between the city and the journey, the tradition and the future, is the metaphor of the absolute present. To speak in the spirit of this metaphor, living in the railway station is the resolve to live in the present.

Resolve is a choice; the resolve to live in the present is equally a choice. In the absence of historical consciousness, one can live in the present without choosing it. But then, one does not live historically, or rather, one's historical existence remains (or becomes) unconscious. Ever since historical existence became a matter of reflection, the philosopher's scorn turned against the man who lived only in the present, and justly so. Living in the present unconsciously is a pre-reflective attitude. However, living in the present by choice is post-reflective. Such a choice can only be made when people have already developed an elaborate historical consciousness.

Since historical consciousness is the central imaginary institution of the spirit of the modern congregation, moderns perceive their present as a kind of railway station. There were many railway stations, that is, cultures, in the past, and there will be many again in the future. As long as this consciousness prevails, modernity also prevails. As long as modernity prevails, we are going to live on the – metaphorical – railway station. But to this life, and to this consciousness, one can develop very different attitudes. One can insist that our railway station is a very special one, because it is from the belfry of this station that we can come to know all previous stations and also all future ones. One can also pay attention to the fast trains which stop – if they stop at all – on our railway station only for a few minutes. This state of mind gives rise to the desire that one should not remain on this station, rather the whole station should board the train in order to run with express speed towards the future. Caught by this spirit, liberals promised infinite progression, Marxists a de-alienated society and, together with many other moderns, also paradise on earth. But after it turned out that these famous trains could be manipulated by devilish machinists and that the locomotive of history can come to a halt in a terminus called Auschwitz and the Gulag, the self-complacency of the nineteenth century was lost. The alternative grand narrative of the modern age, that of decadence and decay, seemed to be thus corroborated. Our railway station will be then abused as the worst of all cultures, and life without or prior to railway stations, that is, pre-modern life, will be idolized. At the same time, it will be forgotten that our railway station can be rejected only from the platform of this railway station. The attitude is deeply inauthentic. The believer in infinite progression and the man-made paradise on earth on the one hand, and the romantic modernity-basher on the other, do the same thing. They continue to live in the railway station of the present, for they cannot help doing so. They live there, yet they prefer living somewhere else; they turn away from the 'here and now' in order to turn toward the other railway stations of which we know next to nothing.

People who choose the life in the railway station choose their present – we can indeed choose our present. In opting for the present, one does not say that this is the best possible world. Surely, one does not say that this is the worse possible world either. What one says first and foremost is as follows. This is our world. It is into this world (this railway station) that I have been thrown by accident; I will conduct my life here, and in this, I have no choice. I can re-choose, however, what I do anyway, or, alternatively, I can choose something that I am incapable of doing, namely to live somewhere else. On the level of the absolute spirit, one can certainly live somewhere else. Absolute spirit also transfigures the railway stations of the past, the present and the future, but it cannot modify the radius of action of those people who are living in this particular, and not in another, railway station. One acts with responsibility within the sphere of one's radius of action. The radius of action of present actors reaches back to the past of the present, and certainly ahead, to the future of the present. But the past of the present and the future of the present are the past and the future of our own railway station, and they have very little to do with those stations in ruins, nor with those not yet built.

The historical consciousness of reflected generality (which can also be termed the post-modern historical consciousness) transforms the spatial analogy of time from the previous metaphors such as lines, trees and spirals into a field resembling a map zig-zagged by railway lines. There are many stations on the map, some we see, others we just surmise. We also know that new stations will also join this republic of all railway stations. The republic of all railway stations makes up the human condition that is the human world.

Each railway station of the human world is different from the rest, although the historian will point out that there are styles here, too. There are continuous railway lines, but also lines which end up nowhere. And although the republic of railway stations is mentioned here, the conclusion need not be drawn that all those stations (known or unknown, past and future) are of the same grandeur or worth. Where we notice lines on the map, we invariably deal with railway stations and with trains, carrying their constantly changing passengers from one particular point of departure to a terminus, where some experience accumulated en route is going to be preserved. One cannot figure out a system on this map. This is the riddle of history which cannot be solved, perhaps because there is no such riddle, just sheer contingency, or perhaps because some intelligence gave up the riddle, wanting it to remain unresolved.

The choice to live in the railway station is not determined by the recognition that history is not linear, progressive or regressive, or, for that matter, spiral-like, that no model of universal regularity can describe what history is, that a funny and always incomplete railway map would do a better job. The resolve to live in the railway station of the present is an original move. But the two together (the new spatial representation of forms of life and cultures on the one hand, and the choice to live in our railway station on the other) are manifestations of the shift in the spirit of our congregation. So, we, men and women of the post-modern era, settle down in the railway station of the present. We can make it liveable; we can also transform it into a hell. Our contemporaries who choose themselves under the category of the universal, make the railway station more liveable by virtue of their choice alone.

When one receives a present on one's birthday, one can accept it with grace. One can also get angry, because one expected something bigger, more expensive, more representative. But begrudging the present does not help, it rather spoils the pleasure and enjoyment drawn from the present that one actually received. But the stupidest of all things is to smash our birthday present out of rage because our expectations have been betrayed. The present is the birthday present that all denizens of our culture have received. There can be more beautiful, broader, lighter, richer, safer railway stations. It is just that this station happens to be ours.

2 World, Things, Life and Home

Arendt's book *The Human Condition*, can also be read as an historical narrative. If read in this way, it becomes a kind of *Verfallsgeschichte*. Each of the three main forms of *vita activa*, that is action, work and labour, have dominated, one after the other, the three major periods of European history: action was the the highest form of active life for the ancients, whereas the worth of work stood highest for the early moderns; in the contemporary modern world, again, labour became the dominating type of human activity. Labour, as the activity of mere reproduction, is necessary for survival, whereas work, and especially action, are luxuries. Luxury is not that what is above necessity in terms of consumption, but what is above the sphere of necessity in general; put bluntly, the acts of freedom are such luxuries. Political action is free, insofar as it is absolute initiative and brings forth something entirely new for its own sake, work is free insofar as it immortalizes action and brings about a world that endures, yet labour is preeminently unfree.[6]

If read as a narrative, Arendt's story is the reversal of the Hegelian; European history is not about the successive extension of freedom in the world, but about the successive elimination of freedom from the world. But these two stories can also be seen as complimentary. For Hegel, 'maximum possible freedom' in the world is tantamount to maximum possible freedom for all'. Hegel describes the modern world in these terms; the modern world offers the best (optimal and maximal) conditions for the free activity of all, yet by no means the best conditions for the intensive (or absolute) free activity of the few.

Whenever Hegel speaks about free activity in Arendt's sense, he unhesitatingly describes its demise. *Ex nihilo* initiative in action requires that a few should stand above the others owing no (institutional) responsibility to anyone but themselves.[7] If one read Hegel's and Arendt's narratives together, one could come to the conclusion that if it were possible to compare the 'amount' of freedom in representative periods of European history, the result would be that it remained the same, but was allocated in different ways. For example, freedom can be intensive, but allocated to a few, or extensive and allocated to all. Yet this would be true only about *vita activa* in Arendt's sense. At any rate, freedom cannot be quantified.

Hegel would object to the dissociation of political (or social) freedom from the freedom of the soul which consists in beholding the absolute spirit and acts performed towards that spirit. Arendt would object to counting the conditions of freedom as freedom, for these conditions can also remained unused. Moreover, the principle of representation and the representative government, which for Hegel are the most fundamental political conditions of freedom, stand for just the opposite in Arendt. They are the conditions of the demise and of the disappearance of political action and of the true republican spirit.

Hegel's position looks more sound. Once the conditions of the freedom for all have been established, the possibility of maximum freedom exists also. Moreover: the possibility of maximum freedom is absent under any other conditions. If we read Arendt's book as a typology of human activities and not as a *Verfallsgeschichte*, we could add, in her spirit, that since political actions cannot be explained by the principle of sufficient cause, all kinds of free initiatives can be taken in the modern world too – moderns can 'begin' no less than the ancients could.

Yet there is an issue on which Arendt and Hegel always speak in unison. Neither Hegel nor, more than one and a half centuries later, Arendt, seem to believe in the world-creating capacity of moderns. Arendt can invest her hope in the rebirth of the republican spirit, and she actually does, but there are no signs that she would have had much hope in the rebirth of the grandeur of the second greatest of all free human activities, that of the World-Creating Work. In Hegel's vision the world is now ready. It does not externalize anything else but its own conditions; it internalizes, that is, it recollects/remembers. Our world contains all the past worlds that it recollects/remembers; creative imagination turns towards the past.

This astonishing coincidence makes us think about the world. What does it mean to have a world? What does it mean to create a world? Do the moderns have a world? Do they still create a world?

When we begin to think about the world we think first of the world in which we have been thrown by the accident of our birth. Bodies surround us; some have faces, some not; some talk to each other and us, the others not. The world consists of men and things; different men and women, different things. Men and women do something with each other and with these things, they do things repeatedly. These are the customs that we must learn. Language helps us discover what action goes with what other action, with this or the other thing, and sometimes also why. Things began to make sense. The more we can do what we are supposed to, the more familiar things become, the more familiar things become, the more we are supposed to do exactly the things we are doing.

World (*mundus*) is the spatial equivalent of history, or rather history (including mythological historical narratives) is the temporal equivalent of world. World and history are our parameters. Human groups locate themselves in the world-space as well as in the history-time of their genesis. Time comprises past-present-future. Similarly, there is a world 'here' and another world 'there'. 'Our world' is different from 'theirs', and, at least since recently, 'my world' is also different from 'yours'. Both in our world and in theirs, 'this world' is juxtaposed to 'the other world' – the world of the living to the world of the dead, the world of the heroes to the world of the gods, the dwarfs and the giants. In Christian vocabulary, 'worldliness' denotes activities and interests vested in the 'lower' world, this world, instead of another, higher, spiritual one.

Our world (as contrasted to 'their world') is like the present time; hence the expression 'hic et nuno'. It is from the vantage point of our world that one distinguishes between worlds that are located on the same level as ours and those located on a lower or a higher level. Similarly, it is from the vantage point of 'this world' that one locates the 'other' worlds either above us or below us – like Heaven and Hell.

All these worlds together are 'the world' people normally know about, but not the world people know. Throughout life, one learns many things about the world, but even more remains unknown. Old men and women were once considered wise because they experienced much in their own world, and heard many a thing also about the worlds of others.

The distinction Kant made between 'having a world' and 'knowing the world'[8] is relevant on all levels of being-in-a-world. Knowing the world requires the attitude of the spectator. Yet only actors have a world. Their world extends as far as their actions, or, perhaps, as far as the results of their actions reach. Everyday knowledge encompasses much, far beyond the scope of everyday activity. Yet it is only in and through everyday activity that one has an everyday world. Similarly, one can know many a political institution one does not have. Yet the centre point of one's world is the world one does have.

One can have one's own world (our world) whereas one normally does not have 'their world'. On the contrary, the distinction between 'this world' and 'that world' cuts across the above dividing line. We have *both* this world and that world, given that all our symbolic actions are performed towards 'other world(s)' – be it the tree where the ancestors' spirits dwell or the highest sphere of the Hegelian Absolute Spirit. The differentiation of this world and the other world is the precondition of having a world at all. Without symbolic action, no action is possible, there is no meaning, no sense, no human life.

Human life is life-in-*a*-world, and not life in-*the*-world. One can know about 'the' world and one can learn many things about it – but one does not have it. But the world that one has can expand, a person can even have more 'worlds' than one, though not too many, and certainly not all of them.

Our own world is called Home. Having a world begins at home. Expanding the world one already has is to expand home. Home is the centrepoint of life, for one has a world at home.

The world that is ours is not their world, it differs from it. It is our home and not theirs; it is we who have it. We can know their world – but we cannot have it.

Men and women are born into *a* world, not into *the* world. Their world is already here; it stands; it awaits the newborn, it invites them, it works harshly upon them so that they should be able and ready to have it. The members of the adult generation are the representatives of this world, for they have it, although they are not identical with the world they have. The world is present (*hic et nunc*) in the objectivations which had been left behind by many previous generations: in their language, in their customs and in their things.

Arendt remarked that only people who leave behind *things* that endure, ever had a world. But every world leaves something behind, though not every world cherishes the ambition to immortalize itself. People can create things for their successors without caring for anything else beyond. The tree they plant can grow very old and in its shade many generations can find relief – they have a world without reflecting on it. But statues of gods, pyramids, temples, churches, castles and sacred writings differ from such trees. They are created as the significant things of a world to immortalize the significant persons of the world together with all that they believe in and so the world they have. Significant persons are mortals even if they strive for immortality. But significant things are immortal, or at least, they are conceived of as immortal after the first stirrings of conscious historicity. Deeply touched by the mysterious greatness of the temple of Karnak, Germanicus once pondered that if a people that created these wonders succumbed to mortality, the same fate can await Rome also. When in the jungle of Guayana the ruins of a magnificent Maya temple emerge before our eyes, we feel the same way. Significant things of a bygone world arouse the feeling of mortality precisely through their immortality. This is how they keep resurrecting the significant persons whose world that world had once been.

Significant things are but the tip of an iceberg. The utensils and the dresses, the household wares and the toys, the vehicles and all those artifacts that have recently been so diligently collected and placed in museums by anthropologists, fill the space of each and every world. As a *topos*, as a place, a world needs to be filled. There is a thing everywhere. Things belong to the place as well as they can also be out-of-place. Things are used, worshipped, applied, cherished, feared, improved, destroyed – thousands of different things are done with all those things. Our world is filled with things different from yours. What is in place here, is out of place in yours.

Human life is life-in-a-world. Life-in-a-world is life amidst things, or rather, a life with things that are used, worshipped, cherished etc. according to customs, in the language of the ancestors and of the generations to come.

A world is here to stay; a home is here to stay; the middle of the circle remains the middle of the circle. A culture lives in its own 'here' that expands beyond its own horizons.

One can hardly put the question of whether modern men and women have a world seriously. Had they none, they could not live. Another question needs to be raised instead: what kind is the world that modern men and women have?

History was said to be the temporal equivalent of the world. Apart from junctures and cataclysms, history – before our times – just reinforced the endurance of the constantly present 'here'. But since History writ large, that is, modern historical consciousness, entered a World, this world has lost its stability. Space is now going to be temporalized and Time is going to be spatialized. The new historical consciousness strongly reinforces the kind of historical intuition that once gave rise to the well-known gloomy premonition in young Germanicus' mind, but with hindsight. Once captured by the spirit of History writ large, men and women will not be grasped by terror at the sight of the spectre of the eventual doom of their own world. They might also warmly welcome their world's coming demise. For the conviction that our world is here to stay is gone; on the contrary, the conviction that our world is bound to vanish, and that it should rather vanish, have spread. Nothing spatializes Time more than the vision of the March of History, or the more general conception of steady progression (or regression). History is the Time that is supposed to move forwards or backwards.

Modernity relativized the *hic et nunc*. In the perception of the moderns, this time is not the kind of present time where we stay, but a present from which we pass into another, and yet another. Simultaneously, the belief became widely accepted that there is, or at least there should be, just one single world instead of many, a kind of universal mankind where the difference between 'our world' and 'theirs' will, or must, disappear for good. Finally, attempts were made to annul the juxtaposition of 'this world', and the 'other world': God and metaphysics should be thus dethroned. It remained sometimes unnoticed that one cannot have a world at all without the distinction between this world and that world, ours and theirs. An undifferentiated world is not a world, for one cannot look at this world from the perspective of another one.

Whenever one has a world that is supposed to stay, and that one juxtaposes to 'their' worlds, one has a home; a home is first and foremost a dwelling place. The dwelling place is a constant, although it changes, whereas the inhabitants are variable, for they come and go while the dwelling place remains. All other things that fill the place, used according to customs, are also constants. They belong to the space, such as musical instruments, weapons, footwear or ceremonial tools.

In the modern world, by contrast, things come and go faster than men and women grow. A watch was still a family heirloom a century ago; grandsons inherited it from their ancestors. Today, one buys a new watch every year. Furthermore, the dwelling place also became a thing among other things. Moreover, it is not the things-that-fill-their-world that people have, but general or Universal Things that are supposed to perform the same (universal) Function. One always picks new things and throws out the old ones, supposing that they perform the same or a similar function. The modern world is the cemetery of things that had been used but not used up, just replaced and thrown away.

Any thing that represents for the time being the Universal Thing (with a similar function), can be carried along, wherever we go, for two interconnected, reasons. First, because such things are not of the kind that fill a concrete world (our world), second, because the self-same things are used in all worlds, that is, in the Universal World.

Where the International of men failed, the International of Things carried victory.

The famous Bauhaus, this pride of modern architecture, symbolizes the demise of the dwelling place. It was in the Bauhaus that the idea of functionalism at its best and usefulness was implemented. The habitat was supposed to be a place where everything is at hand, where people can live comfortably and relatively cheaply, in a limited space. After a half of a century, the Bauhaus buildings strike us as spiritless, drab and grey. They are the typical transit stations of a homeless generation. And what happened since is even worse. Matchboxes of five prototypes are being built and squeezed upon one another. 'To each urban dweller their matchbox' is the slogan, so that they can all hide their private affairs in such a small abode which lacks even the spark of beauty. One has built houses from which one knew ahead that they are going to stay for fifty years and no longer; for the poor because it costs less, for the rich, because fashion changes fast.

It seems as if Arendt's fears would be confirmed – Labour had been substituted for Work. But if we think of it, all the things that fill our world and all the universal Things that fill all the contemporary worlds, are the offsprings of imagination of sorts, namely of technological imagination. Technological imagination is productive and creative (after all, what Arendt calls Work is also the technological imagination in practice). The reason why technological imagination results in the cult of Labour rather than the cult of Work cannot be explained by technological imagination alone. Furthermore, although technological development requires technological imagination, or, in reverse, technological imagination promotes technological development, the domination of one kind of imagination does not need to be taken for granted, especially not in a pluralistic universe. After all, one can choose a fridge functionally, without choosing a lodging functionally, one can use up a system of telecommunications and replace it with a newer and more efficient brand, without doing the same with a citysquare. What has happened yesterday does not need to happen today also.

And what actually happened yesterday was rather interesting. The more Labour (in the Arendtian sense) began to dominate future-oriented phantasy, the more Work began to dominate past-oriented phantasy. As a result, technological imagination expanded in two different directions. On the one hand, the newest was considered always the better or the best, be it a poem, a work of philosophy, a building or a scientific discovery, on the other hand the oldest got the preferential treatment. Archeological zeal is nothing but the reverse side of innovative zeal. As long as everything that is old has a patina

On the Railway Station · 233

due to its oldness, the fusion of History and World, the spatialization of time and the temporalization of the space is still rampant. And this belongs to the core of technological imagination.

Had technological imagination drawn its strength and appeal from the modern technological/scientific development alone, it could not in all probability, have attained to the status of the model of universal rationality. Yet the patterns of modern, *functional* stratification reinforce technological imagination and so does the recently won freedom of making experiments in state-craft, of inventing a great variety of stateforms and of following the political rules suggested by *raison d'état*.[9] Technological imagination was the fountainhead of all the things and acts that can perform a universal function. So it stood for Rationality. Mainstream philosophers actually identified technological imagination and rationality. Their opponents who dismissed technological imagination, or at least refused to grant the royal crown of supreme rationality to it, were seeking for a relevant and strong competitor. The most successful competitor of *Techné* for such a strategic position is *Logos*, this time interpreted as the kind of Rationality that dwells in Language and Speech.

Language, understood as supreme Rationality, is not the mother tongue of poetry and of everyday communication, but Language as such; it is not the language of *a* world, but the language of *the* world, a kind of odd international/cosmopolitan tongue. It seemed as if only absolute universalism could beat the other absolute universalism. Yet this well-considered philosophical gambit runs into a serious difficulty.

Technological imagination can attain to empirical universality for three reasons. First, the things that technology produces are the things which, among other things, can fill all possible home- spaces, as well as they can occupy the place of the home-space itself. Second, a major inspiration and also a fundamental training ground of technological imagination, functional stratification (one of the main features of modernity) became already widespread all around the world. Third, even if not one single concrete form of a state is empirically universal, the technological experience in crafting states is. Trust in the makability of the world feeds on technological imagination and vice versa; so does *raison d'état*. Entirely different states can be crafted, such as totalitarian, autocratic, liberal democratic and so on, yet one still believes that states need to be, and can be, successfully, crafted.[10]

But Rationality qua Logos, as a Universal that dwells in Language as Speech, can rely upon *one* imaginary institution of modernity alone, upon the combination of liberalism and democracy. And, although all liberal democracies share certain features, they are also all different in kind, for in *their concrete uniqueness they are always the institutions of a world and not of the (universal, undifferentiated) world*. A particular liberal democracy is shared by its citizens alone – this is the world they have. For example, America could easily implant its technology, and all the goods this technology produces, from Ireland to Mali. A car, a fridge, a TV set are universal things, they are the same wherever they are used. But the same United States could never implant its own brand of democratic institutions, not even in a single country. These institutions belong to the world of American citizens, and not to the world of others. Liberal democracy belongs to a world where one can dwell.

As a consequence, the strength of a liberal democracy grows in proportion with the evaporation of universal narratives. Democratic and liberal political imagination is not subjected to technological imagination, not even in its more abased forms. It is indifferent from this respect whether technological imagination takes the shape of (Arendtian) Labour or of creative Work. Democratic and liberal political imagination thinks of freedom in an entirely different way. It is the phantasy of men and women who are aware both of their freedom to initiate actions, and of their frailty and ignorance, both of the possibilities of their (own) world and all the uncertainties the present and future may bring. They use their reason, but they are also aware of the fragility of this reason. Communicative reason as liberal-democratic imagination is misunderstood if it is enthroned in lieu of technological imagination, for liberal-democratic imagination is, by definition, republican; and there are more republics than one, for there are more worlds than one.

I call post-modern men and women those of our contemporaries who have resolved to settle down on the railway station of the present. But there are many ways of settling down. The differentiation between 'my world' and 'their world' cannot be constituted by technological imagination, since the latter is empirically universal and undifferentiated. The things produced by this imagination are the same everywhere, and they fill one or another part of all worlds. How big a part, and what significance people attribute to this part, is again another matter.

It seems as if liberal-democratic political action could take care of the differentiation of worlds – as long as there is politics of a liberal-democratic kind, there remains the difference between 'our' world and 'theirs'; and if there remains a difference between 'our' world and 'theirs', we can see (regard) ourselves from the standpoint of the other also, and thus we *have* a world of our own and still *know* the world that is broader than the one that we have. And if this is so, the

Arendtian distinction between Labour and Work loses its significance – whether the universal things are constantly used and used up or whether they are created to stay forever, does not really matter; speech, action alone can become the fountainhead of our (different) worlds. But there are some doubts whether this is really so.

Democracy and liberalism are not just naked political institutions and actions – if they were they could easily perform a Universal Function. Liberal democracy can embody difference *because it is embedded in a form of life*. Difference needs to be there in life, in the way we talk about things, in the way we do things – in the things other than the ones that perform the Universal Functions. The difference-making things are the multiple meaning-carrying things, *the* symbolic things. Things for use can also have a symbolic dimension; and the same thing for use can assume different symbolic dimensions. What kind of symbolic things fill a world, and what kind of symbolic dimensions certain things for use assume, are the paramount features of one or another way of life.

Things for use fill the living space of the present. They come and go; functionally equivalent things replace them. New functions are also invented. It is thus that technological imagination works. Soon outdated and worn out, all products of technological imagination are used as tools. Moreover, they are used as temporary, transitory tools; one uses them only until a better brand appears. Everything is produced in order to be consumed, and not in order to stay there as the enduring monument of a world. Whether consumption is productive or not is of secondary importance from this perspective. There are many things that are used only once, others many times, others again for many years, but all in all, the dead bodies of things are heaped up in the necropolis of things. If one compares this necropolis to the necropolis of human burial-places, what strikes the eye immediately is that whereas the necropolis of men – which contains the things of their world – remains a place of magnificence and worship for all future generations and is thus constantly resurrected from this death, the necropolis of things remains dead forever. There is no magnificence here, but ugliness, dirt and stink. Abandoned factory buildings are not places of worship; there is nothing left here to be resurrected. It seems as if our things had never belonged to our worlds.

The things that had once filled the world (because they were the things of a world) can be reclaimed by nature. The white body of the stone of ruins, overgrown by trees, invites us for a friendly visit to the past. But the dead bodies of useful things are spit out by nature. The burn-out skeletons of concrete or synthetic material are the disgusting vestiges of an inorganic world. Since nature cannot take them back, they are better destroyed, if possible. Yet whether unde-stroyed or destroyed, they will not invite denizens of a remote future to engage in a nostalgia trip into their past, our present. The bodies of the dead things for use do not even implant the horror of mortality into the soul of the spectator. For these things become dead without dying – they are not mortal, for they never lived. Yet they do not stand to endure either, for be they as indestructible as they may, they cannot endure. Only meaning endures.

Things for use can make life more pleasant. Suppose, for simplicity's sake, that they all do. One always prefers the more pleasant ways to get things done to the unpleasant ones. Only fools would abandon the use of things that get things done in a more pleasant way than others, unless we have very serious reasons to avoid them. Romantic bashing of things-for-use is rarely sincere.

There are useful things that do more than get things done in a more pleasant way – they are pleasant themselves. They can appeal to us, to our senses, precisely in that aspect of their being what is not merely for use. This is hardly the case with a TV set with a blank screen, but it can be the case with a car. And there are other useful things which, although not pleasant in themselves, not only get things done in a more pleasant way (as a washing powder), but bring about something that delights for its own sake, something that we might desire to endure (for example, a record player).

Whatever is there on a thing to be perceived beyond and above its usefulness, makes this thing the thing-of-a-world in a small way. The more things are enjoyed for their own sake (and not as means or tools), the more their *being-here* (whether spatial or temporal or both) is an end-in-itself, the more they become the things-of-a-world, home-makers.

Whenever we pass a judgement of taste ('this is beautiful') on a thing, we know that this thing belongs to our world, because it fills this world in a more enduring way than its mere use. In Kant, pure judgements of taste can be passed only upon things of nature.[11] In this context, it is not a decisive question whether the judgements of taste that are passed on things for use are pure. In fact, in a Kantian sense, they are mostly impure, for even if one enjoys a thing for its own sake, one cannot entirely abstract from the perfection of the thing, and sometimes not even from its function. Still, judgements of taste passed on things can get very close to pure judgements of taste passed on the things of nature. Thus, in passing aesthetic judgements on things, one behaves towards man-made things almost as if they were organic bodies of nature; but not quite.

Passing aesthetic judgements on nature is a modern gesture. In all probability, Petrarca was the first who discovered natural beauty during his famous climb to a hilltop. Climbing to the hilltop is a metaphor that stands for ethical perfection. The pure enjoyment of the beauty of nature and ethical perfection were associated at the outset. The more modernity developed, the more the enthusiasm for nature grew. To discover nature's beauties is a gesture of home-making in a world that ceases to be a natural habitat. As long as the world is still a genuine natural habitat, things of nature as things of nature are not yet beautiful. They are too much taken for granted for being beautiful. Judgement of taste requires *thaumadzein* and reflection.

Yet aesthetic judgements were passed on things in the remote past; the beauty of things, artificially prepared things of nature included, has a far longer record than the beauty of wild nature. Yet moderns began to assimilate the aesthetic of man-made things to the aesthetic of nature. Moderns feel less strongly about the representative character of a thing in reflecting upon its beauty. A peasant head-wear can be perceived as beautiful a thing as a royal crown; and for post-moderns, the representative things of an old-bourgeois way of life have lost their specific lustre through and during the movements around 1968. All in all, one makes things beautiful now (by the gesture of an aesthetic judgement) in a very similar way as one makes nature beautiful – by enjoying them for their own sake, and by wishing, desiring that those very things should not be worn out, for they must remain as they are as the enduring sources of delight. The presence of a flower on earth is shorter than of several things for use – but they are both beautiful insofar as, and in the aspect that, they are not used.

Certainly, the difference strikes us. For things for use can also be created as things for enjoyment and pleasure – after all, enjoyment and pleasure are also modes of use, and one can also wear out things while enjoying them. The impure judgement of taste performs in this respect a critical function also: by passing such a judgement, one rejects or affirms the judgement of taste of those who created the things as pleasing, while adding the dimension of beauty to the dimension of usefulness. When I said that Bauhaus buildings are ugly and drab, I have passed a judgement not only on a thing, but also on an architectural taste.

However, my judgement is not only a judgement of taste but also a judgement passed on the ideology, the ideal, the high value placed on usefulness. Only a fool rejects the value of usefulness when contrasted to harmfulness. But the harmful is not the sole opposite of the useful; so is the useless. One has a world if there are useless things there, one inhabits a world if one does things beyond that which is useful. What is beyond the usefulness of common things is *the beauty* of those things. In this sense, beauty is associated with freedom.

A thing for use is a stimulus. As long as it appeals to me as a thing of use, I am under constraint to consume it, to have it or to use it. The constraint can be vague, it can become a strong compulsion, but it is always present. Insofar as I relate to the thing as to a thing of beauty, the 'stimulus' does not trigger a 'response' – for they are identical.

The world-constituting potential of beautiful things does not warrant, however, that men and women achieve freedom in the contemplation of beauty. Beauty itself can become the source of secondary use. Collectors can enjoy the beauty of their things, but the beauty of those things serves a purpose above and beyond itself. The collector is also under constraint, and often under compulsion to add a beautiful thing to his or her collection.

Shakespeare's King Lear insisted that he be surrounded by things beyond that which is necessary. Beauty is always beyond the necessary, even for the poorest, the most downtrodden. In this one respect, he who has a world where he or she can dwell is a king or a queen. It is, after all, not a necessity of life to enjoy the beautiful whiteness of the first snow.

Speaking about end-in-itself, Greek philosophers had first virtuous actions in mind. Plato also mentioned beauty (mainly human beauty). Virtuous action in a stricter sense is also a kind of luxury. Few people are virtuous in this way; only few enjoy moral freedom.[12] Thinking for thinking's sake, the activity of Aristotle's divinity, is also luxury, insofar as it is practised beyond necessity. A world of mere usefulness is not a habitat. Where there are only useful things and actions, one cannot dwell.

The strict distinction between the useful, understood as efficient and functional, and the useless, understood as non-efficient and non-functional, is without doubt modern, and yet another manifestation of technological imagination. A transit-station has to be useful and functional. Yet, provided that men and women desire to settle in on the railway station of the present, they need to embark also on doing useless things, doing certain things just for the sake of doing them.

Yet not all kind of things one does just for their own sake belong to the essential identification marks of a homey dwelling-place. Acts and things are 'wordly' in the sense that they fill a world as the home of their inhabitants, provided that the 'other world' participates somehow in those acts and things. The real luxuries of life are not diamond rings or fur-coats – they are just things for use that cost much. No one has ever achieved freedom of the soul or the mind through them. They are not worn for their own sake, but for the sake of showing off or pleasing others. Real luxuries are not easy to attain or to enjoy. Yet one is free in attaining and enjoying them, for we can choose to have them or to refrain from them. There is no such level at which they would be necessary for survival or for advancement. Studying ancient Greek language is a luxury (except for Classical Philologists), learning modern English is (almost) a necessity. Reading medieval Latin or Sanskrit poetry is a luxury, studying the textbooks of our profession is necessity. Designing a bathroom for each apartment is a necessary aspect of apartment-house architecture today, but designing houses worthy of our greatest aspirations is a luxury.

All the things invented in our age for mere use end up in the cemetery of bodies and will never be resurrected. Furthermore, the things of mere use that fill our spaces do not fill a world, within the framework of modernity, they are world-indifferent, and as such, utterly unsuited for providing subsequent generations with a dwelling place or for leaving anything enduring behind. And also things for use can be transmuted into things of beauty, things of a world, if one just lets them be for their own sake too, and not only for the sake of their technological purpose. In John Cage's composition, *Living Room Music*, commonplace things, newspapers, empty boxes and glassware are made to sing and sound. The music says: music is hidden everywhere; just let things find their voices and they become sources of beauty.

The modern age elaborated strict criteria to distinguish between the useful and the useless, such as rationality, efficiency and the like. Yet the same world cries out for 'luxury' for all the meaning-providing things and acts which are done for their own sake.

In thinking about the world, a world, or our world, I began to think with Arendt and with Hegel, with both of them. It seems as if my Arendtian concerns were steered towards a more Hegelian position; after all, liberal democracy is dependent for meaning on the symbolic power of things – and where do the symbolic powers of things come from? Just from *the other world*, the world of the absolute Spirit. The world of the absolute spirit on its part is reinforced and kept alive now by *vita contemplativa*, by the activities of thinking and beholding. It seems as if, in modernity, *vita activa* depended on *vita contemplativa*, even for just having a world.

The imaginary institution of democracy and technological imagination are essentially different, for what they share (their own reason) they also unshare (between one another). Yet they still have something in common, namely a weakness: the maintainance work vested in them requires a far less, and far less intensive and dense, network of symbolic actions than other imaginary institutions. This phenomenon is sometimes termed 'rationalization' or 'disenchantment of the world'.[13]

It is here that the difficulties in the distinction between 'our world' and 'their worlds' gets entangled with the distinction between 'this world' and 'that (the other) world'. As technological imagination tended to lift the distinction between 'our world' and 'theirs', it also aspired to annul the other distinction between this world and that other (higher) world. The ambition of this negative utopia cannot be achieved since it is self-defeating; in the absence of symbolic actions there is no faith, and no passion or emotion is vested in that what is commonly shared.

There are many ways to regain some of the networks of symbolic actions; the most obvious among them, modern nationalism, was born as a reaction to the attempt to abolish the distinction between 'our world' and 'theirs'. Religion, ethnicity, race, gender etc. can serve as reference points of a passionate and purely symbolic over-identification. With the sole exception of religious fundamentalism, all others draw their magic images from the sphere of the objective spirit, not from that of the absolute spirit. In order to maintain their network of exclusive symbolic actions, they have to create new religions, appeal to pagan myths or try to invent new ones. Those myths can also induce a challenge to technological imagination in a world where the things created by modern technology continue to fill all of the world-spaces.

The difficulty of maintaining the distinction between 'this world' and 'the other world' has been faced since early modernity, and alternative remedies to fundamentalist closure were soon sought. The most promising contender to salvage 'the other world', was Art, the so-called 'world of art', rather than philosophy. Art was eminently suitable for the position of a mobilizer of emotion, faith and desire and for that of a commonly shared imaginary institution for both devotion (*Andacht*) and *Kultus*. All the then available cultural traditions (from Indian to African, from Pacific to Chinese) were mixed and blended into a single kingdom of 'the world of art', the separate world of this new brand of universalism. This 'world of art' became for a while a common text of a cultural elite, yet never much more.

Wittgenstein said that the world of a happy man is different from the world of an unhappy man.[14] This is an extremely disquieting statement.

Our world is the space where we locate ourselves; it is our home. Being-in-a-world also means to share a home where one dwells. Yet, if the world of the happy person is different from the world of the unhappy person, the expression 'being-in-a-world' is unmasked as yet another formula of deception. For in fact, it is not *our* world that is confronted to *theirs*, but *my* world that is confronted to the world of every other single '*I*'. There are as many worlds as persons: a world is subjective.

'Being subjective' can have quite different meanings, depending on the philosophical vision that surrounds the category, or the everyday context in which the use of the adjective is embedded. By 'subjective' I mean here a strictly personal, and as such unshared, yet still conscious and up to a degree reflected, perception, vision, understanding, experience of a world. For example, a dream is unshared, but not subjective, unless the dreamer's reflection transmutes the dream into a part of her world. Reflectivity is not necessarily the kind of infinite self-reflection Kierkegaard discussed.[15] Infinite self-reflection is supposed to deepen the 'internal space' of the personal soul, to speak in a Hegelian metaphor. The world of a person can become idiosyncratic without infinite self-reflection. My world and your world can be different even if neither you nor I are carrying a deep 'internal space' in our respective souls.

Under closer scrutiny, Wittgenstein's dictum underlines that we both, the happy and the unhappy alike, have a world. But, having a world implies being able to live in it, act in it, communicate in it. So if both the happy and the unhappy have a world of their own, they must also share one. For if we did not share a world we could not have a world of our own, neither the happy nor the unhappy.

We seem to have ended up in a commonplace. One cannot find two identical leaves on a tree – how could one possibly find two people with exactly the same world-experience? Yet Wittgenstein's dictum is not the confirmation of a commonplace. It is an emphatic statement. The philosopher asserts that there is nothing philosophically suspect in the happy man's world being different from the unhappy man's world. It is perhaps not philosophy's task to abolish the separateness (subjectivity) of the happy and the unhappy world in order to constitute 'the world' which is neither happy nor unhappy, but entirely shared by the happy and the unhappy alike. Put bluntly, the suggestion that the world is subjective (in the above sense) guides us in direction of a new concept of understanding which is not based on the assumption that reason is something which is entirely shared and that everything that is unshared is fraudulent, or wrong or a mere opinion, or a deception by the senses, a sheer dream, just because it is idiosyncratic.

Nor is it assumed that both the happy and the unhappy are somehow deceived and 'betrayed' because their worlds do not match.

Whether a happy man experiences the world in a different way from the unhappy man is not a question in need of proof. Even children know that this is so. Yet the question whether the world of the happy *is* different from the world of the unhappy is a philosophical question. The 'is' refers to being, not to seeming. If the world of the happy is a world that is different from the world of the unhappy, as every (personal) world is different from every other (personal) world, then 'the world as such' cannot be constituted by philosophy in the usual way, through the elimination of the fraudulent aspects of subjectivity from each and every world to arrive at a common one, but rather by taking all single worlds together. The 'world of art' has always been open for such an interpretation. All past, present and future 'art-works' together are the 'world of art', whereas this 'world of art' consists of many separate worlds. The Truth of the world of art is not that what is shared, and certainly not 'what the case is'. For each and every work of art conveys its truth to the message-eager recipient who wants to know what the Truth is – the Truth for her or him.[16] Every work of art is supposed to be unique, personal, although not equally valuable, and the world of the happy author is always different from the world of the unhappy author. Taking all single works (worlds) together is not a matter of addition, neither is it a Hegelian kind of reconciliation through the unification of difference. Every single world can be thought of as a Leibnizian monad that encompasses the whole of the universe, yet from a single, and entirely unique, perspective. One does not need to think also the Grand Reason, who unifies all those pespectives. The unity is there, it is within each monad, and in all of them if they could be taken together, yet the difference between 'your world' and 'my world' remains, and so does the idiosyncratic character of every single world; difference and singularity are not sublated.

One can experience and one can also think *a* world in this manner. A world *is* then the mosaic of all the subjective worlds, and it encompasses all that is shared and all that is unshared. This 'is' ('the world is a mosaic') refers to an imaginary horizon (the spirit of our congregation) which points at the inscrutability of a World into which History has already entered.[17] This 'is' is the 'is' of the present and of the 'here', the 'is' of *hic et nunc*, of our railway station where we begin to settle in. We may perhaps make it our home where we can dwell.

A world leaves traces that endure. It is questionable whether our world does so.

Pre-moderns do not see beyond the horizons of their world; only their world can endure. If their world collapses, *the* world goes down. In the modern age, where History has entered the World, it became commonplace wisdom that nothing particular endures. The dwellers of a modern world are contingent and they are aware of their contingency. They have no fate. To pretend that they still have one is the sign of inauthenticity. The sole authentic gesture they are capable of is to enter the cosmic wager and (or) make an existential choice.

Single persons can enter a cosmic wager and they can make an existential choice, but groups cannot. Neither can a world. Yet all the persons who choose themselves, and thus their destiny, *choose also a world according to them.* There is a world according to everyone, because we are contingent and we perceive the 'elimination' of contingency from truth, goodness and beauty as alien and oppressive attempts at robbing men and women of what is their own, their dearly acquired luxury – freedom. The world of people who chose themselves existentially is a significant world. A world where modern men and women can settle in and dwell is composed of the worlds of significant subjects. Every work stands for itself in the friendly company of other works. One thing might still be shared: the 'common thing', *res publica,* a world as a political habitat. But nothing else, or very little beyond this.

Can a world like this create something that endures?

The voice of the things in Cage's music sounds for me and you, for our contemporaries, for the fellow subjects in an absolute present. My world is a happy world and your world is an unhappy world.

No major tapestry can be woven from the mosaic of difference. No single-minded idea raises its pyramids here, and no grand style creates cathedrals on the soil of our homes. This may be still ahead, but we have no knowledge about it. At the moment, we keep digging into the past. We dig deep, we collect traces, we restore the ruins of the past to resurrect bygone worlds. Our work is maintenance and preservation. It is done for the others' sake, for they are the ones to be immortalized by us, not us. Yet it is also done for our own sake, for it is like blood-transfusion; we, free people of a free age, give meaning to our life by infusing the blood of the dead into our anaemic veins.

There is no certitude. Nothing can be predicted. The game is open. The croupier expects us to bet right now: so,

'faites vos jeux'

Some put their stakes, others defer, yet no one can run away.

Notes

Chapter 1 Contingency

1 As the remark also indicates, Kierkegaard shared the Platonist interpretation of Hegel's philosophy with all of his significant contemporaries, among them Feuerbach. See Kierkegaard, 1980.
2 Adorno did this earlier, yet with less sympathetic eye, in Adorno, 1973 and 1983.
3 Hans Jonas, in *The Gnostic Religion* (Boston: Beacon Press, 1958), interpreted the Valentinian formula in this spirit.
4 Many modern phenomena appeared in a great variety of pre-modern societies – on the margins of, or in the interstices within, the dominant social arrangments. Foucault has stressed emphatically that every novel thing appears on the margins and, sometimes, also remains there – especially in his essay 'Nietzsche, Genealogy, History' in Foucault, 1977.
5 Hans Jonas discussed this shift from the margins towards the centre in detail in Jonas, 1966.
6 Contrary to the 'classical view', contemporary philosophers share the dark interpretation of the Greek experience of the cosmos. This is also true of authors who have no sympathies with Nietzsche and entertain a great admiration for the Athenian democracy.
7 *De Anima* 407b 20.
8 Kierkegaard made the point that Paul cannot be described as a 'genius'. The work of an apostle draws its significance not from the content of the text, which could be entirely insignificant, but from the authority that it carries. Yet Paul's 'text' has carried a significance – otherwise its authority would have hardly been accepted: 'The Difference between the Genius and the Apostle' in Kierkegaard, 1962.
9 The Augustinian discovery of the Will has been discussed by Hannah Arendt in Arendt, 1971, volume 2: *Willing*. I am going to speak about Will, as a philosophical character, in chapter 3.
10 VI.B. Der sich entfemdete Geist. Die Bildung. (In Hegel, 1977: Self-alienated Spirit; Culture.)

11 K. Löwith speaks about a total adjustment; this is, in my view, an exaggeration. See Löwith, 1966.
12 Toulmin, 1982.
13 We are 'thrown' (*geworfen*) – it is Being that 'throws'.
14 Pascal, 1977, Series Two: The Wager.
15 Hegel repeats his dictum in several variations, from the Introduction to *The Phenomenology of the Spirit* to the Preface of *The Philosophy of Right*.
16 One could argue that Leibniz's principle of sufficient reason (ground) has anticipated the Hegelian solution.
17 There is a similar distinction, though without reference to Aristotle, in Kant, 1990, especially in the first Introduction.
18 That Hegel has presupposed the absoluteness of the absolute was one of the major critical points formulated by Heidegger. To this question I will return in chapter 6.
19 Georg Lukács, 1974, p. 21.
20 Pascal, 1977, Series Two: The Wager.
21 Ibid.
22 Ibid.
23 Hans Jonas uses the expression *Necropolis* to denote nature as perceived by modern natural sciences, (Jonas, 1966).
24 Lucien Goldmann conjured up a 'tragic' Kant, a kind of follower to Pascal. One does not need to agree with him in order to discover that the three 'postulates' of pure practical reason are equivalent to the Pascalian wager.
25 Nietzsche, F.: *Use and Abuse of History*. Translated as *On the Advantage and Disadvantage of History for Life* by P. Preuss (1980).
26 Rorty, 1989.
27 Pascal, 1977, B.819.272.
28 Sartre, 1956, pp. 440–1.
29 'What is Metaphysics?', in Heidegger, 1977, pp. 91–112.
30 Sartre, 1956, p. 444.
31 Hegel elaborates this topic in his lectures on the *Philosophy of Religion*. In his mind, it was Christianity that sublated the accident of birth by declaring the salvation of all humans.
32 Hegel insisted that the sentence 'all men are born free' is but a thoughtless generalization of the pre-modern state of affairs. In pre-modern times some people were free just because they were born free. In modern times this is, however, not so. In spite of his (justified) philosophical objection, Hegel still made occasional use of the well-known phrase.
33 To be made does not stand for being 'ready made'. One can fulfill traditional (inherited) tasks in many different ways; they may be grand or petty, grey or colourful. Greatness of a pre-modern provenance shows some plastic propensities. Yet even the greatest of characters cannot be termed self-made if he inherits, at least socially, the conditions of his greatness, if his destiny is not self-destined.

34 Obviously, if we insist that modern men and women are born free we do not mean that the newborn baby can do as she pleases. There are several, equally valid, interpretations of freedom which cannot be substituted one for the other. Born free means (in the well-known phrase) to be born free in a *social* sense, that is, to be born contingent. To be born contingent is not tantamount to being born free morally, politically, psychologically or even physically. I discussed contingency as the result of the modern social arrangment in 'Rights, Modernity, Democracy' in Heller, 1990, pp. 160–75.

35 The expression as well as the idea of 'the significant other' was conceived by G. H. Mead, the contrast between the 'outer-' and the 'inner-' directedness was pointed out by D. Riesmann.

36 One-dimensional man and one-dimensional society are well-known metaphors coined by H. Marcuse.

37 In Kierkegaard, 1941.

38 In Riesmann, the inner-directed man is oriented towards a task and not towards itself. In everything beyond this similarity, my use of the term differs from that of Riesmann. See Heller, 1984, 1985 and 1990.

39 Epicurus, in *Hellenistic Philosophy*, eds. B. Inwood and L. P. Gerson (Indianapolis: Hackett, 1988), p. 29.

40 I have elaborated one aspect of this idea in Heller, 1990. I will return to it in my forthcoming book, within the framework of a moral psychology.

41 On Kierkegaard's dictum that truth is subjective, see chapter 4.

42 Collingwood, R. G. *Autobiography* (Oxford: Oxford University Press) s.a., pp. 4–5.

43 Although Rorty does not make reference to the concept of the existential choice, he discusses the relation between the novel and the novelist in terms of such a choice. See chapter 5, 'Self-creation and affiliation: Proust, Nietzsche, Heidegger' in Rorty, 1987.

44 It is in Heller, 1990, that I discuss the possibility of choosing ourselves as decent persons, and the main theoretical/practical connotations of such a choice.

45 Modern philosophers normally use two different words to make a distinction between life lived in contingency and self-destined (essential) life. This is so in Kierkegaard, in Nietzsche, in Dilthey (as generally by all philosophers of life – *Lebensphilosophie*) in the young Lukács and Heidegger, to mention only the most representative thinkers.

46 Lukács, ss. 1971, follows the logic of an existential choice.

47 In Merleau-Ponty, understanding in history is a category of Weberian provenance, it refers to people who conduct their business in history both theoretically and practically, whereas reason in History comes from the Hegelian-Marxian legacy – which, as a quasi-mythical subject, shapes the ways of history according to an unknown but firm plan.

48 In Goldmann, the Marxian promise cannot be based on knowledge; one needs to put one's stakes on it. This is how Goldmann secularizes Pascal.

49 Reflective judgement is *a priori* only as aesthetic judgement; as teleological judgement it becomes functionally equivalent to purposiveness as the idea of reason, as already formulated in 'The Idea of History from a Cosmopolitan point of View' and other political writings.

50 Marx's theory could also be described as the application of the old Aristotelian concept of internal teleology, or as the mere recapitulation of the Hegelian narrative. What exists as *dynamis* unfolds as *energeia/ergon*, what exists in-itself unfolds as in-and-for-itself. However, Marx also enumerates all the constituents of the human essence, which happen to be exactly those of a modern self-made man in the terms which he chose himself as well as his world (to come).

51 The Kierkegaardian Exister is what became later Heidegger's *Dasein*. The exister is the individual person (not only the individual consciousness) for whom existence as such became the (main) problem. The Exister is the individual, who, as an individual, is the universal.

52 I discuss this problem in detail in the second and third parts of *A Theory of History*.

53 To juxtapose thinking to philosophy (or, as Kierkegaard did, the 'existing thinker' to the philosopher) was a provocative gesture. Now that the provocative colour has worn off, Derrida and some other philosophical provocateurs return to the term 'philosophy'.

54 The 'existing thinker' is an exister who practises infinite reflection (thinking), that is, who reflects upon the problem of existing.

Chapter 2 Lived History, Utopia, Apocalyse,. Marche Funèbre

1 Yet even a small modification in the mythical story can matter much, e.g. Seneca's Oedipus is almost identical with Sophocles' Oedipus: and yet, the few modifications eliminate the tragic grandeur, and transform the drama into a kind of bloodsoaked *Trauerspiel*.

2 T. Mann introduces his Joseph tetralogy with the sentence: 'Tief ist der Brunnen der Vergangenheit.' And he adds: 'Sollte man ihn nicht unergründlich nennen?'

3 One can speak about *a priori* imagination provided that one dismisses the Kantian distinction of faculties and their functional division.

4 Collingwood, 1946, makes a case for the *a priori* character of historical imagination Foucault, 1972, speaks about the 'historical a priori'.

5 This is a slight modification of Castoriadis' conception. According to Castoriadis, 1987, imagination bursts out from the depth of the Psyche; in the world of society, this imagination can be institutionalized.

6 The problem that ensues from the absence of chthonic deities in modern cultures is discussed by Blumenberg. See Blumenberg, 1976.

7 I borrowed the term 'sublunar region' from Veyne, 1983.

8 Hegel, G. W. F., Werke, volume 17, p. 191 (Frankfurt: Suhrkamp, 1976). The English one-volume edition of Hegel's *Lectures on The Philosophy of Religion* (University of California Press) is based on the

lectures from 1827. I use the far broader and more substantial two-volume edition of 1840 (by Bruno Bauer). Volume 17 of *Werke* is the second volume of *Lectures*. All the quotations from this book are mine.

9 I made a few allusions to the phantasy-images attached to the 'underground' in a culture where there are no chthonic deities. The underground man is historically extremely significant creature of Dostoyevskij.

10 The ruin is one of Benjamin's main images – or metaphors – of history, in several of his works. The discussion here will be based mainly on two of them, namely 'Ursprung des Deutschen Trauerspiels' and 'Ueber den Begriff der Geschichte'; both from Walter Benjamin, Gesammelte Schriften (I.l and I.II)
(Surhkamp, Frankfurt, 1974) The first is translated as *The Origin of the German Tragic Drama* (London: NLB, 1977). The second is collected in *Illuminations* (New York: Schocken Books, 1968). I return to Benjamin's philosophy of history at the end of this chapter.

11 Apocalyptic imagination is both the radicalization and the negation of history (and of historicity).

12 Benjamin, 1968, urges the apocalyptic liberation of the 'repressed past' in 'Theses on the Philosophy of History', XII. It is difficult to give an idea of all the implications of the verb '*unterdrückt*' by simply translating it. They are (among others) repressed, dominated, inhibited, pushed into the underground, forgotten.

13 Kierkegaard made the connection between Socratic irony concerning knowledge on the one hand, and Christian (Protestant) self-reflection concerning sin, on the other hand. The first increases the consciousness of one's ignorance, the second increases the consciousness of one's sinfulness.

14 I owe this observation to Paul Carter.

15 In 'The Esthetic Validity of Marriage' in Kierkegaard, 1987, V.2, pp. 5–154.

16 I speak about the hermeneutical dimension of ethics, and among others about the ethical aspects of forgetting, in greater detail in: 'The Role of Interpretation in Modern Ethical Practice' in 'Philosophy and Social Criticism'. V. 17:2, pp. 83–102

17 Ernst Bloch, 1986.

18 In Spinoza, *Ethics* (III, 12 and 13), fear and hope ensue from the inadequacy of ideas. Goethe, in the second part of *Faust*, puts both Fear and Hope in the pillory.

19 It was not hope but mistrust that characterized the (ancient) Greek mind. Maybe Plato was the first (in his interpretation of the Myth of Er in book 10 of *The Republic*) who invoked something like hope as an otherworldly reward, to give a greater weight to his argument in favour of strict morals.

20 The messianistic/apocalyptic character of the Marxian vision of the future was frequently pointed out, but maybe first by Karl Löwith. See K. K. Löwith: *Weltgeschichte und Heilgeschehen* (Stuttgart, 1953), trans-

lated in English as: *Meaning in History. The Theological Implications of the Philosophy of History* (Chicago: University of Chicago Press, 1949). Michel Löwy (1989) pointed out the messianistic message in the works of twenthieth century Marxists, among others, of Lukáacs, Bloch and Benjamin

21 Without denying the connection, Blumenberg criticizes Löwith's attempt at overstretching the idea of secularization in the understanding of modern political philosophies and institutions; see Blumenberg, 1983.

22 William Shakespeare: *The Tempest*, Act II, Scene 1.

23 Joachim of Floris might have been an exception. See my discussion of consciousness of unreflected and of reflected universality in Heller, 1982, Part I.

24 Kant, 'Perpetual Peace', in Kant, 1957, pp. 85–137.

25 'The End of all Things', Kant, 1957 p. 75.

26 In Kant's *Critique of Judgement*, teleological judgement is introduced to take over the philosophical function that was performed earlier in Kant's system by the regulative idea of reason.

27 This point will be discussed in chapter 4.

28 This how Lukács discusses works of art in his *Philosophy of Art* (Darmstadt: Luchterhand, 1974).

29 Karl Mannheim, in his *Ideology and Utopia* (New York: Harcourt, Brace & Jovanovich, 1936), chapter IV, speaks, in similar context, about utopian mentality.

30 Nozick, *Anarchy, State and Utopia*, 1974.

31 Kant writes: '[I] cannot do good to anyone according to *my* concept of happiness . . . but only according to that of the one I intend to benefit', Kant, 1964, p. 122 (emphasis by Kant).

32 Lewy, P., *Survival in Auschwitz* (New York: Collier, 1961), p. 111.

33 *The Zohar*, Parashat Pinhas, 242/b, 568 and 569. Translated and edited by Philip S. Berg (Jerusalem/New York: Kabbala Press, 1987).

34 Hegel, *Vorlesungen über die Philosophie der Religion*, II, Werke 17 (Frankfurt: Suhrkamp, 1986), p. 251 (*Lectures on the Philosophy of Religion*).

35 This is especially emphasized in *The Genealogy of Morals*. A proper genealogy is to put together the erased moral text from a few available traces.

36 Caputo juxtaposes the *free* circulation of letters to the circulation of letters, where the former stands for the dream of the present as 'eschatology now', a dream that the author associates with the name of Derrida; 1987, p. 170.

37 It is Hans Jonas who censures certain Christian philosophers for trying to 'Christianize' a 'pagan' like Heidegger; see 'Heidegger and Theology' in Jonas, 1966.

38 I discuss these matters in details in Heller, 1990.

39 Kierkegaard, 1980, distinguishes between these two kinds of anxiety.

40 I make this distinction in Heller, 1990. Only they choose themselves absolutely under the category of the universal choose themselves as

decent (good, righteous) persons. The choice of decency is meant to be universal for the simple reason that everyone and anyone can live up entirely to this kind of self-choice.

41 These are the lines of Hölderlin's poem that serve as the trampoline for Heidegger's interpretation of the artwork in 'The Origin of the Work of Art', in Heidegger, 1977, pp. 143–88.

42 J. W. von Goethe, *Faust*, Part II. This is the last sentence of the drama, spoken by the Chorus Mysticus. The Chorus's message is Platonizing ('Alles Vergaengliche ist nur ein Gleichnis', that is, everything transitory is but a simile), so there is some ambiguity about that eternal-femininity, the source of the 'saving power'.

43 Isaiah I: 27–8.

44 Revelation IX.

45 Revelation XXI.

46 Kant, in his 'Ideas for a Universal History from a Cosmopolitan Intent' (Kant, 1983), describes the progressivist universal history as a kind of hope-motivated fiction that narrates a possible story.

47 Sorel, 1969.

48 Revelation I.

49 This is how Lukács pondered the end of WW1. If the West is going to win the war (he saw this as a positive result in itself), what or who will *save* 'us' from Western Civilization. The 'us' stood for radical intellectuals', yet also for the 'world'. Only a kind of saviour (or saving power) can 'save us' from 'décadence'. Décadence means going down, collapsing; it is the antechambre of apocalypse as End-of-a-civilization. So, a kind of redemptive apocalypse is juxtaposed to the other apocalyptic vision of an ungraceful End.

50 Castoriadis, 1986, p. 7.

51 For Castoriadis, Plato is the founding father of theology – yet certainly not of an apocalyptic kind.

52 Derrida, 1982.

53 *The Zohar*, Parashat Pinhas, op. cit.

54 'The End of Philosophy and the Task of Thinking' in Heidegger, 1977, p. 377.

55 Ibid., p. 379.

56 Benjamin, 'Theses on the Philosophy of History' XVI, in Benjamin, 1968.

57 Heller, 'Death of the Subject?' in Heller, 1990.

58 Thomas Mann, *Doctor Faustus*, *Werke*, volume 6, p. 513–14 (H. T. Lowe-Porter translation, 1971, pp. 378–9).

59 Benjamin, 1968, p. 262. Reference to thesis XVI.

60 Ibid., p. 261. Reference to thesis XV.

61 Ibid., p. 260. Reference to thesis XII.

62 Ibid., p. 255. Reference to thesis IV.

63 Ibid., p. 255. Reference to thesis V.

64 Lessing, *Emilia Galotti*, (trans. Edward Dvoretsky, New York: Ungar, 1962) Act V, Scene 7.

65 In the discussion on force and violence, if not otherwise indicated, references are to Walter Benjamin, 'Critique of Violence', in *Reflections*, Edmund Sephcoh (NY: Schocken Books, 1986).

66 Kant, 1965, p. 39.

67 Benjamin, *Reflections*, p. 297.

68 Sorel, 1956.

69 Benjamin, *Reflections*, p. 300.

70 Benjamin, W. *Gesammelte Schriften*, I.3, p. 1245 (Frankfurt: Suhrkamp, 1974) (not translated).

71 Ibid., p. 1244.

72 Ibid., p. 1236.

73 Ibid., p. 1239.

74 Ibid., p. 1242.

Chapter 3 Introducing Reason, Will and Other Characters

Preliminary Remark After having delivered a lecture based on the abbreviated version of this chapter at the Cardozo Law School in October, 1991, J. Derrida drew my attention to Deleuze's recent book that contains similar views. It was due to his remark that I became cognizant of the existence of Deleuze and Guattari, 1991. I was very pleased to see that there are some familiarities between their conceptions and mine, although we differ in many essential points. Let me introduce the characters of the French co-authors in their own words: 'Le personnage conceptuel n'est pas le représentant du philosophie, c'est meme l'inverse: le philosophie est seulment l'enveloppe de son principal personnage conceptuel . . . les personnage-conceptuels sont les "hétéronymes" du philosophe, le simple pseudonyme de ses personnages.' (p. 62) Their main examples are the Cogito of Descartes, the Idiot of Cusanus, Dionysos of Nietzsche and so on. On my part, I rather speak of a common pool of philosophical characters, and of a few shared protagonists (like Reason or Will). Although I agree with the French authors' contention that much in a philosophy is autobiographical, a kind of presentation of the self of the philosopher (I wrote about this issue in Heller, 1984), I would be very reluctant to make such a flatly direct connection between author and work as they do.

1 Plato, *Theaetetus* 189/c.

2 G. W. F. Hegel, *Encyklopaedie*, paragraph 556. In English, *Encyclopedia* (NY: Continuum, 1990).

3 In his autobiography, Collingwood describes how he discovered that philosophy is about asking fresh questions rather than about answering 'perennial' ones.

4 According to Whitehead, all philosophies are footnotes to Plato's work.

5 This point was made by Blumenberg, 1979, and by Jean-Pierre Vernant. Vernant concludes his book Mythe & pensée chez les Crecs Éditions La Découverte: Paris, 1985 by emphasizing the rupture between myth on the one hand, and both major types of Greek philosophy on the other

hand. In English, *Myth and Thought among the Greeks* (London/Boston: RKP, 1983).

6 When Aristotle, in *Metaphysics*, Book I (983b), ponders from where Thales could get the notion of making water the first principle, he mentions, among the possible explanations, natural ones, and also the ancient myth according to which Ocean and Tethys are the parents of creation 'and described the oath of the gods as being water, which they themselves call Styx' (p. 30).

7 The unfinished work of Maurice Merleau-Ponty, 1968, challenges this tradition from a post-phenomenological point of view.

8 Derrida, in his booklet *Chora*, affirms that philosophical characters are not metaphors.

9 Definition I.

10 Though Hegel termed Napoleon the world spirit on horseback, the same Napoleon never became a philosophical character in his system.

11 In the third sub-section of this chapter (on will) we shall see how Augustine coined the formula 'Will wills' on the analogy of 'Reason reasons' – Heidegger just follows in the footsteps of this tradition.

12 Kant, Hegel, and Kierkegaard also, used the philosophical character-configuration of the Fall purposefully as a rich metaphor.

13 Instead of *De libero arbitrio*, Luther titles his work *De servo arbitrio*. This is meant as a polemic not only against the content of works by Boethius or by Valla, but also against the metaphorical aspect of their treatment of theological truth.

14 The theory of possible worlds (and possible Adams) is a necessary component in the argument for the principle of sufficient reason (Cause). The complexity of Leibniz's theory requires the staging of all the characters in question.

15 See Blumenberg, 1979

16 Lukács's essay, 'The Metaphysics of the Tragedy' in Lukács, 1974, is a masterpiece, yet the tragedy it discusses, *Brünhilde* by Paul Ernst, is an entirely unreadable and overpretentious piece. Whenever Sartre tried to induce into his dramas an existentialist-metaphysical dimension, they turned out to be artistic failures, like *The Flies*.

17 G. Lukács, *A modern dráma Keletkezésének története* (Budapest: Magvetö, s.a.) (*History of the Modern Drama*, not translated).

18 Lukács has pointed out this innovation of the novel in contrast to epic poetry, especially the epopeia.

19 The abandonment of the common pool is normally connected to the emergence of individual authorship, especially in the fine arts. But in philosophy, authorship had always been essential, so much so, that the first histories about philosophies were always intertwined with the life-histories of philosophers – for example in Diogenes Laertius.

20 I will return to the discussion of the hermeneutical turn in modern culture in general, and modern philosophy in particular, in chapter 6.

21 Rorty has collapsed these two, and entirely different, understandings of being private. See his essay, 'From ironist theory to private allusions:

Derrida' in Rorty, 1989. Derrida is certainly not a 'private' philosopher in the first sense: he does not appeal to the so-called private sensitivities of his readers. But he is a private, or rather 'personal' philosopher in the sense that his oeuvre is idiosyncratic.

22 See Jonas, 1966.

23 Harold Bloom, in his Introduction (or Commentary) to Bloom, 1990, convinces us of the literary superiority of this biblical author, but not of her philosophical (speculative) superiority. Without invisible characters no philosophical play can be staged – and first and foremost the Main Character needs to be invisible. The more moral and rational this Supreme Being is, the better from a metaphysical point of view.

24 This is certainly also the case in the writings attributed to the biblical author of J.

25 In tragedy, both deception and self-deception must be present. One can, however, notice an interesting change in their proportion from the ancient tragedy through Shakespeare to modern tragedy, especially Ibsen. At first deception outweighs self-deception, in Shakespeare they are outbalanced, whereas in modern tragedy it is self-deception that outweighs deception – this contributes to the increasing comic elements in modern tragedies.

26 One can pass only a very few generalized sentences about human experience. But one can confidently say that all cultures invent devices to fence off the powers that betray and deceive us as much as possible, from magic (sorcery) through philosophical hermeticism up to the beliefs in Divine Providence, or the all-encompassing power of Science.

27 I have borrowed here some rhetoric elements from Derrida, but nothing from the substance of his interesting work. See Jacques Derrida, 'Plato's Pharmacy' in Derrida, 1981.

28 The expression 'imaginary institution' is an abbreviation and stands for 'imaginary institution of signification' in Castoriadis, 1986 and 1987.

29 Aristotle, *Metaphysics*, Ross translation. In my book on *philosophy* I maintain that the relevance of philosophy is warranted by all those people who utter the sentence: 'I want to know the Truth'; Heller 1984.

30 There really was a Grand Hotel Abyss (Grand Hotel Abgrund) in the Alps. Lukács used to say that whoever prophsies doomsday yet (or and) lives comfortably and well from a self-complacent theoretical exercise, dwells in this Hotel.

31 Fear and trembling from being deceived is one of the most forceful motivations that pushes Descartes towards the philosophy of the cogito, towards God and towards the establishment of a foolproof method – according to his own stories, especially the story of the first Meditation.

32 Plato, *Symposion*, 207/a.

33 Ibid., XXV.

34 Ibid., 221c.

35 See Hume, 1951, volume two. In addition to asserting that reason is slave to passions, Hume also asserts that this ought to be so. There are

a few philosophers, however, who do not find remedies in Plato's Pharmacy, among whom Pascal is the most significant – Kierkegaard follows in his footsteps.

36 I discuss the basic categories of value-orientation elsewhere. See especially Heller, 1985.

37 Mutual understanding does not stand here for consensus, but for the very simple fact that I understand what you mean, what you are up to, to what you are refering and vice versa, to the extent necessary for meaningful interaction, including to attend a common business of any sort.

38 See also Blumenberg, 1987.

39 I discussed this issue in Heller, 1985.

40 I will return to the problem in chapter 6.

41 Castoriadis, 1987.

42 This is how Hannah Arendt gives an account of 'pure thinking' when exploring the life of the mind.

43 This is so in Aristotle. See *De Anima*, 427b, 428a, 429a, 432b, 433a.

44 Descartes contrasts imagination and rule-following reason radically, e.g. in the well-known and frequently quoted *A Discourse On Method* (London: Dent, 1989), Part Four, op. cit.

45 Foucault discusses interpretations of the sexual meaning of dreams in ancient Greece, in Foucault 1985.

46 Martin Jay discusses the end of 'isms' in his lecture delivered at a conference on Reason and Imagination, organized by Monash University, August 1991, Melbourne.

47 See Derrida, 1982.

48 Silone satirizes Soviet communism and its Italian following who had to know every time how to answer these two questions 'correctly', that is, according to the then party line.

49 I return to this issue in the following chapter.

50 For example Habermas, by making the distinction between instrumental reason on the one hand and communicative reason on the other hand. Instrumental Reason does evil whenever it is substituted for Communicative Reason.

51 There is Evil in the world as the man-made Apocalypse of the twentieth century bears out. In Heller, 1985, I speak about Evil as something that is brought forth whenever evil maxims mobilize the 'underworld' (of the soul and of society).

52 This point was argued by Hannah Arendt very convincingly in Arendt, 1971.

53 MacIntyre translates *prohairesis* as 'rational desire', obscuring thereby the fact that here a decision is made. The decision follows deliberation (*boulesis*), so it is not choice 'between' but choice 'for', a kind of a leap – one takes one's hand off the rail, and begins. The translation 'rational desire' preempts the dynamic propensity of *prohairesis*. (See MacIntyre, 1988.)

54 Augustine, 1964, I: 3. 'It would not be just to punish evil deeds if they were not done wilfully'.

55 Ibid., II: 1: 'we have freedom of the will'.

56 Ibid., II: 194–5: In the same way as we know by reason everything that we know, nevertheless even reason itself is numbered among the things we know by reason. Have you forgotten that when we asked what is known by reason, you admitted that reason is known by reason? Do not wonder then that we can use the free will by means of itself, if we use other things through our free will. As reason, knowing other things, also knows itself, so the free will, which makes use of other things, also makes use of itself.'

57 After Nietzsche, who put a self-created character termed will-to-power at the centre of the cast, no one of high philosophical standing staged it again.

58 Theologically-inspired philosophers, especially Protestant philosophers, certainly continue to talk about Sin. Reinhold Niebuhr, for example, speaks about the sin of idolatry (thinking that out perception of Truth is the Truth), and of the moral sin of the ego who make itself as the centre of the universe, etc. But I am not familiar with an attempt by a contemporary theologically-inspired philosopher to re-stage (in this context) the story of the fall with all its ancient props in a non-metaphorical sense. In the radical literature, the term guilt (*Schuld*) begins to replace sin (*Sünde*), though still with explicit theological connotations. See Lukács' frequent reference to the story of the biblical Judith.

59 This is obvious in Kierkegaard who made moderns conscious of the existential choice. He distinguishes between guilt and sin, sin and anxiety. And still Sin becomes rather an internal state, the state of suffering, in Kierkegaard, 1941.

60 I discuss this problem in Heller, 1988, Chapter 3, 'From Voluntary Action to Moral Autonomy'. I am indebted here to Wittgenstein, who has radically reassumed the Aristotelian position.

61 I speak about moral autonomy as resulting from the existential choice of ourselves under the category of the universal in the first chapter of Heller, 1990.

Chapter 4 The Question of Truth

1 John, XVIII: 37–8.

2 There is no social (human) life possible without the distinction of true and false, right and wrong. I elaborate on this problem in Heller, 1985 and 1988.

3 It was the unique feature of the Jewish God that his might was reconfirmed not by victory alone, but also by defeat. This is one reason why Nietzsche linked the Jewish and Christian religions to *ressentiment*. Yet from Plato onwards, philosophy too got close to this 'Jewish' perception of the world. Socrates' daimonion has not 'failed' Socrates by

letting him die by the injustice of his fellow-citizens, for dying was preferable to committing injustice.

4 Kierkegaard discusses this paradox in 'The Historical Point of View', Kierkegaard, 1941.

5 Ludwig Wittgenstein, *Zettel*, p. 461. In *Schriften* 5 (Frankfurt: Suhrkamp, 1970). In English, *Zettel* (Berkeley: University of California Press, 1967).

6 See Kierkegaard, 1980, and 'Ueber den Begriff der Geschichte', in Benjamin, 1968.

7 Veyne, 1983.

8 See 'Everyday Life, Rationality of Reason, Rationality of Intellect' in Heller, 1985.

9 This is an obvious reference to Heidegger's 'ontological difference' between Being and beings (*Sein-Seiende*).

10 It is difficult to outbalance the tension between the commitment to One and Only Truth on the one hand, and the assertion that there is a hierarchy of truth according to the spheres of truth, on the other hand, but most philosophers faced this difficulty, although in quite different ways, and none of them as radically as Hegel did.

11 Foucault, 1972. Foucault, 1984 encompasses several interviews where this topic is explained.

12 Heidegger writes, 'Art then is the becoming and happening of truth. Does truth, then, arise out of nothing? It does indeed if by nothing is meant the mere not of beings . . . the question is decided whether art can be an origin and then must be a forward spring . . .' Quoted, from 'The Origin of the Work of Art' in Heidegger, 1977 pp. 183, 187.

13 Derrida, 1987. Derrida radicalizes Heidegger in having recourse to an idiosyncratically 'interpreted', that is, 'deconstructed' kant of the *Critique of Judgement*. See sections 1, 'Parergon' and 4, 'Restitutions'.

14 According to Albrecht Wellmer, truth in art is a metaphor that stands for both representation and '*Stimmigkeit*'. See Wellmer 1985.

15 Derrida, 1987.

16 Sigmund Freud, 'The Future of an Illusion,' in Freud 1955.

17 Certainly, the Nolan did not die for physics, but for a totally new vision of the world into which his person became totally involved. (For a beautiful discussion see 'The Nolan', in Blumenberg, 1983.

18 The correspondence theory of Truth provokes four main reactions. Either one accepts it but refines it and makes it more sophisticated (e.g. through the paradigm of language), or one accepts it, and for that reason rejects the question of truth as a banal and subaltern, aphilosophical issue (like Arendt) or one discusses it as one, yet only one, manifestation of Truth (like Heidegger), or one rejects it entirely.

19 In his 'New Thinking. A few afterthoughts to *The Star of Redemption*', Franz Rosenzweig differentiates among truths by the criterion of how much they cost for the person who holds them. He speaks about a 'Messianistic epistemology'; Truth is One only for God.

20 This point is strongly advocated in Collingwood, 1946.
21 Blumenberg, 1983, attributes the claim of Science to absolute Truth (which is not in any way a necessary condition of successful scientific enquiry), to the competition with Christianity.
22 More and more scholars who come from the analytical tradition now acknowledge the plurality of truth, e.g. Hilary Putnam and Richard Rorty.
23 I have explored the themes of truthfulness, frankness and authenticity in Heller, 1990. 'Authenticity' as a new philosophical character was to be added to the older ones in our discourse on morals, due to the modern condition of contingency.
24 Kierkegaard, 1987. The quotation reads: 'for only the truth that builds up is truth for you'; II, p. 354.
25 Kierkegaard, 1941.
26 In Apel, the *a priori* speech-conditions of the question of truth do not prejudge the answers. In Habermas, they prejudge them insofar as truth is defined as consensus concerning theoretical claims, but not insofar as the content of such a consensus is concerned.
27 Both Hume and Hegel have dismissed the contract theory; they have not needed it for the sake of world-construction.
28 Wittgenstein's well-known dictum that there is no private language needs to be remembered here.
29 Total consensus can come about only in trivial issues, and would close the search for truth. Habermas' consensus theory of truth runs against not only our common-sense observations, but also against our present perception of the development of sciences. *Kuhn* (and also *Feyerabend*, whether one agrees with him or not) made us look at the 'question of truth' in natural sciences with fresh eyes. It is not only that consensus cannot be achieved, but that to achieve consensus is not even desirable. Certainly, the problem of consensus in case of rightness (good) differs from the consensus concerning truth – but here, as I argued elsewhere, consensus concerning one supreme value suffices. I made a point against full consensus in the case of justice in Heller, 1987, where I insisted that a completely just society is not only impossible but also undesirable.
30 'Opening of Truth' (*Lichtung der Wahrheit*) is Heidegger's beautiful and telling expression.
31 'Restitutions', in Derrida, 1987, p. 381.
32 In Heller, 1984, I explained with a few examples that whenever someone exclaims 'Tell me the Truth – I want to know the truth', his or her existence is entirely involved in this knowledge. 'Entirely' can stand for 'momentarily entirely' ('Doctor, tell me . . .'), for if I learn that I am not going to die, this truth immediately re-transforms itself to information, as it can also stand for 'entirely during my lifetime', as, among others, the truth that manifests itself in an existential choice.
33 This is why I emphasize that there is an existential choice under the category of the particular, too. The Truth that manifests itself in this

choice is by no means necessarily connected with morals. See Heller, 1990.

Chapter 5 *Culture, or Invitation to Luncheon by Immanuel Kant*

1 'Eine grosse Stadt . . . wie etwa Königsberg am Pregelflusse, kann schon für einen schicklichen Platz zu Erweiterung sowohl der Menschenkenntnis als auch der Weltkenntnis genommen werden . . .', footnote to the Preface, *Anthropologie pragmatischer Hinsicht, Kant Werke*, Band XII. (Frankfurt: Suhrkamp Verlag, 1964), p. 400. 'A big city. . .such as Königsberg on the river Pregel . . . is a suitable place for broadening one's knowledge of man and the world . . .', Kant, 1974, p. 4.

2 Kant, *Die Religion innerhalb der Grenzen der blossen Vernunft*, Part II, 'Von dem Hange zum Bösen in der menschlichen Natur', *Werke* VIII, pp. 675–80. In English, *Religion within the Limits of Reason Alone*, II 'Concerning the propensity to evil in Human Nature', tr. T. M. Greene and H. H. Hudson (NY: Harper & Row, 1960), pp. 23–7.

3 Kant, 1974, p. 147.

4 The conception of the ruse of nature first appears in Kant, 'Idee zur einer allgemeinen Geschichte in weltbürgerlicher Absicht', *Werke* XI. pp. 33–50. In English, 'Idea for a Universal History with a Cosmopolitan Intent', op. cit.

5 Kant, 'Über den Gemeinspruch: Das mag in der Theorie richtig sein, taugt aber nicht für die Praxis', part II 'Im Staatsrecht', ibid., pp. 143–64, 'On the Proverb: it may work in theory but not in Practice', in Kant, 1983.

6 Kant, 1974, pp. 339–400.

7 Ibid., p. 32, translation corrected.

8 Kant, *Anthropologie*, p. 485 (text not included in the English translation).

9 Kant, *Kritik der Urteilskraft, Werke*, X (Frankfurt: Suhrkamp, 1951), para. 41. In English, Kant, 1990).

10 Arend, 1982. I disagree with Arendt on this point. The close relation between politics and morals as elaborated by him in the first Part of *Metaphysics of Morals* is a crucial (if not the most crucial) aspect of Kant's political philosophy. Para. 40 (in *Critique of Judgement*) discusses the cognitive mentality of the political author, one, yet only one, important aspect of political philosophy. Artur Jacobson, in his fine study on Hegel and jurisprudence (*Cardozo Law Review*, 1990) emphasizes the other aspect of Kant's political philosophy, namely Kant's commitment to what Jacobson calls the 'jurisprudence of duty'.

11 Kant, 1951, para. 60.

12 Ibid.

13 Kant, 'Beobachtungen über die Gefühle des Schönen und des Erhabenen', *Werke*, III ('Observations concerning the feelings of the beautiful and the sublime', not translated).

14 Kant, 1951 (in 'General Remark upon the Exposition of the Aesthetical Reflective Judgement'), para. 29.
15 Kant, 1974, 'On Egoism', p. 10.
16 Kant, 1951, para. 40.
17 The third kind of pluralism, namely the ethical one, will be discussed immediately afterwards in para. 41, ibid.
18 Kant, 1974, p. 412.
19 Ibid., para. 66.
20 Ibid. Translation slightly corrected.
21 Kant, 1951, para. 29, 'General Remark . . .'.
22 Kant, 1974, para. 59.
23 Ibid.
24 This feature of the life and teaching of Jesus of Nazareth is beautifully analyzed in Sheehan, 1988.
25 Kant, 1974, para. 88.
26 Ibid.
27 Ibid.
28 Kant, 1951, 'Dialectic of the Aesthetical Judgement', para. 56.
29 Kant, 1974, para. 88.
30 Ibid.
31 Ibid.
32 Khrushchev, 1971, pp. 262–9.
33 Goffman, 1959.
34 Not even to enjoy food. See Finkelstein, 1988.
35 There are differences between power-games, though. When Foucault discusses the Platonic dialogues, especially the Symposium, he shows how the roles can be reversed, and that the 'dialectics of love' 'calls for two movements exactly alike on the part of the two lovers; the love is the same for both of them, since it is the motion that carries them towards truth', Foucault, 1985, p. 240.
36 E.g. Mappelthorpe's sexually explicit photos are defended on the grounds that in art it is alone the beauty of the form that matters, but also on the grounds that his art is the manifestation of a 'correct' 'sexual politics'.
37 I discussed this problem in some detail in 'Hermeneutics of Social Sciences', in Heller, 1990.
38 To render (new) meaning to concepts, stories and thoughts is just fundamental in philosophy; otherwise one could not juxtapose 'true knowledge' to mere opinion, essence to appearances. Philosophical characters are constantly re-groomed, re-interpreted to assume new and different shades of meaning. Yet Meaning as a philosophical Character results from second-order reflection; philosophy reflects upon its condition, calling, performance and limits. Meaning as a protagonist has no place in 'naive' but only in 'sentimental' philosophies.
39 Hegel, 1990, para. 554.
40 Ibid., para. 662.

41 Goethe collected folk-poetry, and he also created Lieder in folk-style, transforming it through refinement, but preserving the simplicity of the form.

42 The ambiguous character of the prophecies of Delphi that played such an important role in both tragedy and philosophy is well known.

43 I discussed this matter in 'Hermeneutics of Social Sciences', Heller, 1990.

44 The 'fusion of horizons', as Gadamer discusses it, can mean an actual fusion of two different horizons, yet also the illusion of such a fusion (a subjective fusion).

45 The difficulties cultures have in understanding one another is enormous. Since I have realized that people who grew up in Western Europe or America would never really understand what a Eastern European meant when saying something (as long as they lived under totalitarian rule), and vice versa, I began to doubt whether we are able to 'fuse' our horizon with that of remote people, like the ancient Greeks.

46 Here I refer back to chapter 2.

47 I will distinguish between the meaning of these three terms in chapter 6.

48 The romantic streak in the third Critique appears together with the problem of Meaning.

49 The paradigm of communication maintains the Kantian duality between reason and feelings, or rather radicalizes it – for it does not know of reflective aesthetic judgement. Authenticity (of expression) that manifests itself in speech acts is an inferior version of Kant's subjective purposiveness. See Habermas, 1984.

50 See Heller, 'Death of the Subject?' in Heller, 1990.

51 'Die Welt des Glücklichen ist eine andere Welt als die des Unglücklichen. Die Welt des Glücklichen ist *eine glückliche Welt*. Kann es also eine Welt geben, die weder glücklich noch unglücklich ist?' (author's emphasis), Wittgenstein, *Tagebücher 1914–16*. From L. Wittgenstein *Schriften* 1 (Frankfurt, Suhrkamp, 1969), p. 70. In English, 'The world of the happy is a different world than the world of the unhappy. The world of the happy is *a happy world*. Can there be a world that is neither happy nor unhappy?' (my translation).

Chapter 6 The Absolute Spirit

1 Hegel, 1990. Third Part of the Philosophy of the Spirit (Mind): The Absolute Spirit (Mind) para. 554.

2 Ibid., Commentary (*Zusatz*).

3 I have termed this sphere 'the sphere of objectivation for-itself' in Heller, 1984 and 1985 (in the study 'Everyday Life, Rationality of Reason, Rationality of Intellect').

4 In Hegel Truth emerges out of recollection (*Erinnerung*). The word *Erinnerung* is rich in connotations. It means also appropriation by the subject (contrasted to *Entausserung*) and make it 'deep'. Whatever is forgotten is no object/subject of *Erinnerung* (Recollection), and, by de-

finition does not partake in Truth (does not even contribute to Truth). Yet Truth is also the Whole. Actually, Hegel notices that which Heidegger terms later 'ontological difference', and he decides consciously to sublate it.

5 This is the concluding sentence of para. 563.

6 The English translation of *Gemeinde* as 'community' can be misleading.

7 Jews caused a theoretical problem for Hegel. After the world-spirit had left the Jewish people and began to dwell with the Greeks, and finally after Christianity came into being, Jews should have ceased to exist. But they did not. This was a flaw of universal history.

8 MacIntyre, 1988, discusses the attempt of liberalism to include every human being, culture and community into the universal discourse on justice and rationality. Yet what is maintained in this discourse (if it is maintained at all) is certainly not a *cultural* identity, that includes substantive aspects also, but a merely formal identity.

9 See Heidegger, 1970.

10 Feuerbach, Kritik des Anti-Hegels (Leipzig: O. Wigard, 1844).

11 See the chapter on 'Dynamic Justice' in *Beyond Justice*.

12 G. W. F. Hegel, 1977 Band II (*Werke* 17), p. 343. In English, *Lectures on the Philosophy of Religion*.

13 Ibid.

14 Of course, one could maintain, that philosophers are the representative individuals (subjects) of modernity. Hegel's reluctance to accept such a conclusion is obvious.

15 For simplicity's sake, I speak here a neo-Kantian language.

16 Among the three Kantian *a priori* cognitive faculties, understanding and reason constitute a world (that of nature and that of freedom), yet judgement does not. In the mind of Lukács (in the *Heidelberg Philosophy of Art*) this leaves judgement – and the aesthetic domain – void of authentic autonomy. Deleuze, 1984, argues the other way around – in his mind the 'anarchic' state of faculties and the freedom of imagination secures the superiority of the aesthetic domain as against the other two.

17 For details, see chapter 3.

18 Para. 577. 'Der dritte Schluss ist die Idee der Philosophie, welche *die sich wissende Vernunft*, das Abolut-Allgemeine zu ihrer *Mitte* har, die sich un *Geist* und *Natur* entzweit . . .' (emphasis by Hegel).

19 *Andacht* is a-temporal because of the absence of historical time, that is external time, the time of external events. The distinction between past-present-and-future disappears. This is why it is 'presencing'. Moreover that which it is presencing is the eternal (the unchanging meaning, the absolute). But the same *Andacht* is also temporal, insofar as it is an internal event, and the subject undergoes changes through it.

20 Modern men and women could recognize their life-experiences far better in the Kantian distinction between pluralistic and egoistic language. See previous chapter.

21 Niklas Luhmann, *Soziologische Aufklärung: Aufsätze zur Theorie Sozialer Systeme* (Köln-Upladen: West-Deutscher Verlag, 1970).

22 In Habermas, 1974, pp. 25–75.

23 I discussed this issue in greater detail in 'The Concept of the Political' in Heller, 1990.

24 Ibid., p. 51.

25 The relationship between the experience of contingency and meaning-deficit had been discussed in chapter 1.

26 The personalization of contemporary philosophy has been discussed in chapter 2.

27 Exactly the same question can be (relevantly) asked from the standpoint of the Wittgensteinian language-game theory.

28 See 'Death of the Subject?', in Heller, 1990.

29 MacIntyre, 1981, ascribes both the intuitivist and the emotivist moral theories to particular ways of life of particular groups of modern (or rather modernist) men and women.

30 H. Bloom's discovery of the author of the Book of J as the genius-writer is a case in point.

31 The emergence of social sciences had been discussed as one of the escape routes from this impasse in 'Hermeneutics of Social Sciences', in Heller, 1990.

32 See chapter 7. In Castoriadis; 1987.

33 'Everything is language' is an omnivorous cultural statement.

34 The core of the spirit of our congregation becomes a kind of 'a thing in itself' – we can talk confidently about its phenomena alone. For one, the core is suspect (it can exist yet also not); and secondly, if there is a core, one can only allude to it, hint at it, for it is shrouded in mysteries.

35 The vertical chain of determination (substance-attributes-modes), and the horizontal chain of determination (modus cause of other modi) are strictly differentiated in Spinoza's *Ethics*. This has an important impact on Spinoza's ethic proper, for the vertical chain is responsible for freedom (goodness, reason) and the horizontal chain for slavery (evil, suffering, being subject to passions).

36 I refer here to Heller, 1985 and 1990.

37 This issue will discussed in chapter 7.

38 This interpretation can be challenged on the grounds that it is not Nietzsche who says that God is dead, but Zarathustra, who is not a philosopher but the founder of a religion. It was Nietzsche, after Kierkegaard, who returned to Plato by re-introducing life-characters in addition to the philosophical characters. If Zarathustra is a philosophical character, he is certainly not simply the mouthpiece of Nietzsche. Nietzsche, after all, can talk directly when he wills. Yet still, I would attribute the sentence, 'god is dead' to Nietzsche the philosopher, and read it as a philosophical sentence, that is a sentence that concerns philosophy.

39 Whether one treats ancient texts, or the master text of one's own culture or nation, reverently or irreverently, depends on traditions and attitudes. The latter are changing (so are the former, though at a slower pace). National classics, for example, are treated as sacred texts in a devotional

manner by people with the tradition of cultural nationalism, yet not by others. Classics can be put on an invisible altar, and touching them or criticizing them is often perceived as blasphemy.

40 See 'The Human Condition' in Heller, 1988.
41 See Elias, 1978. There is a roll-back in self-discipline in certain sectors that underwent the 'civilizing process' in early modernity, especially concerning dressing and the encounter of the sexes, yet a kind of tightening in some others (like eating habits).
42 I have read in a New York magazine the answers of local celebrities to the question about their greatest and most joyful experience in life. The overwhelming majority mentioned giving a diamond ring to their beloved (or receiving one), the same with a fur coat, and first and foremost the great hours when they were drinking pink champagne, especially while riding in a horse-drawn carriage with their lover in the Central Park at night. Only a very few had other remembrances worth mentioning, e.g. one who spoke about his father's return from WWII. Is kitsch-fantasy also retrospective?
43 See the sub-section on utopia in chapter 2.
44 Ibid.
45 The kind of humanism that placed humanity at the top of the value-hierarchy did not necessarily dismiss humility; e.g. in Kant humility is due to the rational humankind in us, and not to our own empirical person or the empirical person of the other. The empirical person should bow before no one but the Moral Law. Certainly, the idea of the deification of man gathered momentum, and landed, as usual, in hero worship. See also 'The Power of Shame' in Heller, 1985.
46 It is here that I return to the question raised at the end of chapter 4. This question is now answered in the affirmative.
47 This is the summary of the conclusion I drew in 'Death of the Subject' in Heller, 1990.
48 'Mass Culture' in Arendt, 1968.
49 According to György Márkus, natural sciences played a pivotal role in establishing the specific sphere of 'high culture'.
50 Horace claimed immortal fame because of his rendering of Greek poetry in Latin: 'Exegi monumentum aere perennio . . .'.
51 To seek redemption in the sphere of objective spirit (in history, in political institutions) was an attemnpt that concluded – in our century – in the totalitarian imagination. This is why it is (for the time being?) abandoned. See chapter 2.
52 Hegel, 1990 e.g. para. 571: 'Nur indem die reine unendliche Form . . . die Einseitigkeit des Subjektiven . . . ablegt, ist sie das freie Denken, welches seine unendliche Bestimmung zugleich als absoluten, an und für sich seienden Inhalt und ihn als Objekt hat, in welchen es ebenso frei ist. Das Denken is insofern selbst nur das Formelle des absoluten Inhalts.'
53 So the 'bad grammar' of *Alice in Wonderland* will also be the object of curiosity and interpretation.

54 Irony is back again, both in the ancient/Socratian and in the Romantic version. Derrida and Rorty, de Man and Luhmann, are all 'ironists' but they represent different versions of irony.
55 Eco, 1990. In his novel (Eco, 1989), Eco – wittingly, unwittingly – exemplified that there are such limits.

Chapter 7 On the Railway Station

1 Hegel, 1986, *Werke*, XX, p. 120.
2 W. Schadendorf, *Das Jahrhundert der Eisenbahn* (München: Prestel, 1965), p. 17.
3 Mihály Kubinszky, *Vasutak épitése Europában* (Budapest: Müszaki Könykiado, 1965).
4 Thomas, 1981.
5 The reconstruction of the station took place between 1886–9, whereas Monet's paintings originate from 1876–7.
6 Arendt, *The Human Condition* (Chicago: University of Chicago Press, 1958). One does not need to read Arendt's book as a historical narrative, but as a process of thinking about the three fundamental attitudes of active life. All forthcoming references to Arendt are to this work.
7 This is the main reason why, according to Hegel, great tragedies are matters of the past. The single modern man is not free enough an actor to challenge a tragic fate.
8 Kant, 1974. See chapter 5.
9 To the discussion of *raison d'état*, see Maurizio Virolli, *The Reason of State* (in manuscript).
10 I distinguish between three relatively independent logics of modernity, such as functional division of labour, manufacturing industry and the crafting of states. These logics can be filled with various contents, yet not all of them produces a socio-political arrangement fit for longevity or even survival. For the most decisive formulation of this theory see Feher-Heller, *Modernity's Pendulum* forthcoming.
11 In the case of the appreciation of human beauty (which was not 'pure' aesthetic judgement in Kant), one can hardly speak of 'nature' alone, for this 'nature' is already transformed to meet aesthetic expectations. Self-ornamentation is a case in point.
12 Though the distinction between functionally appropriate and inappropriate is already there in Plato (*ergon* means for him result, work, function, and also perfection adequate to *energeia*), he relates the functional to the good; the representative example is the product of *paideia*, the virtuous person accomplished.
13 Whether one juxtaposes communicative reason to instrumental reason, political discourse to technological discourse, political imagination to technological immagination is not of decisive importance for the issue under discussion. It is widely accepted that the two are different, or at least, that they ought to be.

14 See note 48 of chapter 5.
15 Especially in the manner Frater Taciturnus discusses it in *Stages on Life's Way* (Princeton: Princeton University Press, 1988).
16 See chapter 4.
17 See chapter 6.

Bibliography

Adorno, Theodor 1973: *Jargon of Authenticity*, tr. Knut Tarkowki and Frederic Will. Evanston: Northwestern University Press.
——1983: *Negative Dialectics*, tr. E.B. Ashton. New York: Continuum Press.
Arendt, Hannah 1968: *Between Past and Future*. New York: Penguin.
——1982: *Lectures on Kant's Political Philosophy*. Chicago: University of Chicago Press.
——1971: *The Life of the Mind: Willing*. New York: Harcourt, Brace & Jovanovich.
Augustine 1964: *On the Free Choice of the Will*. Indianapolis: Bobbs-and Merrill.
Benjamin, Walter 1968: *Illuminations*, ed. Hannah Arendt; tr. Harry Zohn. New York: Schocken Books.
——1977: *Origin of the German Tragic Drama*, tr. John Osborne. London: NLB.
Bloch, Ernst 1986: *The Principle of Hope*, tr. Neville Plaice, Stephen Plaice and Paul Knight. Cambridge, Mass.: MIT Press.
Bloom, Harold 1990: *The Book of J*. New York: Grove.
Blumenberg, Hans 1987: *Das Lachen der Thrakerin*. Frankfurt: Suhrkamp.
——1976: *Höllenausgaenge*. Frankfurt: Suhrkamp Verlag.
——1983: *Legitimacy of the Modern Age*, tr. Robert M. Wallace. Cambridge, Mass.: MIT.
——1979: *Work on Myth*, tr. Robert M. Wallace. Cambridge, Mass.: MIT.
Caputo, John 1987: *Radical Hermeneutics*. Indiana: Indiana University Press.
Castoriadis, Cornelius 1986: *Domaines de l'homme*. Paris: Seuil.
——1987: *The Imaginary Institution of Society*, tr. Kathleen Blamey. Cambridge, Mass.: MIT.
Collingwood, R.G. 1946: *The Idea of History*. Oxford: Clarendon Press.
Deleuze, Gilles 1984: *Kant's Critical Philosophy*, tr. Hugh Tomlinson and Barbara Habberjam. Minneapolis: University of Minnesota Press.
Deleuze, Gilles and Guattari, Felix 1991: *Qu'est-ce que la Philosophie?* Paris: Les Editions de Minuit.

Derrida, Jacques 1981: *Dissemination*, tr. Barbara Johnson. Chicago: University of Chicago Press.

——1982: *D'un ton apocalyptique adopte naguere en philosophie*. Paris: Edition Galilee.

Derrida, Jacques 1987: *The Truth in Painting*, tr. Geoff Bennington and Ian MacLeod. Chicago: University of Chicago Press.

Eco, Umberto 1989: *Foucault's Pendulum*. San Diego: HBT.

——1990: *The Limits of Interpretation*, tr. William Weaver. Bloomington, Indiana University Press.

Elias, Norbert 1978: *The Civilizing Process*, tr. Edmund Jephcott. New York: Urizen Books.

Finkelstein, Joanne 1988: *Dining Out*. Oxford: Basil Blackwell.

Foucault, Michel 1972: *The Archeology of Knowledge*, tr. A.M. Sheridan. New York: Pantheon.

——1984: *The Foucault Reader*, ed. Paul Rabinow. New York: Pantheon.

——1977: *Language, Counter-memory, Practice*, ed. Donald F. Bouchard; tr. Donald F. Bouchard and Sherry Simer. Ithaca: Cornell University Press.

——1985: *The Use of Pleasure*, tr. Robert Hurley. New York: Vintage Books.

Freud, Sigmund 1955: *Civilization, Society and Religion*. Harmondsworth: Penguin.

Goffman, Erving 1959: *The Presentation of Self in Everyday Life*. New York: Doubleday.

Habermas, Jürgen 1984: *The Theory of Communicative Action*, tr. Thomas McCarthy. Boston: Beacon Press.

——1974: *Zwei Reden*. Frankfurt: Suhrkamp.

Hegel, G.W.F. 1990: *Encyclopedia*. New York: Continuum.

——1977: *The Phenomenology of Spirit*, tr. A.V. Miller. Oxford: Clarendon.

——1986: *Vorlesungen über die Philosophie der Religion*. Frankfurt: Suhrkamp.

Heidegger, Martin 1977: *Basic Writings*, ed. David Krell. New York: Harper & Row.

——1970: *Hegel's Concept of Experience*. New York: Harper & Row.

Heller, Agnes 1990: *A Philosophy of Morals*. (Oxford: Basil Blackwell. 1990).

——1982: A Theory of History. London: RKP.

——1987: *Beyond Justice*. Oxford: Basil Blackwell.

——1990: *Can Modernity Survive?* Berkeley: University of California Press.

——1984: *Everyday Life*. London: RKP.

——1988: *General Ethics*. Oxford: Basil Blackwell.

——1984: *Radical Philosophy*. Oxford: Basil Blackwell.

——1985: *The Power of Shame*. London: RKP.

Hume, David A. 1951: *A Treatise of Human Nature*. Edinburgh: Nelson.

Jonas, Hans 1966: *The Phenomenon of Life*. New York: Harper & Row.

268 *Bibliography*

Kant, Immanuel 1974: *Anthropology from a Pragmatic Point of View*, tr. M. Gregor. The Hague: Martinus Nijhoff.
——1990: *Critique of Judgement*, tr. Werner S. Pluhar. Indianapolis: Hackett.
——1964: *The Doctrine of Virtue*. Philadelphia: University of Philadelphia Press.
——1965: *The Metaphysical Elements of Justice*. Indianapolis: Bobbs-Merrill.
——1957: *On History*, ed. Lewis White Beck; tr. Robert Anchor and Emil Fackenheim. Indianapolis: Bobbs-Merrill.
——1983: *Perpetual Peace*, tr. Ted Humphrey. Indianapolis: Hackett.
——1960: *Religion Within the Limits of Reason Alone*, tr. T.M. Greene and H.H.Hudson. New York: Harper & Row.
Khrushchev, Nikita 1971: *Khrushchev Remembers*, tr. Strobe Talbott. Boston: Little, Brown and Co.
Kierkegaard, Soren 1980: *The Concept of Anxiety*, tr. Reider Thomte and Albert B. Anderson. Princeton: Princeton University Press.
——1941: *Concluding Unscientific Postscript*, tr. David Swenson. Princeton: Princeton University Press.
——1987: *Either/Or*, tr. Howard V. and Edna H. Hong. Princeton: Princeton University Press.
——1962: *The Present Age*, tr. Alexander Dru. New York: Harper & Row.
——1941: *Sickness unto Death*, tr. Walter Lowrie. Princeton: Princeton University Press.
Lessing 1962: *Emilia Galotti*, tr. Edward Dvoretsky. New York: Ungar.
Löwy, Michael 1989: *Rédemption et utopie*. Paris: Presses Universitaire de France.
Löwith, Karl 1949: *Meaning in History*. Chicago: University of Chicago Press.
——1966: *Nature, History and Existentialism*. Evanston: Northwestern University Press.
Lukács, Georg 1971: *History and Class Consciousness*, tr. David Livingstone. Cambridge, Mass.: MIT.
——1974: *Soul and Form*, tr. Anna Bostock. London: Merlin Press.
MacIntyre, Alasdair 1981: *After Virtue*. South Bend: University of Notre Dame Press.
——1988: *Whose Justice? Which Rationality?* South Bend: University of Notre Dame Press.
Mann, Thomas 1963: *Doctor Faustus*. New York: Knopf.
Merleau-Ponty, Maurice 1968: *The Visible and the Invisible*, ed. Claude Lefort; tr. Alfonso Lingis. Evanston: Northwestern University Press.
Nietzche, Friedrich 1956: *The Birth of Tragedy and the Genealogy of Morals*. Garden City, NY: Doubleday.
——1980: *On the Advantage and Disadvantage of History for Life*. Indianapolis: Hackett Press.
Nozick, Robert 1974: *Anarchy, State and Utopia*. Oxford: Basil Blackwell.

Pascal, Blaise 1977: *Pensées*. Paris: Gallimard.

Rorty, Richard 1987: *Contingency, Irony and Solidarity*. Cambridge: Cambridge University Press.

Rosenzweig, Franz 1971: *The Star of Redemption*, tr. William Hallo. New York: Holt, Rinehart and Winston.

Sartre, Jean-Paul 1956: *Being and Nothingness*, tr. Hazel E. Barnes. New York: Philosophical Library.

Sheehan, Thomas 1988: *The First Coming*. New York: Vintage Books.

Sorel, George 1969: *The Illusion of Progress*, tr. John and Charlotte Stanley. Berkeley: University of California Press.

——1956: *On Violence*. Glencoe, I: Free Press.

Thomas, D.M. 1981: *The White Hotel*. New York: Viking.

Toulmin, Steven 1982: *The Return to Cosmology*. Berkeley: University of California Press.

Vernant, Jean-Pierre 1983: *Myth and Thought among the Greeks*. London: RKP.

Veyne, Paul 1983: *Did the Greeks believe in their Myths?*, tr. Paula Wissing. Chicago: University of Chicago Press.

Wellmer, Albrecht 1985: *Zur Dialektik der Moderne und Postmoderne*. Frankfurt: Suhrkamp.

Wittgenstein, Ludwig 1967: *Zettel*, ed. G.E.M. Anscombe and G.H. Von Wright; tr. G.E.M. Anscombe. Berkeley: University of California Press.

Index

compulsory, 124; correspondance of, 213; discourse about, 206; as edifying, 129, 130, 131, 132, 134; as end, 69; factual, 124–5; and falsity, 123; for me, 133; for us, 194; of history, 125–6, 194; idea of, 132, 133, 134; of philosophy, 119, 183; pluralization of, 117; rational, 124–5; relative, 130; in religion, 117, 122; scientific, 122, 126; as subjective, 128, 129, 132, 206, 207, 211; as whole, 116, 134, 177, 183, 211
Turner, 216

universal claims, 173; functions, 231; thing, 231; validity, 148, 165, 174
universality, comparative, 148
usefulness, 232, 237
utopia, 51, 173; absolute, 58, 60, 113; cultural, 163; incarnate in good person, 59; major, 57, 58, 60; minor, 57; modern, 53, 54; of the past, 156; social, 52, 53, 56, 57; unity of freedom and happiness, 163
utopian reality, 154, 159, 161, 162

Valla, Lorenzo, 87
Veyne, Paul, 117
Vico, 131
violence, 74, 75; saving power of, 66
Virgil, 137
vita active, 226

wager, existential, 11, 12, 13, 14, 15, 22, 25, 32, 33, 35, 45, 64, 73, 133, 187, 197, 243
Wagner, 75
Weber, Max, 103
western civilization, 68
'White Hotel, The', 217
Whitehead, 82
whole, 61, 63
will, 6; good, 162; philosophical character, 106, 107, 108, 109, 110
will-to-power, 108
Wittgenstein, 116, 240, 241
work, 226, 232, 234, 235
world, 227, 230; 'a', 229; enduring trace of, 242; fusion with history, 233; as spatial equivalent of history, 228; 'the', 228; 'the other', 240; 'this', 240; universal, 231
world-constitution; idiosyncratic, 192; intersubjective, 173, 174, 193; secondary, 192
world-creating capacity of moderns, 227; work, 227
world-picture, 187
worship, secondary, 208

Zeitblom, Serenus, 73
zero, 10, 11, 12, 16
Zeus, 83
Zohar, 60